WA

*Warfare and Society in Europe, 1898 to the Present* examines warfare in Europe from the Fashoda conflict in 1898 in modern-day Sudan to the recent war in Iraq. The twentieth century was by far the world's most destructive century, with two global wars marking the first half of the century and the constant fear of nuclear annihilation haunting the second half. Throughout, this book treats warfare as a function of large political, cultural, social and economic issues and includes discussion of:

- the alliances that led to the outbreak of World War I
- World War I
- World War II
- the increasing role played by the United States in Europe's twentieth-century wars
- Eastern European wars, such as the Russian Civil War and the Greco-Turkish war
- new technologies and weapons.

Combining a traditional survey of military history with a survey of social issues, Michael S. Neiberg examines both how social changes have impacted the nature of war fighting and how war has shaped the basic patterns of European society.

**Michael S. Neiberg** is Professor of History at the United States Air Force Academy in Colorado. He is the author of *Warfare in World History* (2001) and *Making Citizen-Soldiers: ROTC and the Ideology of American Military Service* (2000).

# Warfare and History
## General Editor
## Jeremy Black
### *Professor of History, University of Exeter*

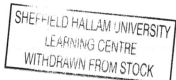
# WARFARE AND SOCIETY IN EUROPE

## 1898 to the Present

*Michael S. Neiberg*

Routledge
Taylor & Francis Group

NEW YORK AND LONDON

First published 2004
by Routledge
29 West 35th Street, New York, NY 10001

Simultaneously published in the UK
by Routledge
11 New Fetter Lane, London EC4P 4EE

*Routledge is an imprint of the Taylor & Francis Group*

© 2004 Michael S. Neiberg

Typeset in Bembo by
Keystroke, Jacaranda Lodge, Wolverhampton
Printed and bound in Great Britain by
The Cromwell Press, Trowbridge, Wiltshire

*Library of Congress Cataloging in Publication Data*
Neiberg, Michael S.
Warfare & society in Europe: 1898 to the present / Michael S.
Neiberg.
p. cm. — (Warfare and history)
Includes bibliographical references and index.
ISBN 0–415–32718–0 — ISBN 0–415–32719–9 (pbk.)
1. Europe—History, Military—20th century.  2. War and
society—Europe.  3. World War, 1914–1918—Social aspects.  4. World
War, 1939–1945—Social aspects.  5. Politics and war.  6. Military
history, Modern—20th century.  7. Nuclear arms control.  I. Title:
Warfare and society in Europe.  II. Title.  III. Series.
D431.N45 2004
303.6′6′094—dc22    2003014632

*British Library Cataloguing in Publication Data*
A catalogue record for this book is available from the British Library

ISBN 0–415–32718–0 (hbk)
ISBN 0–415–32719–9 (pbk)

# CONTENTS

# INTRODUCTION*

The history of Europe in the twentieth century is inseparable from the history of warfare. The twentieth century was by far the world's most destructive and Europe felt the brunt of its impact. Two major global wars characterized the first half of the century and the threat of nuclear annihilation haunted the second half. Under the surface of these great power conflagrations raged several smaller wars, many of them fought by Europeans at a great distance from the continent. Even those societies that tried to remain neutral during these wars, such as Holland, were radically transformed by the wars fought around them. To be European in the twentieth century was, by definition, to be impacted and shaped by war.

The peoples of Europe, technologically sophisticated, thoroughly modern, and divided by ancient animosities and hatreds, killed one another on the battlefield in the twentieth century in sheer quantities theretofore impossible. They also projected their military power in greater force and at greater distances. The image of the "civilized" world tearing itself apart in such a manner continues to speak to us as a dire warning, raising questions about the definitions of "modernity" and "progress" that are difficult to answer. Many Europeans avoid facing these questions by erroneously attempting to look away from Europe's uglier side and imagining that the ferocity of twentieth-century warfare was somehow an aberration from "normal" European patterns. Others live in the hope that the barbarity of the twentieth century has receded into a distant past from which Europe is now somehow immune.

Neither of these approaches solves the essential problem of understanding the century as it was. To truly understand Europe in the twentieth century, one must, inevitably, return to the study of warfare. Victory or defeat on the battlefield determined the shape of European societies more than any other single factor. Europe's other patterns – political, cultural, economic, and social

---

*   The views expressed in this book are those of the author and do not reflect the official policy or position of the United States Air Force Academy, the Department of Defense, or the United States Government.

1

– are direct or indirect products of its military history. One could cite thousands of examples to prove the point. It is no coincidence that France's Third Republic began in the wake of one military disaster and was finally destroyed by another. Similarly, its Fourth Republic collapsed as a result of its inability to deal with the consequences of war, this time in Algeria. One could argue that the current Fifth Republic has thus far been more consistent than its predecessors in large part because it has not yet had to contend with a major war.

Moreover, it is inconceivable that the current forms of Europe would have evolved without the tragic events of the twentieth century. The development of the integrating institutions of the continent such as the European Union and NATO have their origins in preventing another large-scale war through cooperation, whether military, economic, political, or cultural. Thus far, they have succeeded. If they are to continue, it is imperative to remember the reasons why they were created in the first place and why so many people believed that Europeans had to create these institutions to contain and control their own bellicose passions.

The primary focus of this brief analysis of European warfare is on wars between European states. Wars between Europeans and non-Europeans necessarily receive less attention. Thus I have made no attempt to include an in-depth analysis of the Boer Wars (1899–1902), the Russo-Japanese War (1904–1905), and other smaller wars except where they are important for the overall picture. Analyzing the operational and tactical features of Europe's wars against anti-colonial forces in the post-1945 period is also outside the scope of this study. I am not suggesting that these wars were unimportant. Rather I am keeping the focus squarely on the wars that most directly impacted European society and the European continent as a whole.

The traditional manner of analyzing the history of warfare has been, under-standably enough, from a military perspective. Such studies attempt to explain victory and defeat based upon military factors such as levels of force, command decisions, and the development of weapons and ancillary technologies. This approach is eminently logical, as the fates of societies are often decided on the battlefield, at what military officers sometimes call the sharp end of the stick. Indeed, it is impossible to write military history without an examination of these factors; this book will not attempt to do so.

While this book does not attempt to denigrate or downplay military factors, it nevertheless belongs to another approach. The following chapters will examine the dialectical relationship between warfare and European society more generally. This approach, sometimes called the "new military history" assumes that military factors are themselves products of larger, not always military, factors, such as dominant cultural beliefs, political structures, and economic systems. In other words, this book will work backwards from the sharp end to analyze the strengths and weaknesses of the stick behind it.[1]

This book is therefore informed by two schools of historical thought. The first, military history, examines the nature of war as it pertains to victory and defeat. Its usual modes of analysis are operational and focus on factors such as leadership and technology. Military historians, in general, are less concerned with the social and cultural impacts of war. By its nature, military history is most comfortable with events that occur on the battlefield and in the halls of power. What happens after the guns stop firing often sits outside the purview of strictly military history.

Social history, on the other hand, normally concerns itself with the "long durée." By this phrase, social historians mean the long, often unseen processes that produce change, such as ethnicity, class, and gender. Most social history, therefore, concerns itself much less with individuals and isolated events like battles and wars. Social historians often show a poor understanding of the history of warfare. They have, however, done excellent work in examining how wars and their consequences have shaped the development of societies and created altogether new patterns.

Traditionally, these two fields of analysis have had little in common. It is not my intention in this book to somehow merge the two fields. Rather, I hope to use both military and social history to present a slightly different way of seeing war in twentieth-century Europe. This approach should present a fuller picture of both how social changes have impacted the nature of war fighting and how war has shaped the basic patterns of European society.

The following chapters will thus examine the ways in which warfare either enhanced patterns of European development already underway or fundamentally altered them. The wars of the twentieth century, I argue, were not aberrations to an otherwise progressive and peaceful history of European development. Rather they were essential (and often popular) products of the fundamental nature of European society. There is a great deal of continuity to the patterns of twentieth-century European history, patterns that are often lost when wars are analyzed separately. By seeing the century as a seamless whole, the larger patterns become more evident.

This problem of understanding the twentieth century as a period of continuity is especially acute when analyzing the seemingly prosaic period between the world wars. Rather than standing apart as a period of total peace between periods of total war, the years 1918–1939 were fraught with wars and international tensions. The absence of war between France and Germany should not confuse the student into believing that the period was either peaceful or of secondary importance. War plagued large and small states such as Russia, Turkey, and Poland in this period and the threat of another general war was always just below the surface. The great powers themselves used this period to wage "war through peace," finding diplomatic, economic, and cultural ways to strike at one another, even in times of peace. This process often left tensions high across the continent even before Hitler's remilitarization of Germany after 1933.

Two patterns deserve special mention. First, over the course of the period under study here, European societies came increasingly to rely on cooperation with one another. From the signing of a German–Austrian alliance in 1879 and first rumblings of an Entente Cordiale between Britain and France at the turn of the century, the basic structures of international military cooperation had been formed. Theretofore, those arrangements had been based on little more than the good will of diplomats and heads of state. Even the pre-1914 arrangements were loose, informal, and often failed to function properly when the shooting began. They came, perforce, to be replaced by more effective and more formalized alliances that foreshadowed the international cooperation by rough equals in the post-World War II period as exemplified in structures such as the European Coal and Steel Community (1953), the European Parliament (1979), the single Euro currency (2001), and the still unrealized attempts to create a single European defense force (first proposed in 1949).

These structures derived in part from the military continentalism that characterized the twentieth century. French general Ferdinand Foch's command of a joint French–British–Belgian Northern Army Group in 1915 began the process. French general Robert Nivelle's mishandling of a joint command in 1917 nearly killed it. Only the crisis caused by the advance of German forces toward Paris in 1918 resuscitated the idea, again with Foch at the head.[2] Beside him sat an inter-allied governing body, the Supreme War Council, at which politicians and generals of numerous nations made critical political and military decisions.

This pattern repeated itself in World War II. The Americans, the British, and the Dominions created and nurtured a Chief of Staff of the Supreme Allied Commander (COSSAC) that divided responsibilities between the nationalities and formed a joint body for study and debate. Together, they worked with their Russian ally, albeit on a much less formal basis, and coordinated activity with a host of governments in exile. A similar organization governed Allied operations in Asia. Alliance warfare, with all of its foibles and problems, had become (and largely remains) the dominant paradigm of modern warfare. This pattern relied, in turn, on the willingness of the combatant societies to cede some of their own autonomy and swallow some of their national pride in the larger interests of achieving a common goal. The process was not easy, but the side that did it best usually emerged victorious.

To prove the point further, Germany's failure to take alliance warfare seriously played a major role in the nation's two battlefield defeats in the twentieth century. This failure derived from distinct German patterns that made the prospect of sharing power unlikely in the extreme.[3] As the German army advanced in 1939–1941, several "jackal" states tried to ally with the Germans to collect scraps, but this system never developed into an alliance with synergistic power. On the other hand, the Americans, British, and Soviets were able to work through significant disagreements to create one of the most potent alliances in the history of the world. After the war, the creation of two powerful peacetime alliances, the North Atlantic Treaty Organization (1949) and the Warsaw Pact (1955) continued the pattern.

The entrance of the Americans into the affairs of Europe represents the second major pattern. Long a society that envisioned itself as the new, purer alternative to Europe, since 1917 the United States has played a central role in the affairs of the continent. To be sure, not all Americans and Europeans have welcomed this role; the creation of continental organizations has often been prompted by a desire to compete with or even replace the Americans. Nevertheless, there is no denying the astonishing change in the relationship between the Old World and the premier power of the New World.

German Chancellor Otto von Bismarck once remarked that God must have a special place in His heart for drunkards, idiots, and Americans. At the time of his statement in the late nineteenth century, few Americans cared much for playing a role in European affairs. No American president had ever even visited Europe while in office and the United States had just a handful of formal embassies overseas. In the late nineteenth and early twentieth centuries, however, the economic power of the United States quickly translated into military power and a greater willingness on the part of the American people to use it. The nation's decisive defeat of Spain in 1898 (while a clash between French and British forces in far away Sudan threatened war in Europe) seemed to many Americans to signal that a quantum leap in America's role on the world stage was imminent.

That leap came twenty years later with American contributions to allied victory in World War I and the appearance of President Woodrow Wilson at the Paris Peace Conference. While American politicians largely rejected Wilson's aggressive and idealistic internationalism, American society did not retreat into the absolute isolation that conservatives wanted. Rather, the United States remained a key player in European affairs and drifted slowly toward war again by the early 1940s. The relative ease with which a Japanese attack on a Pacific possession led to a massive American military effort in the European war demonstrates the dynamic changes in American attitudes during the first half of the twentieth century.

From 1941 on, it became impossible to speak any longer of American isolationism. Through NATO and growing American economic and cultural influence, the United States exercised a decisive role in European military affairs. While this book is not a history of the military and American society, it is inevitable that the United States should become a major actor, especially in the book's final chapters. The relationship between the United States and an ever more integrated Europe has often been a difficult one. Anti-Americanism has never been far below the surface, especially among the political left in Europe. Similarly, American desires for unilateralism remain, especially on the American right. Still, the two partners operate with the knowledge that their shared history overrides periodic differences.

The dominant role of the Americans in European military history and of Europe in American military history seems to me to argue strongly against the notion of a separate "exceptionalist" course of American development. In

5

military terms, the Americans and the Europeans have but one history in the twentieth century. Even America's most unilateral major war, that in Vietnam, had roots in Europe. America's escape from isolation was itself a direct result of the turmoil and chaos of the continent and American beliefs that only the New World could redeem the sins of the Old.[4]

America's motives have not always been altruistic. Still, it seems inescapable to me that, disagreements and allegations of American hegemony notwithstanding, the Old World is significantly better off as a result of American participation. The United States, too, has become a nation that is stronger, wiser, and better served by alliances than by isolation. The shrinking world we now inhabit will only intensify these patterns, if at times uneasily.

I have taken the historian's liberty of starting this study of the twentieth century in 1898.[5] In that year two events transpired that later impacted the entire course of European history. The first, and seemingly much more important to contemporary Europeans, was the ability of the French and British to resolve peacefully a clash over a minor strongpoint in the Sudan at Fashoda. That event formed the basis of what eventually became the Anglo-French alliance that fought World War I, began World War II, and formed an important core of NATO. It thus receives a great deal of attention in Chapter 1. The other event, as mentioned briefly earlier, was the American victory over Spain. That "splendid little war" gave the Americans confidence, wealth, power, and a desire to use them.

Until 1917, however, the Americans preferred to use their newly found global power in the western hemisphere and in the Philippines. Chapter 2 thus covers World War I as it was fought in Europe by Europeans. It is not my intention to try to review all of the major military campaigns of the war. Rather, I examine the development of the alliance system used by Britain, France, Belgium, Italy, and, after 1917, the United States, to defeat Imperial Germany. Alliances are, of course, creations of diplomats and soldiers. In order to understand the war, one must understand how it developed into a "people's war" and how it grew beyond the control even of those powers prosecuting it. Before it was over, the war had radically changed the political, economic, social, and cultural landscape of Europe and, consequently, much of the rest of the world as well.

Europe's attempts to rebuild, in part with American help, form the focal point of Chapter 3. The failed peace process begun in Paris in 1919 has received a great deal of blame from historians for making World War II and (in some minds) the Cold War inevitable. Indeed the Treaty of Versailles, a hodgepodge of unworkable stopgap measures and compromises, is easy to vilify. For all the attention that historians have given to its consequences, however, few historians have attempted to analyze and explain fully the social conditions that produced it. Most scholars of the period study the treaty as a process of discussions among the "Big Three" heads of the French, British, and American governments. This avenue of study is the diplomatic equivalent of the military sharp end of the stick. In this chapter I attempt to look at the societal factors that influenced the Big Three (all representing governments answerable to electorates) at Paris.

Historians have also paid insufficient attention to the period between the world wars. This period, covered in Chapter 4, is worthy of intense analysis both for what it reveals about the impact of World War I and the origins of World War II. But it is also important because of the massive Russian Civil War (which may have killed more people than World War I did) and the smaller wars fought by Europeans in Turkey, Morocco, Spain, and elsewhere. Seeing this period as a time of peace between two horrible periods of war very much misses the point of these years. The origins of World War II do not simply begin with Hitler's rise to power in 1933 nor even with the end of World War I in 1918. Recent attempts by some historians to see the period 1914–1945 as "Europe's Second Thirty Years' War" help to clarify some patterns of the period. Here I take my cue from them in trying to see the period as a whole rather than as discrete and unconnected parts.

Chapter 5 examines the outbreak and origins of World War II less from the perspective of diplomacy than through the lens of societal values. It is my contention in this book that one cannot understand a society's military and strategic decisions without understanding that nation's fundamental systems of belief. Nowhere is this pattern more evident than in Nazi Germany. Germany's entire war was based on the extension of a series of core ideas, most of them built upon the belief that as members of a supposedly superior race, the Germans had a right to do whatever they wished to do to members of lesser races. Without an understanding of these beliefs, Germany's behavior in World War II makes little sense.

Chapter 6 addresses the end of World War II and examines it by analyzing the nature of alliances. Here, as elsewhere, I examine the impact of war on less well-studied nations such as Holland, Poland, and Norway. Their histories were shaped every bit as much by war as those of the major combatants. Rather than trying to cover the entire history of warfare within these nations, I have used them to explore themes such as collaboration, resistance, and the impact of war on historical development. This chapter also examines the growing power of the United States and the Soviet Union. The years 1941–1945 saw them grow from powers to superpowers.

Chapter 7 examines the development of two separate sets of conflicts. The first is the European wars to retain colonial empires and fight communist-inspired revolutions. The second is the Cold War. Although the second half of the century saw much less fighting on European soil than did the first half, the years since 1945 have not been entirely peaceful. They have seen the extension of alliance warfare into peacetime (with the formation of NATO and the Warsaw Pact) and the continuing intrusion of warfare into the general economic, social, and political patterns of European society.

Finally, the book concludes with a brief discussion of warfare since 1989. This section is necessarily brief and speculative because the patterns have not yet fully emerged. Historians normally treat the recent past with a great deal of trepidation and I am no exception here. Nevertheless, I link warfare since the end of the Cold War to the patterns I have explored in this present volume. It is, of course, possible that between the time I finish this book and the time you read it events may transpire to call into question my conclusions. Such is the nature of writing the history of the recent past.

One further word of explanation is important. I have attempted to be as precise as possible in my use of language. I have tried to use "German" when I mean "German" and "Nazi" when I mean "Nazi." I have also tried to use "Russian" and "Soviet" in the same manner. Nevertheless, here and elsewhere it is often difficult to make distinctions. Is, for example, a Ukrainian who loathes the Soviet system but nevertheless lives inside the boundaries of the USSR a "Soviet"? Here I have used a political definition and assumed so. As discussed in Chapter 7, the rhetorical division of Nazi and German has served an important historical and political function since 1933 though in reality making the distinction is difficult to do. I have tried to be as careful as I can be when choosing my terms.

At the end of each chapter, I have presented the reader with a brief list of works to consult for further reading. I hope that these selections will serve as a starting point for those interested in particular topics. Good general introductions to the history of warfare that include a focus on the modern period include Jeremy Black, *Warfare in the Western World, 1882–1975* (Bloomington: Indiana University Press, 2002) and *War: Past, Present, and Future* (New York: St Martin's, 2000). See also Michael Howard, *War in European History* (Oxford: Oxford University Press, 1977); Brian Bond, *War and Society in Europe, 1870–1970* (London: Sutton, 1984); Hew Strachan, *European Armies and the Conduct of War* (London: Routledge, 1983); and Michael Neiberg, *Warfare in World History* (London: Routledge, 2001).

In writing this book, I have relied heavily on the archival and primary research of many fine scholars. I have made every effort to cite them and their works either in the notes or in the suggestions for further reading. I would like to thank Jeremy Black for inviting me to write this book and for his family's gracious hospitality during my visit to Exeter. I also wish to thank John Abbatiello and Dave and Dawn Jardini for their equally gracious hospitality in London. William Philpott and one anonymous reviewer provided me with helpful suggestions.

As always, Dennis Showalter provided me with a sounding board and a keen set of eyes. I thank him and William J. Astore for reading this manuscript and for providing outstanding commentary. John Jennings shared his immense knowledge of the Russian Civil War with me. Ed Kaplan helped me clear up the finer points of the Cold War. Balkan veterans Vance Skarstedt and Mark Witzel helped me understand the complexities of that troubled region. If any errors remain they are mine alone.

My deepest debts are, as always, to my wife Barbara and my daughter Claire for putting up with my periodic absences both in Europe and in front of a book or a computer. As I conclude the writing of this book, we are awaiting travel permissions to go to China to adopt our second daughter. I dedicate this book to that little girl, wherever she may be, with love.

# 1

# FROM FASHODA TO
# SARAJEVO

## Africa, alliances, and Agadir

On July 10, 1898 a French force of seven European officers and 120 Senegalese soldiers under the command of Major Jean Baptiste Marchand arrived at the fortified oasis of Fashoda in modern-day Sudan. Marchand had risen from the ranks and therefore was almost custom-made for fame in a Third Republic France suspicious of its own entrenched military officers. He had played a key role in the French conquest of West Africa and had taken charge of the expedition to extend French influence east to the Nile River. His arrival at Fashoda created a surge of patriotism badly needed in a country still suffering from its humiliation at the hands of the Germans in the Franco-Prussian War of 1870–1871, the aftershocks of the bloody civil war known as the Paris Commune that followed, and the enduring scandal known as the Dreyfus Affair. Marchand's arrival at Fashoda seemed to usher in a new era of French glory at the expense of France's long-standing rival, the British Empire.

If Marchand was the ready-made hero, Britain seemed an equally ready-made foe. Anti-British sentiment had been rising in France, partially due to colonial rivalry in Africa. German policy after 1871 encouraged French expansion in Africa, both to shift France's focus from continental issues and to strengthen existing Anglo-French tensions. By encouraging French expansion in Africa at the Berlin Conference of 1884–1885, Germany placed two of its main rivals on a potential collision course with one another. This policy seemed to be paying dividends as French and British interests clashed at Fashoda.

Horatio Herbert Kitchener, one of Great Britain's rising military stars, was an ironic choice to change that situation. In 1898 he seemed to be acting in Germany's interest by challenging the French position at Fashoda, but in 1870 he had volunteered to fight for France against the Prussians. Since then, he had become a veritable stereotype of the British colonial officer; his image later graced countless World War I recruitment posters. Between 1871 and 1898, he rose to become the commander of the Anglo-Egyptian Army and won a major victory at Omdurman in September, 1898, recovering Khartoum from the anti-imperial Mahdists. One of his junior officers in this campaign was a young volunteer named Winston Churchill. After that victory, Kitchener turned a small part of his force toward Fashoda, determined to win it back for the British Empire.

The stage seemed set for a major clash of French and British forces. Popular opinion on both sides of the English Channel clamored for war. Anglo-French relations deteriorated to their lowest point since Waterloo. Kitchener and Marchand both received orders from their respective governments not to back down. France's foreign minister, Théophile Delcassé, had been one of the organizers of the Marchand mission and supported a wider French sphere of influence in Africa. Like most Frenchmen, his initial response to the crisis was to dig in his heels and prepare for the worst. As the two nations began preparations for battle, Europe seemed ready for war once again.

Delcassé wanted to remove the British barrier to a French African empire, but he was more fearful of Germany. He was therefore a vigorous supporter of closer French links to Russia as a means of creating a two-front problem for the German military. A crisis between Britain and France could lead the former into an alliance with Germany, the nation virtually all Frenchmen saw as their most insatiable enemy. An Anglo-German alliance was a far more dangerous prospect for France than losing Fashoda. How, then, could Delcassé get France out of this predicament with its self-image intact, especially with French popular opinion in favor of war as the best method by which to recover its honor? "The problem," Delcassé insightfully wrote during the crisis, "is to harmonize the exigencies of national honor with the avoidance of a naval war we are in no position to fight."[1]

Paul Cambon, France's ambassador in London, found a way out. He convinced Delcassé to accept a British proposal that promised to resolve the Fashoda impasse without war. France agreed to withdraw from Egypt and the Sudan in exchange for British recognition of Morocco as a French sphere of influence. The bargain cost Britain almost nothing, as they had little influence in Morocco anyway. In return the British were now masters of the Nile River and its Sudanese watersheds. Although they had to cede Fashoda to the British, France had been able to gain a Moroccan foothold that was much closer to home than the Sudan. Despite public clamor for an armed resolution to the crisis, cooler heads had prevailed. The two sides then began talks designed to lead to an agreement that would balance out the Triple Alliance (signed in 1882) of Germany, Austria-Hungary, and Italy. The result was a tectonic shift in European affairs that completed the alliance system that went to war in 1914.

The alliance that emerged from the "Spirit of Fashoda," the Entente Cordiale of 1904, fell far short of a mutual defense pact. Nevertheless it formalized friendly relations between Britain and France and thereby revolutionized European diplomacy. "With this act old animosities were buried, past humiliations forgotten, new cooperation and support pledged."[2] The British and French navies could now look upon one another as potential allies rather than as a rivals.

11

Moreover, because the Dual Alliance of 1894 linked Russia and France, the Entente Cordiale opened a door for Anglo-Russian cooperation as well. In 1907 the Triple Entente linked all three nations into a system that reduced colonial tensions around the globe in the hopes of avoiding future misunderstandings like the one at Fashoda. Militarily, the continent's largest army and the world's most powerful navy had forged a linkage. It also linked France to both, vastly increasing French power and security.

Despite the alliance's unpopularity with the British left (which distrusted the Tsar's despotism) and the British right (which feared that an alliance might be accompanied by restricted freedom of action), the Entente Cordiale had much to recommend it. During Britain's frustrating war in South Africa against the Boers (1899–1902), the British found that their "splendid isolation" policy of not involving themselves in alliances had left them alone and increasingly unpopular. It took the British nearly three years and 500,000 men to defeat a guerrilla force that was never one-tenth as large as their own forces in South Africa. British policies of concentrating Boer families into camps made them a virtual international pariah. An alliance with Russia and France provided diplomatic support and helped to return Britain to equal status in the community of European nations.

The Entente Cordiale also gave Britain a chance to absorb the military lessons of the Boer War. British forces in South Africa suffered 30,000 casualties at the hands of determined, though amateurish, Boer rifle fire. The casualties that the British had suffered at the hands of relatively unsophisticated white settlers underscored the potency of modern firepower; the Boers had used modern magazine rifles and machine guns, some of them provided by Germany. In the years following the war, the British reformed their general staff and began making plans to create an expeditionary force capable of being deployed almost anywhere in the Empire or, if need be, onto the continent of Europe itself.

The insurgency in South Africa was just one of the national security concerns facing Britain at the turn of the century. Continental events frightened the British enough to want to avoid a repeat of the diplomatic isolation of the Boer War years. The growth of the German Navy was by far the most important of these events. Around the time of Fashoda, Kaiser Wilhelm II and his ambitious senior admiral, Alfred von Tirpitz, had begun a program to create a German High Seas Fleet that they expected would eventually be powerful enough to challenge and perhaps even defeat the British in a major battleship clash. German naval growth frightened the British public enough to support dramatic increases in naval expenditures. A wave of popular fiction that riveted the British public with vivid tales of German amphibious landings on the south coast of England stirred popular fears and helped to reenergize traditional British navalism.

The British were willing and able to meet the Germans ship for ship and even increase their edge, both quantitatively and qualitatively. In 1906, the British introduced the most powerful ship yet built, HMS *Dreadnought*. This revolutionary ship had modern nickel-steel alloy armor that was lighter than previous armors, enabling the ship's powerful diesel engines to propel it at record speeds. Its 12-inch rotating turret guns could destroy any ship in the water without even getting within range of the guns on enemy warships. British opinion demanded even more dreadnoughts (as all ships of this type became known) than the admiralty had originally planned to build. Britain had already developed a "two power standard" that pledged them to build a navy equivalent to the combined fleets of Europe's next two largest powers. *Dreadnought's* ability to render obsolete all other warships changed this calculus, but Britain's desire to maintain its naval superiority did not change. Thus as Germany built dreadnoughts, Britain outbuilt them until the Royal Navy had a 20 to 13 advantage in dreadnoughts by 1914. The Royal Navy also enjoyed advantages of 102 to 41 in cruisers and 301 to 144 in destroyers.

Nevertheless, lavish spending on the Grand Fleet did not solve the problem of projecting power onto the European continent. As the French were fond of reminding their British allies, the Royal Navy would not be worth a single bayonet in a land war on the continent. The British therefore sought agreements with continental powers such as Russia and France, whose sizeable armies could balance their own naval strength and compensate for the small size of their professional army.

Because the Franco-British alliance lasted (albeit at times somewhat uneasily) through two world wars and a cold war it seems almost natural in retrospect, but its achievement was both surprising and unlikely. France and Britain were longstanding rivals. Although they had fought on the same side in the Crimean War (1854–1856), the experience had been less than pleasant, characterized by endemic Franco-British squabbling and a rather impolitic British decision to launch a major offensive on the fortieth anniversary of Waterloo. Great Britain had stood neutral in the Franco-Prussian War, angering many in France who had expected Britain to help mediate more lenient terms. Colonial rivalry further increased the tensions. French sentiment remained anti-British for many years after Fashoda, partly as a result of British conduct in the Boer War. Still, the advantages of working together and avoiding future Fashodas appeared manifest to both sides. In 1903 King Edward VII symbolized the new era of Franco-British amity with a high visibility state visit to Paris, where he was met by enthusiastic crowds wherever he went.

An alliance between Russia and Britain also had much to recommend it. Both nations were experiencing "imperial overstretch" and looked to reduce their global commitments. Furthermore, as noted earlier, Russia's tremendous army nicely complemented Britain's powerful navy. The combination, many hoped, would deter Germany both on land and at sea. The Triple Entente also led to the resolution of Anglo-Russian disputes in Persia, allowing the British to reduce the amount of military resources needed to defend India. Russia could also remove a potential threat to their Central Asian interests and regroup and rebuild following their catastrophic defeat in the Russo-Japanese War of

1904–1905. Each side could now rule out the other as a potential rival and focus on new challenges.

It is an axiom of diplomacy that alliances hold together only in the face of a sufficient common threat. For the signatories of the Triple Entente, that threat was Germany. As a result of the Wars of German Unification, a new, powerful state existed in central Europe. Lightning victories over Denmark (1864), Austria (1866), and France (1870–1871) had united the German states and principalities under Prussian suzerainty. Relatively lenient treatment of Austria had left Germany not with a bitter foe, but an ally, solidified in the Austro-German alliance of 1879. In the years that followed, German industrial growth combined with an unusually influential military to remake the balance of power in Europe. This tremendous and rapid growth intoxicated German leaders, most notably Kaiser Wilhelm II, to seek even greater glories. Despite the powerful presence of the Royal Navy in the North Sea, a bitter and resentful France to the west, and a massive, if maladroit, Russian giant to the east, Germany dreamed of further conquests.

Kaiser Wilhelm II, who assumed the Hohenzollern throne in 1888, was the inheritor of the proud Prussian military tradition, but he lacked the skills necessary to follow in that tradition. He was blustery, indecisive, and committed to personal rule. He was also childishly envious of the power and wealth of his British cousins. The Kaiser's decision to build his High Seas Fleet emerged partly from his own insecurity in relation to the British. His grandmother, England's Queen Victoria, once described him as "a hot-headed, conceited and wrong-headed young man."[3] It was an opinion that many in Europe's ruling class shared. He dismissed Germany's masterful diplomat and chancellor Otto von Bismarck in 1890 and, as a result, his relationship with nations that Bismarck had carefully courted (most importantly Russia) suffered. French diplomats saw the Russo-German rupture and gladly stepped in to become Russia's principal alliance partner. If the Kaiser thus complained that Germany was "encircled," it was largely by a noose of his own creation.

To slip that noose, the Kaiser set his expansionist aims on Morocco, where a major diplomatic coup might achieve spectacular results at home and abroad. In 1905 the Kaiser arrived in Tangier and spoke in favor of independence for Morocco. He had hoped to pressure Britain into backing off from its Fashoda era commitments to French control of the area and therefore show the Entente Cordiale to be worthless. With Russia absorbed by its war with Japan, the Kaiser hoped that his timing would isolate France from its other main ally as well. Moreover, by supporting Moroccan independence, he also hoped that Moroccan goodwill might help to establish a German naval base on the Atlantic Ocean, thus providing another outlet for the large navy that the Germans were then in the process of building. That navy needed an Atlantic port because of the ease with which the Royal Navy could bottle it up from the North Sea.

Social and domestic factors played a role in the Kaiser's thinking as well. Germany's left-leaning parties had been gaining significant ground (they became a majority in the Reichstag by 1912) and with that growth came opposition to a budgetary process that led to a 142 percent rise in defense spending between 1905 and 1914. The Kaiser and conservative groups inside Germany hoped that an international crisis could unite the nation behind the monarchy.[4]

Because of the Kaiser's diplomatic clumsiness, German policy in Morocco produced almost the direct opposite result from what the Kaiser and his advisors had sought. Britain, France, and Russia presented a united front, rejecting American President Theodore Roosevelt's offer of mediation and allowing France to continue its predominant role in Moroccan affairs. German bellicosity had frightened Britain enough to induce the first Anglo-French military staff talks in January, 1906. The following year, the British formally created the British Expeditionary Force (BEF) designed to facilitate the rapid deployment of an army onto the continent. Beginning in 1909 senior French and British officers visited one another's staff colleges each year and attended annual maneuvers. While they shied away from direct joint planning, these visits allowed the leaders of the two armies to develop relationships that paid important dividends during World War I.

The Kaiser's dispatch of a German warship to the Moroccan port of Agadir caused a second Moroccan crisis in 1911. Once again, France and Britain held firm together amidst widespread fears of war. The crisis revealed that the preparations made by France and Britain were inadequate should a similar future crisis spark war. While formal joint military planning was still anathema to both Britain and France, the two alliance partners took a significant step forward in 1912 when they signed a naval agreement that gave Great Britain the responsibility of securing the North Sea and France the responsibility of securing the Mediterranean. Britain could thus shift significant naval assets from the Mediterranean to the North Sea, increasing the already substantial force it had there and making any German forays out of their bases even more risky than before.

The two Moroccan crises had important ramifications on the domestic front as well. German failure to break the Entente only strengthened the power of the socialist opposition, threatening future military appropriations and forcing the Kaiser to find ways around his own legislature. By World War I he had managed to make the Reichstag virtually impotent in matters of military budgeting. He also came to rely on the advice of his generals much more than did any other European head of state. Germany was well on its way to the autocratic, military dictatorship that it had devolved to by the end of World War I.

## Nationalism, alliances, and war plans

Nationalism, nineteenth-century Europe's most important intellectual force, had many meanings in pre-war Europe and all of them contributed to the rising tensions of the period. Nationalism was a flexible ideology, useable by both the left and the right. All forms of nationalism argued for the distinct nature of a given group based on similarities such as religion, ethnicity, language, and history. Some Europeans, such as the Italian Giuseppe Garibaldi and French Emperor Napoleon III, believed that Europe could not enter into a period of true peace and prosperity until each nation attained self-determination; thus (ironically enough) Napoleon III at first supported German unification. Garibaldi extended his ideology across the globe, fighting in South America and receiving acclaim from Abraham Lincoln, who offered him a command during the American Civil War.

Nationalists were most outraged by political boundaries within which fellow nationals were living under regimes that did not represent them. Thus Slavs opposed Austro-Hungarian rule over Slavic areas and sought to establish a Slavic state in southern Europe. Of course, this logic posed a mortal threat to the very existence of the Austro-Hungarian Empire, based as it was on a dizzying variety of mutually antagonistic ethnic groupings. Many senior Austro-Hungarian officials argued that a centrally controlled empire was the only way to prevent these groups from turning the Balkans into a perpetually war-torn area. To them, nationalism had to be stopped and Serbian support for a Slavic state had to be crushed.

Nationalism served as the most important cause of the two Balkan Wars, fought in 1912 and 1913. The First Balkan War in 1912–1913 pitted Bulgaria, Serbia, Montenegro, and Greece (together called the Balkan League) against the Ottoman Empire. The Second Balkan War in 1913 pitted Bulgaria against its erstwhile allies. Building upon past glories and mythic histories, the nations of the Balkan League united to expel Ottoman forces from what they saw as their rightful territory. Bulgaria's large, well-trained army and the Greek navy's control of the Aegean Sea proved too powerful a combination for the extended Ottomans, who had also recently lost Libya to the Italians. The Ottoman Empire, the so-called "sick man" of Europe, appeared increasingly weak and unable to control their far-flung empire.

Once the expulsion of the Ottomans from most of Europe had been completed, however, the members of the Balkan League began to fight among one another for the spoils. Their alliance had been a temporary marriage of convenience at best. Even as they fought alongside one another against the Ottomans, they were squabbling over the exact boundaries of their "national" territory. For most Balkan nations, World War I was just another round in the fighting that had characterized the region for years. It is perhaps more accurate to describe World War I in this region as the Third Balkan War.

The end of hostilities in 1913 therefore put only a temporary halt to military action in the region. A reform movement in the Ottoman Empire, called the Young Turk Movement, gained popularity by calling for an aggressive rebuilding of the Ottoman Army in order to revive Turkish glory. The Ottomans invited Western European advisors to help reshape their nation's economic and military infrastructures. The increasing dominance of Germans among these advisors furthered Great Power rivalries. Neither Great Britain nor Russia

16

looked favorably upon a seamless "Berlin to Baghdad" link that could threaten their spheres of influence in Central Asia.

Consequently, tensions in the Balkans remained high. The Ottomans, Austrians and Russians all had direct interests in the region. After 1912, these traditional pressures combined with increasing interest from Germany, France, and Great Britain. Several statesmen believed that the instability of the region had the potential to spark a continental war. Germany's iron-willed chancellor, Otto von Bismarck, coined the phrase "Balkan Powder Keg" as early as 1877. He later spoke for many when he responded to a question about what might start the next large European war; he replied "some damn fool thing in the Balkans."

Almost by definition, nationalists in the Balkans and elsewhere were xenophobes who argued for the inherent superiority of their cultural identity. Insults, perceived and real, to that identity thus took on the character of an insult to an entire people. Individuals, for instance Paul Cambon, felt national tragedies like the loss of Alsace and Lorraine "as a personal loss, a kind of dis-honor."[5] Moreover, national borders (unlike state borders) were impossible to define. Discerning the line between an ethnically "Bosnian" area and an ethnically "Serbian" one was not possible because no reasonable consensus between rival groups could be reached. Thus familiarity continued to breed discontent. The Balkan Wars became a grand stage for avenging age-old insults. One international commission that examined the Second Balkan War concluded that it had been unusually cruel, especially to civilians. The commissioners noted that the conduct of the war was "as desperate as though extermination were the end sought."[6]

In many respects the trend toward alliances was rather at odds with the ascendant nationalism of the pre-war years. Alliances require a state to yield some of its own decision-making ability in the interest of honoring its commit-ments to its alliance partner. Most alliances required a signatory to come to the aid of an alliance partner if attacked, whether that signatory's direct interests were threatened or not. As the events of 1914 later showed, such alliances can drag a reluctant nation into a war not in its own direct interests. For these reasons, extreme nationalists across Europe often voiced their opposition to alli-ances, especially in Great Britain, where the Royal Navy served as an important shield from the sullied affairs of the continent.

Alliances can also create uncomfortable domestic situations. Many French and British socialists, for example, objected to an alliance that bound them to the strategic goals of autocratic Russia. Indeed, nationalism made some alliances impossible. An alliance between Austria-Hungary and Russia, the protector of the Slavic minority inside the Austro-Hungarian empire, would have been unacceptable to nationalists on both sides. Similarly, Italy's joining of the Triple Alliance in 1882 could never resolve that state's core discontent with Austrian possession of two ethnically Italian areas, the Trentino to the north and the cities of Trieste and Fiume to the east. To the surprise of no one in Europe, Italy failed to fulfill its treaty obligations in 1914, arguing that since Austria-Hungary had been the aggressor against Serbia, they had no commitment to honor. In 1915 Italy instead signed the Treaty of London and declared war on Austria. In return, Britain and France were pleased to promise Italy the lands they desired since these areas came at Austria-Hungary's expense. Britain and France later reneged on these promises, sowing the seeds of Italian discontent and the post-war rise of Fascism.

Despite their unpopularity with many domestic constituencies, alliances seemed to promise the best protection from potential foes. As long as Germany seemed sufficiently threatening, the Triple Entente held together despite the obvious compromises and tensions inherent in the relationship. Charles Péguy, a prominent intellectual critic of the French army during the Dreyfus Affair, had cause to reconsider his opposition to military preparedness after the first Moroccan crisis. "Everyone suddenly realized that the menace of a German invasion exists," he wrote, "that it could really happen."[7] Alliances seemed the best way either to deter such an invasion or help a nation survive one.

Alliances could also lead to profitable business arrangements. France invested heavily in Russian railways in order to improve Russian mobilization times. The French made money and improved their alliance relationships while the Russians received a modern rail network to facilitate movement across their vast spaces and also created thousands of jobs to calm their restive working classes. Germany's dream of a Berlin-to-Baghdad railway promised the same for its allies, though it fell short of the goal of creating a seamless link from Germany through Austria-Hungary to the outer reaches of the Ottoman Empire.

From the German perspective, the Triple Entente confirmed perceptions of an "encirclement" that threatened further German expansion. An alliance with Austria-Hungary offered only modest support as the Austro-Hungarian empire was rife with problems of its own. Military preparations there had to be approved by both the ethnically German-dominated parliament in Austria and the Magyar-dominated parliament in Budapest. The empire's officers were disproportionately German, a dominance that the Magyars, theoretical equals in the empire, particularly resented. Both armies relied heavily on ethnic minorities to fill out the ranks, with the Austrians forced to employ large numbers of Czechs, Ruthenes, Poles, Slavs and Croats, none of whom they completely trusted. The Austro-Hungarian armed forces were thus fragile instruments, a factor that played heavily in Emperor Franz Joseph's decision not to intervene in the Balkan Wars.

Nationalism could also be defensive in character, with, to cite one of Europe's most incendiary examples, the French always on the lookout for "Prussian" aggression. They had to look no further than Alsace and the parts of Lorraine seized by the Germans in 1870. The Germans there had banned the teaching of French and stamped out as many elements of French culture as they could. Alsace and Lorraine became terrible harbingers to French nationalists, who saw in German treatment of the two provinces a German plan for France's future.

18

By the time of World War I, however, Alsace and Lorraine had been in German hands for more than forty years. Young French conscripts had never known the provinces as a part of their nation. Moreover, France had long since abandoned the idea of an offensive war to reacquire the regions. Still, Alsace and Lorraine became ever-present symbols of what could happen to France under German rule. Léon Gambetta's plea to his countrymen, "speak of them [Alsace and Lorraine] never, think of them always" underscored the important symbolic value of their loss. French maps continued to include the provinces within French boundaries and the statue of the city of Strasbourg (Alsace's capital) in Paris's Place de la Concorde remained wrapped in a black shroud. If France was not willing to go to war to reacquire Alsace and Lorraine, the provinces nevertheless remained a potent symbol of the dangers of German nationalism. After the two Moroccan crises, concern over the Lost Provinces increased.

If nationalism could thus unite, it could also divide. Mobilization posters in the Austro-Hungarian empire in 1914 were printed in fifteen languages.[8] The multi-ethnic Ottoman Empire faced similar problems, as did Italy. Although recently united into a single state, the regions of Italy continued to see themselves as culturally and linguistically distinct. Disaffection between southerners and northerns was particularly intense. Southerners resented the dominance of Lombards and Piedmontese at the upper levels of the military and government. Racial stereotypes about Sicilians, Calabrians, and other southerners persisted in the north, leaving Italy with important domestic tensions. The demoralizing trouncing of an Italian force in Ethiopia in 1896 did little to encourage national feeling. Even in nationalistic France, so many soldiers spoke local dialects (or in the case of the Bretons, a Celtic language incomprehensible to most Frenchmen) that NCOs and officers could not always conduct training in the "national" language.

Nationalism also affected debates on how to organize and staff a military to an extent that remains poorly examined. In Britain, for example, lingering fears about standing armies and abiding faith in the Royal Navy combined to resist the general continental trend toward conscription. Although individual soldiers such as Kitchener and Sir Frederick Roberts became great heroes, the British public remained suspicious of an entrenched military and the uses to which it might be put. Even a man of Roberts's folk legend stature could not convince the British to institute conscription despite his vehement advocacy of it until his death in 1913.

Domestic crises also intruded on the public view of the army. In 1914, 57 British officers threatened to resign rather than march against Ulster unionists (many of whose leaders were retired Army officers) in the event of a government declaration of Home Rule for Ireland. Many senior officers not involved in the incident indicated their willingness to resign if the government punished the ringleaders. The so-called Curragh Incident suggested that the British Army was not as apolitical as many had believed. Even the King, himself no friend of Home Rule, called the incident a "disastrous and irreparable catastrophe."[9]

Incidents such as Curragh cast long shadows. Field Marshal Sir John French, who had resigned his post as Chief of the Imperial General Staff in protest against what he saw as the army's mutinous behavior, raised his stock in the eyes of many British politicians by remaining loyal to the government. Upon the outbreak of World War I, he was recalled to duty and given command of the British Expeditionary Force despite his questionable qualifications for such an important post and the disdain in which many senior British officers held him. British concerns about the willingness of officers to obey orders thus played an important, and often overlooked, role in high-level decision-making.

Even in militaristic Germany, which faced a large Russian rival to the east, social and domestic pressures combined to limit army growth. Many conservatives feared that an expansion of the army would require an unacceptable reliance on non-aristocratic officers. The army had become the most important institution for social advancement for the Junkers, German aristocrats whose agricultural estates could not yield wealth to match that of Germany's growing urban bourgeoisie. The army thus became an important means of societal compensation that the Junkers were unwilling to share. They successfully devised ways to limit the bourgeoisie's representation at the highest ranks and effectively banned Jews and other "suspect" groups altogether.

In France, a nation with a long history of suspicion toward centralized authority in general and the military in particular, two important military models emerged. Social conservatives, Germanophobes, and senior military officers preferred a continental-style conscript army large enough and professional enough to deter and, if necessary, defeat, Germany. The Dreyfus Affair, a scandal that lasted from 1894 to 1906, undermined this approach by discrediting the army as a reactionary, anti-republican instrument. As a result, many left-leaning French nationalists came to believe that the French army was as great a threat to French liberty as any foreign force.

With popular opinion running against the army, the French left successfully resisted the wider European trend toward a professional conscript army for fear of developing a large force that could be used to threaten civil liberties. Socialists and even many conservative republicans recalled the heavy-handed domestic use of the military that characterized Napoleon III's Second Empire, when the phrase "militarism" first came into general usage. They therefore mistrusted a large standing army almost as much as their English allies did.

Instead, they supported a militia constituted of men who would compensate for their relative lack of military training and skill with patriotism and élan. Many supporters of this ideal, such as the charismatic and popular Socialist leader Jean Jaurès, also saw the militia's non-professionalism as a benefit. Because of the minimal mandatory training it would require, the young men of the French militia would not be exposed to the allegedly rampant corruption, clericalism, and anti-republicanism of the barracks. Moreover, such an army would be insufficient for building and maintaining an empire, thus appealing to France's anti-imperialists. Jaurès and others successfully limited France's mandatory military service to two years until Germany's 1913 decision to expand its standing army to 200,000 men. In August of that year, after a tumultuous debate, France responded by increasing the mandatory term of service to three years despite Jaurès's continued opposition.[10]

French fears of their own military officers had important ramifications. France did not create a war college until 1876 and did not appoint a true chief of the general staff until 1890. As late as 1911 that chief still did not have the *ex officio* responsibility of commanding the French armies in the event of hostilities. In all of these areas, France was considerably behind its most important potential enemy, Germany. Also unlike Germany, France's civilian war ministry sometimes acted as a governmental check on its own officers, assembling secret folders on their political and religious affiliations and basing promotions in large part on that information rather than on military fitness reports.

Thus one cannot assume that military efficiency was the most important guiding principle in determining military policy. Domestic societal factors played critical roles as well. Fears of standing armies and tensions in civil–military relations limited and guided the choices available to politicians and generals. In some nations, such as Great Britain, they made certain types of military policies, such as conscription, impossible. In others, such as Spain, they virtually forced the leadership to renounce any pretensions to great power status. Austria-Hungary continued in its pretensions, which the events of 1914–1918 showed to be little more than delusions.

Nationalism combined with the ideology of Social Darwinism to create a very perilous mix. In brief, Social Darwinism argued that human races and nations were involved in the same struggle for existence that characterized animal and plant species. Taken to extremes, this ideology argued that those groups that did not expand, by force if necessary, would wither and fade away. It allowed European nationalists to justify their colonial expansions at the expense of Asians and Africans on the basis that they were simply acting within the "natural order" of human activity.

On a larger scale, Social Darwinism provided a rationale for popular support of overseas expansion. By virtue of membership in the white race, any Englishman or Dutchman or Belgian immediately attained superiority over the subjects of their empires. As the nation benefited, they, too, benefited. As a result, gains in the empire reflected a personal triumph and helped to link men and women to their nation and their empire. This linkage helps to explain the explosion of national feelings during crises like Fashoda and Morocco.

The ideology of Social Darwinism had more influence on elites and the bourgeoisie than it did among the peasantry and working classes. Still, the emphasis on competition, what the American industrialist John Rockefeller called "a law of God," had a pervasive influence on turn-of-the-century mindsets. All national disputes, like the ones in the Sudan or Morocco, could therefore seem to be about much more than arcane diplomatic questions or colonial expansion. They could seem vital to the very life or death of the nation. In this way, Social Darwinism and the emphasis on competition between nations, states, and races fanned the flames of controversies of Fashoda, Morocco, and several others.

This perception of mortal threat helps to explain much of the rush to war that every belligerent nation in Europe experienced in 1914. Once the war began, even internationally minded groups such as the Socialists joined in the euphoria. Labor unions, often at odds with the state before 1914, also supported war as necessary to the defense of the nation.[11] Their ability to distinguish between defending the governmental apparatus of the state, which they often abhorred, and the more amorphous nation, which they saw as indissoluble from their most cherished values, proved to be critical. The willingness of men to see war as "a war for justice and liberty, not of imperial aggrandizement" would not have been possible without the powerful influences of nationalism and Social Darwinism.[12] These ideologies made every nation, even the German aggressors, believe that they were fighting for their ultimate survival.

The general mood reflected popular enthusiasm for war. The few opponents of war in the summer of 1914 appeared increasingly anti-patriotic. One of France's skeptics was Jean Jaurès, the Socialist leader of the opposition to the three-year conscription law. On June 29, Jaurès delivered a speech in Brussels denouncing the fervor for war then sweeping the continent. "Humanity is accursed," he said, "if to prove its courage it is condemned to perpetual slaughter."[13] Two days later, he was assassinated in a Parisian café by a fanatical right-wing Frenchman angered by Jaurès's opposition to the war. Oddly enough, the French media turned Jaurès into a national martyr, the first of the war for France. *La Guerre Socialiste*'s headline read: "National Defense above all! They have assassinated Jaurès! We will not assassinate France!"[14] Even the war's opponents had become symbols for its prosecution.

Social Darwinism and the emphasis on competition also affected the nature of war planning. The dominant interpretation of Prussian success in the Wars of German Unification argued that the lightning victories of the Prussian forces between 1864 and 1871 had been due to superior planning. As a result, every nation in Europe created general staffs more or less along Prussian lines (the United States followed suit in 1903). These staffs were responsible for a managerial revolution in warfare. They envisioned the nature of future wars, planned for them, and created synergistic links with relevant civilian agencies like railways and industry. The staffs also brought together the finest (though as we will see still imperfect) minds of a nation's military and created communities within which ideas about the future of warfare could be shared and analyzed.

In the years before World War I each of these staffs created rigid war plans designed to be activated at a moment's notice. When war threatened in 1914, these plans forced political decision-makers to cede considerable authority to their militaries because few politicians understood the intricate details and military technicalities involved. Because their common emphasis was on mobilizing and deploying forces more quickly than their opponents, these plans also sped up the timetables for making critical decisions. Few people foresaw the chain reaction that such planning would create in the event that cooler heads could not prevail as they had during the Moroccan and Balkan crises. Instead, each side's soldiers were obsessed with the belief that to cede the initiative to the other side would be to court disaster. General Joseph Joffre, principal author of France's Plan XVII, warned his government that every day's delay in ordering the execution of his plan would cost France twenty kilometers of territory.

War plans therefore focused on speed. Most important was the period known as mobilization, or the time between a declaration of war and a nation's ability to deploy its armies in the field and ready for combat. During the period of mobilization, reservists had to be informed of the declaration of war and notified of the assembly point for their unit, all in an age before the extensive use of telephones or radios. These men then had to be retrained for war, given weapons with which they may not have been familiar, and rushed to combat zones. Failure to do so as quickly as possible could be catastrophic. As the Prussians proved in 1870, the ability to assemble units rapidly provided a crucial advantage in the early stages of a war.

Germany's war plan counted on speed and efficiency to solve the essential two-front dilemma of the German position. It called for a lightning attack of seven of Germany's eight armies through France with the goal of forcing a French surrender within six weeks. The German army would then be able to avoid a two-front war and turn its attention to the Russians, whom they presumed would be slower to mobilize. After the rapid defeat of the French, the plan called for the German armies to entrain and rapidly redeploy across Germany to the Russian front in time to stop any advance from the east. The plan required absolutely everything to go according to schedule and it presumed that the Austrians would play a major role in slowing down any unexpectedly quick Russian action. In the event, Germany's precise timetable did not hold and Austria proved to be of little help on the Russian frontier.

The emphasis on speed also led the plan's principal author, Count Alfred von Schlieffen, to propose violating the neutrality of Belgium in order to get around the north flank of the French army. His plan necessitated the invasion of a country that was heavily defended, as Belgium possessed some of the continent's best fortifications. Although Belgium's army was small, its fortifications threatened to delay the advance of any invading army. Still, Schlieffen and his successors saw the invasion of Belgium as necessary in order to avoid attacking the French along their front and their impressive line of fortified cities that ran west of the Vosges Mountains from Verdun to Belfort.

The plan was likely to force a response from Great Britain as well, since the British had guaranteed the neutrality of Belgium through an 1839 treaty. The treaty itself mattered considerably less than British desires to deny Germany control of Belgium's ports. That concern was so great that the Belgians considered a British violation of their neutrality almost as likely as a German violation. Any British military response to a German invasion of Belgium was likely to come in one of two forms, either the landing of their small, but highly skilled, army into Belgium or a blockade by the awesome Royal Navy. German planners largely disregarded the former, with the Kaiser dismissing the British army as a band of "old contemptibles," but the Germans had good reason to fear the latter. A British blockade would cause significant problems for a nation that was dependent on imports for a large proportion of both food and industrial goods. The fear of blockade was another reason for the Germans to focus on winning a quick war or risk not winning at all.

Schlieffen's replacement, Helmuth von Moltke, the younger (nephew of his namesake, the architect of Prussia's victories from 1864 to 1871), did not care for many aspects of the plan, but he kept it anyway. Moltke was a good deal more perceptive (and nervous) than Schlieffen and more clearly saw the tremendous risks that his predecessor's plan entailed. He also did not share the blind faith in the German army that Schlieffen possessed. "I will do what I can," he told the Austrian Chief of Staff Conrad von Hötzendorf, "We are not superior to the French."[15] Moltke thus realized that the Germans could not count on a six-week victory in the west. Nevertheless, he, like all German leaders, believed that Germany could not win a long war of attrition. Therefore, like Schlieffen, he felt compelled to gamble.

War plans were also inflexible. In general, soldiers dislike ambiguity, preferring instead clear definitions of "enemy" and "ally" in order to facilitate their planning and training. Thus the soldier's traditional antipathy for diplomats, who have a habit of turning yesterday's ally into tomorrow's enemy. Much of the reason for Germany's ability to seize the initiative in 1914 came from the dominance of the general staff over the diplomats. In France and Britain, no such dominance existed, which made the soldiers less resolute. As a result, senior officers in Germany were in a better position to use the immediate pre-war crisis as an excuse for a war they wanted.

The evolution of two alliance systems seemed to have made the task of identifying enemies and allies much easier by dividing Europe's great powers into two camps. But the actual outbreak of war in 1914 did not conform exactly to the plans. The crisis surrounding the death of an Austrian archduke seemed to threaten the direct interests of Austria-Hungary, Serbia, and perhaps Russia, but not France, Britain, or even Germany. Nevertheless, the German government decided to support its Austrian ally, issuing the infamous "blank check" of support for whatever action the Austro-Hungarian statesmen might choose (to be discussed in the next section).

It is important to note as well that nationalism and the constraints of alliance warfare placed limits and restraints on the types of operations for which each country's army could realistically plan. Once again military considerations were not always primary. France's Plan XVII, although it was more of a mobilization plan than a war plan, represents these constraints as well as any. Most French generals foresaw the dangers of a German violation of Belgian neutrality, but the French government forbade any consideration of a preemptive French march into Belgium in order that France should be able to depict themselves (and, less importantly, the Belgians) as victims of German aggression. Such a stance stood a much greater chance of gaining British help. A French violation of Belgian neutrality, even if done at the same time as a German violation, might result in British ire rather than assistance.

French public opinion also made close contacts with the British military politically hazardous. Joint war planning might have given the appearance that the French were preparing for an offensive war, an image that the French military took pains not to adopt, both at home and abroad. As a result, Plan XVII did not include contingencies for cooperation with the British Expeditionary Force, even though the French were counting on Great Britain to send such a force. The generals and politicians did, however, understand the need to give the Russians time to mobilize fully. They therefore sought an early offensive to force the Germans to divide their efforts between two distant fronts.

But the single most important factor influencing French strategy was domestic. Although France was unwilling to go to war for Alsace and Lorraine, most Frenchmen nevertheless believed that if war did occur, France should seize the opportunity to recapture the Lost Provinces. While a preemptive thrust into Belgium would smack too much of French aggression, an invasion into Alsace and Lorraine would merely represent the return of French forces to territory that was rightfully French to begin with. Such an operation would not threaten the official French line that the nation was fighting a defensive war, nor would it damage French relations with either of its main allies. Such an operation would also have the additional advantage of forcing Germany to fight on the defensive and, if executed quickly enough, might disrupt whatever offensive the Germans had planned.

Plan XVII also deployed the left wing of French forces in the general direction of the Belgian border, giving French commander Joseph Joffre, the plan's chief author, the option of moving into Belgian territory the instant that the Germans first broke that country's neutrality. Thus Joffre could move his forces into this critical region quickly but still meet the French government's demand that France not be the first nation to violate Belgian neutrality.[16]

Still, the main French goals remained the recovery of the Lost Provinces. Accordingly, on the outbreak of the war, the French planned an attack by 80 percent of the French army's units into the Lost Provinces. German generals, able to read the domestic and international situation in France quite clearly, counted on the French to attack in Alsace and Lorraine. The Germans thus directed the Sixth and Seventh armies to give ground slowly, inflicting heavy French casualties, while allowing the French to advance into Alsace and Lorraine. The French armies would then be too far east to redeploy to resist the bulk of German forces (the First through Fifth armies) as they moved through Belgium toward Paris. If such planning was, in the words of Geoffrey Wawro, "bad strategy," it is difficult to envision how French social and political constraints could have produced a radically different plan.[17]

Similar problems existed in the already troubled Austro-Hungarian Empire. Most senior Austrian leaders saw the expansion of Serbian nationalism as the most immediate danger to the future of the empire. The empire's senior military planners had vigorously argued that the empire should have used the Balkan Wars as an excuse to eradicate Serbia from the map of Europe. They became convinced that should another opportunity present itself, Austria-Hungary could not afford to miss it. Time, they believed, was not on their side because the Russian army continued to recover from its defeat at the hands of Japan in 1904–1905, and the British navy continued to increase its dominance over the German navy. Austria-Hungary, they argued, had no choice but to use the next Balkan crisis as an excuse to declare war on Serbia and settle its scores with the menace of Serb nationalism once and for all.

In order to do so they might also have to settle with Russia, a state with deep sentimental, ethnic, and religious ties to Serbia. Despite the menace of Russia's huge army, Conrad von Hötzendorf and the Austrian military leadership could not escape the empire's visceral hatred of Serbia. Their war plan called for Austria-Hungary's army to be divided into three groups. Minimalgruppe Balkan, ten divisions strong, would invade Serbia at the earliest available opportunity while the thirty divisions of Staffel-A would head into Poland to delay any Russian advance. The twelve divisions of Staffel-B would act as a reserve to be rapidly deployed to whichever theater seemed to need them most, though Conrad envisioned sending them to help Minimalgruppe Balkan. Once again, speed was of the essence as the Austrians counted on a quick defeat of Serbia in order to allow them to counter the 72 divisions that the Russians would have available in the first weeks of the war alone.

Russia's war plan was influenced by similar considerations. To fulfill their commitments to France, Russia's Plan 19 promised an early offensive into East Prussia to ensure that Germany could not focus too much of its strength on the French front. For that offensive to have any chance of success, Russia would have to mobilize its vast, but widely dispersed, army quickly. The Russians devised a complicated phased mobilization plan that included a "period preparatory to mobilization" and advance mobilization centers in European Russia. As a result, Russia's enormous army was in the field much more quickly than the Germans and Austrians had believed possible, leaving just 13 German and 27 Austro-Hungarian divisions to face the initial wave of 72 Russian divisions and the certainty of many dozens more to follow.

War planning required rapid decision-making, both to seize initiative and to complete mobilization in as little time as possible. Nationalism and Social Darwinism ensured that, once declared, war would be welcomed by most, grudgingly accepted by a few, and rejected by only the most committed pacifists. Alliances designed to deter aggression backfired and instead ensured that a crisis anywhere in Europe could drag in all of the continent's great powers. All of these factors existed below the surface when Archduke Franz Ferdinand, heir to the throne of the Austro-Hungarian empire, took an official state visit to Sarajevo in 1914. His death produced the spark that set the continent ablaze.

## The death of an Archduke

Archduke Franz Ferdinand's visit to Sarajevo was designed to underscore Austrian control of an area that the Serbs wanted to include in their pan-Slavic state. Franz Ferdinand, nephew of the emperor, was an unpopular man both inside and outside the empire's inner circle. He had openly supported a plan that would have given the empire's Croatian minority equal status with the Austrians and the Magyars. In doing so, he hoped to divide the loyalties of Austria-Hungary's disaffected minorities by elevating the Croatians, thereby furthering the isolation of the empire's Slavs. This plan to change the Dual Monarchy into a Triple Monarchy threatened to dilute the power of the ruling German and Magyar elites. Franz Ferdinand had also angered the Serbs by limiting Serbian gains after the First Balkan War; he had worked with Germany to deny Serbia the port of Skhodër, thus keeping the Serbian state landlocked.[18]

To add insult to injury, Ferdinand entered Sarajevo on June 28, St. Vitus Day. The day was a Serbian holiday, commemorating the defeat in 1389 of a Serbian army at the hands of an Ottoman army at the battle of Kosovo Polje. The slight to Serbian honor was too much for the members of a group known as the Black Hand. Armed with pistols and grenades, they waited for the archduke's motorcade along the main streets of the city. Two assassins had their chance but missed their intended targets, instead wounding passengers in the car behind the archduke's. The archduke's driver, on the way to the hospital so that the archduke could visit the victims, made a wrong turn, placing the car directly in the path of another Black Hand assassin, a surprised teenager named Gavrilo Princip. Princip fired twice, one bullet killing the archduke, the other killing his wife, Sophie.

The incident was more a state tragedy than personal one. Franz Ferdinand's chosen wife had struck many, including his uncle, the aging Emperor Franz Joseph, as far too low in social stature. As a result, Sophie was routinely shunned at official functions. The emperor and those closest to him reacted so coolly to the death of the archduke that some European leaders dismissed the situation altogether. In fact, many members of the Austro-Hungarian elite, including the emperor himself, either did not attend the funerals or made the most perfunctory of appearances.

Still, the assassination gave the extremists in Austria the opportunity they had been seeking. The murder of a member of the Austrian royal family, even if an unpopular one, could provide the pretext for the chance to punish Serbia they had long desired. Sophie's death generated considerable popular sympathy as well, especially since the couple left behind three small children. While some, including Conrad von Hötzendorf, screamed for an immediate war, Austria instead prepared a series of ultimatums to Serbia, whose military intelligence bureau the Austrians believed had links to the Black Hand.

The terms were designed to be unacceptable to the Serbs. They included the demand that Serbia dismiss all officers linked to the Black Hand, suppress all anti-Austrian propaganda, and permit Austro-Hungarian officials to serve on the Serbian investigation. Some, like the Hungarian Prime Minister Istvan Tisza, hoped to find a diplomatic solution. Most, like Conrad, saw the terms as a means to "prepare the way for a radical solution based on military force."[19] The Austrian military waited for Serbia to reject the ultimatums and give Austria-Hungary an excuse to mobilize.

The assassination crisis need not have led to a continental war. In the previous decade, two Moroccan crises and two Balkan Wars had demonstrated that the great powers of Europe could diffuse dangerous diplomatic situations and work together to localize Balkan conflicts. Many important Europeans saw nothing in the crisis that might cause them to cancel summer vacation plans. British Foreign Secretary Sir Edward Grey left on a fishing weekend and the vigorously anti-German French general Ferdinand Foch, commander of the "spearhead" corps of Plan XVII, went on leave to his estate in Brittany. Even Germany's vaunted military strategists did not foresee what the crisis would become. Moltke and Prussian War Minister General Erich von Falkenhayn both continued their vacations as well. The Kaiser went on a cruise.

In western Europe, domestic issues pushed the Balkan crisis to back burners. July 21–24 in Great Britain were consumed by the Buckingham Palace Conference on the future of the Irish Question. The debates surrounding Irish Home Rule seemed infinitely more important to Britons than did the murder of a man few had heard of in faraway Sarajevo. In France, the media remained obsessed with the trial of Henriette Caillaux, second wife of Joseph Caillaux, French prime minister at the time of the Agadir incident. The newspaper *Le Figaro* had acquired, and published, explicit love letters between Mr. and Mrs. Caillaux. *Le Figaro*'s editor, Gaston Calmette, was also leading a campaign to undermine Caillaux's tax reform plan. Believing her honor to have been compromised, Madame Caillaux entered Calmette's office and fatally shot him. Defense witnesses argued that female reason was weak in the face of passions and, just days before France entered World War I, a jury found her not guilty.

The real impetus that drove the continent to war came from Germany. German decision-making changed the complexion of the crisis and eventually led to the general war that most Frenchmen and Britons hoped to avoid. The German military and the Kaiser believed, as did the Austrians, that time was working against them. By 1917, Russia would have completed a rapid modernization program making the Russian army a considerably more formidable foe. A stronger, faster Russia put all of the assumptions implicit in German planning at risk. It was, the Germans believed, better to fight the war in 1914 than at some point in the future when the combination of the more modern Russian army and the even larger British Navy (to say nothing of the French forces) would be too powerful.

Furthermore, Germany did not want to see its most powerful ally humiliated. German diplomats therefore made the fateful decision to issue a "blank check" to the Austrians. The check was a German guarantee of support for whatever action Austria-Hungary might take in the crisis. German honor, they believed, required them to support their ally to the fullest extent possible. Moreover, many senior German advisors to the Kaiser believed that the shaky domestic situation in Russia (where a revolution had occurred in 1905 during the Russo-Japanese War) would prevent the Russians from entering the war. Therefore, the Balkan crisis could be localized, Austrian prestige restored, and Germany's strategic situation improved. If war did come, better that it come in 1914 than in 1917 or even later.

Assured of German support, the Austrians delivered an ultimatum to Serbia on July 20 and, already assuming Serbian rejection, prepared to begin mobilization five days later. The Serbs accepted nine of the ten demands, rejecting only the demand that they permit Austrian officials to be a part of their investigation into the assassination. That rejection was enough for the Austrians as well as the Germans. They would get war, but it was not to be the short war they wanted.

The blank check forced Germany to implement its war plans, which called for a preemptive attack against France, a nation that was not directly involved in the current crisis and might still have remained neutral. France alone among the continental powers was willing to subordinate its military to diplomatic considerations. As the Sarajevo crisis reached its climax, President Raymond Poincaré issued an order that all French forces be pulled back ten kilometers from the German frontier so that France would not accidentally precipitate German belligerence.[20] Only after Germany declared war on France (on the false pretense of an alleged French aerial bombing of Nuremberg) did France order mobilization.

The British were unsure of their intentions. The crisis in the Balkans did not directly concern them and at first they prepared to host a conference (as they had in 1912), not mobilize for war. The British Parliament, a much more influential body than its German or Russian counterpart, was not prepared to vote for war simply to balance out German strength in eastern Europe. German threats to Belgium, however, were much more serious. Germany's dismissal of the 1839 treaty guaranteeing Belgian neutrality as a "scrap of paper" angered and offended British sentiment. Germany's subsequent invasion of Belgium changed the situation dramatically and on August 3, Sir Edward Grey spoke before the House of Commons to urge its members to uphold the nation's "obligations of honour."[21] The next day, the British Cabinet agreed to send the British Expeditionary Force to the continent.

Russian honor was also at stake. Although Serbia and Russia had no formal treaty between them, the Serbs and Russians shared a common Slavic background and a religion, Eastern Orthodox Christianity. These ties combined with Russia's domestic situation to push Russia toward a war that some Germans had supposed they would not fight. Tsar Nicholas II, the Kaiser's cousin, had seen his prestige decline significantly in the face of the humiliating defeat at the hands of Japan in 1904–1905. He and his advisors believed that strong Russian support of Serbia could rally the nation around the Romanov Dynasty. Failure to help the Serbs, they believed, would cause a further lack of faith in the Tsar, perhaps leading to a serious domestic political crisis. The nationalist press in Russia urged the Tsar to make strong statements in support of the Serbs and the Tsar was inclined to listen.

Serbian military success in the Balkan Wars had absolved the Russians of the need to intervene in 1912. By 1914, the Serbian situation looked much more serious and the Russian position much stronger. More importantly, to back down in the face of the Austrian ultimatum to fellow Slavs would have been too unpopular a step for a regime that was already suffering from a lack of support. On the contrary, despite some resistance to mobilization, the crisis led to a rallying behind the state and the Tsar that surprised even many Russians. In the first fifteen days of the war, the Russian army, a notoriously unpopular institution with most Russians, signed up 800,000 volunteers.

It is easy to look back from a century's perspective and argue that the war was not in the direct interests of any of the great powers. To do so, however, is to be unduly simplistic. The question of honoring alliance commitments was about much more than diplomacy. In an age when honor meant a great deal (witness the actions of Henriette Caillaux), a national aversion to honoring commitments meant demonstrating to the world a failure to honor agreements made in good faith. Alliance obligations therefore became questions of national identity. Even in Great Britain, whose formal relationship to France did not require military support unless the French coastline were attacked without provocation, many people saw a failure to intervene in the war as a sign of national cowardice. The nation's self-image and self-respect demanded that Britain not stand by while the Germans overran Belgium and France.

The causes of the war, then, are rooted much more deeply than the actions of diplomats. European leaders knew that their populations would follow them down the road to war because they knew that national honor was not a commodity to be taken lightly. Even in unpopular regimes, as in Austria-Hungary, men went willingly to war. Failures to report for mobilization were surprisingly rare. In Britain, the professional army was soon supplemented by a wave of volunteers that averaged 350 men per hour for two months. Men went to war to fight for honor and country and they did so without a trace of cynicism. They also fully expected to be back home, as heroes, by Christmas.

The enthusiasm with which men went to war in 1914 underscored the belief among almost all Europeans that the war would be short. Those few people who predicted a bloody and destructive global war lasting four years were fringe figures. The two men who came closest were Friedrich Engels, co-author, with Karl Marx, of the *Communist Manifesto*, and a wealthy banker named Ivan Bloch. Bloch, writing in 1897, foresaw that warfare would necessarily be fought from trenches, as the firepower of modern weaponry would leave men little choice but to dig. Engels, writing in 1887, predicted a three- or four-year war

> of never before seen extension and intensity. . . . Eight to ten million soldiers will slaughter each other and strip Europe as bare as no swarm of locusts has ever done before . . . the collapse of old states and their traditional wisdom [will occur] in such a way that the crowns will roll in the gutter by the dozens and there will be nobody to pick them up.

Both Engels, a Communist, and Bloch, a Polish Jew, were on the periphery of European society. Neither had much impact on the military or popular attitudes of 1914. Moreover, both men's works on warfare were more than a decade and half old by 1914. Even Bloch's work could be read as optimistic, as he argued that warfare might be impossible in the modern age because of the intricacies of financing it. Thus most military and political leaders felt safe in disregarding their grim and dire writings.

Nevertheless, many others understood that modern nationalism had made European nations much more resilient and determined. Helmuth von Moltke (the elder) had warned the German Reichstag in 1890 that the age of "cabinet wars," by which he meant wars fought for the narrow interests of a state's political leadership, were impossible in the new, nationalistic Europe. Instead, he argued that the future of warfare would consist of "people's wars," popular struggles that governments would not be able to end by admitting defeat as they had in the 1860s and 1870s. Believing themselves fighting for their very survival, peoples and governments would fight to "renew the struggle" as often as necessary. As had occurred in 1871, the victorious nation would need to defeat not just the enemy's field armies, but the enemy's national will as well. "Woe to him who sets Europe alight," Moltke concluded, "who first puts the fuse to the powder keg!"[22]

As these premonitions suggest, some Europeans understood that modern, nationalistic, and industrial nations would not be beaten in a single campaign, as the Austrians had essentially been in 1866. Many more understood the tactical lessons of the Boer War and the Russo-Japanese War; namely, that frontal attacks against well-trained infantry armed with modern weapons were tantamount to suicide. Moreover, all nations worried about the long-term domestic impacts of a lengthy war. Russia's 1905 defeat had severely undermined the authority of the Tsar and was an ominous harbinger of possible revolution. A long, unsuccessful war might unleash the anti-monarchical forces that Engels had foreseen.

The "short war illusion" of 1914, then, needs to be understood as much more than a lack of vision. On the German side, we have already seen that the Schlieffen Plan had been predicated on winning a short war, but not because of any presumed German superiority. Rather, the Germans believed that they were unlikely to win a long war of attrition against the combined might of the Royal

Navy, the Russian army, and the French army. They had to win quickly, most Germans believed, or risk not winning at all. Short wars therefore required offensive war planning. Although historians have especially criticized the French Plan XVII for its offensive mindset, all of the great powers' war plans called for fighting on (and thus devastating) someone else's soil.

The role of nationalism was even more important, underscoring the fact that war planning responded not just to military factors, but to social and cultural forces as well. Just as pious people in all nations believed in God's blessing for their cause, nationalists on all sides believed in the inherent superiority of their own morality and character. Some went so far as to argue that offensive warfare fit better into national virtue than did defensive warfare. Eager and willing men of strong "national" fiber, they believed, could negate the enemy's advantages of firepower. Recalling a presumed national military legacy, the French Army's "Regulations for the Conduct of Large Units" (1912) summarized the French doctrine of *offensive à outrance* (offensive to the utmost): "The French Army, reviving its old traditions, no longer admits for the conduct of operations any other law than that of the offensive."[23] From a strictly military perspective, offensive warfare took maximum advantage of youthful enthusiasm and national ardor and had the additional virtue of being easy to teach to conscripts and reservists.

A belief in their own inherent superiority, however fallacious it might appear in hindsight, also helped men to rationalize and legitimate their own experiences. Faith in nationalism, and the martial virtues associated with it, gave men confidence in their leaders and in their comrades. It also helped some men to dispel fears about how they themselves would perform when the "test of battle" presented itself. The rude dispelling of these illusions had important effects in 1914–1915, leading to the disillusionment that so many men came to feel by the middle of the war. Their entire constellation of values came to appear not just as spurious, but as a fraudulent lie.

Thus by 1914, a dangerous and volatile mix had been created in Europe. Nationalism had created larger and more resilient armies fighting, they believed, for their own survival and the survival of national traditions. Alliances dragged nations into a catastrophe that, for many, was not in their direct interests. War planning, most notably in Germany, converted the Sarajevo crisis into a general continental war that led Sir Edward Grey to remark: "The lamps are going out all over Europe; we shall not see them lit again in our lifetime."

## Further reading

Any serious study of World War I should begin with Hew Strachan's masterful *The First World War: To Arms!* (Oxford: Oxford University Press, 2001), the first volume of a projected trilogy. James Joll, *The Origins of the First World War* (London: Longman, 1984) and Ruth Henig's book of the same title (London: Routledge, 1993) both provide brief and quite readable accounts. V. R.

Berghahn, *Germany and the Approach of War 1914* (London: Palgrave, 1973); J. F. V. Keiger, *France and the Origins of the First World War* (London: Palgrave, 1984); Zara Steiner, *Britain and the Origins of the First World War* (London: Macmillan, 1977); Douglas Porch, *March to the Marne: The French Army, 1871–1914* (Cambridge: Cambridge University Press, 1981); Samuel R. Williamson, *Austria-Hungary and the Origins of the First World War* (London: Macmillan, 1991); and Richard Bosworth, *Italy and the Approach of the First World War* (London: Macmillan, 1983) all offer country-specific studies.

On war planning and alliances see Paul Kennedy, ed., *The War Plans of the Great Powers, 1880–1914* (London: Allen and Unwin, 1979); Samuel Williamson, *The Politics of Grand Strategy: Britain and France Prepare for War* (Cambridge: Harvard University Press, 1969); and Terence Zuber, *Inventing the Schlieffen Plan: German War Planning 1871–1914* (Oxford: Oxford University Press, 2003). On nationalism see Ian Ousby, *The Road to Verdun: World War I's Most Momentous Battle and the Folly of Nationalism* (New York: Doubleday, 2002); Robert Tombs, ed., *Nationhood and Nationalism in France: From Boulangism to the Great War, 1889–1918* (London: HarperCollins, 1991); Benedict Anderson, *Imagined Communities: Reflections on the Origin and Spread of Nationalism* (London: Verso, 1983); and Eric Hobsbawm, *Nations and Nationalism since 1780: Programme, Myth, Reality* (Cambridge: Cambridge University Press, 1992). Richard Hall, *The Balkan Wars: Prelude to the First World War* (London: Routledge, 2000) is a good start for these conflicts.

# 2

# WORLD WAR I, 1914–1917

## 1914–1915: Fighting an alliance war

Four years before the outbreak of World War I, British general Henry Wilson noted that few of his nation's regimental officers showed much concern for "a funny little country like Belgium, although most of them may be buried there before they are much older."[1] Wilson's grim prophecy, of course, came true during the course of the war, as almost 700,000 Britons died in Belgium and France. If men like Wilson foresaw not only the German invasion of Belgium, but also its likely consequences, then it is all the more curious that the British army did not more fully prepare for that eventuality. From a strictly military standpoint, those preparations would have made good sense. The whole logic of war planning and general staffs inclined professional military officers toward thinking about exactly the kind of problem that landing a force in Belgium presented. Since an alliance already existed between France and Britain, joint war planning could have been a routine matter.

Some joint planning did occur, but it fell far short of preparing the BEF for the crisis of 1914. After the two Moroccan incidents, British war planning became, in the words of John Gooch, more "extroverted." As early as 1906, British planners had begun to think about a deployment on the right flank of the Belgian army.[2] From 1909 British army planners worked from the assumption that any general war in Europe would happen much too quickly for a blockade to have much effect. Therefore, they reasoned, the army would need to be prepared to quickly dispatch five divisions near the French left wing. French planners welcomed these conclusions. Still, joint war planning did not follow, in part because of unresolved debates inside Britain. Much of British army planning, for example, lacked proper coordination with the Royal Navy, which feared that an aggressive army deployment onto continental Europe would compromise their own blockade plans.

Generals and politicians therefore understood the need for better joint planning, but, as we saw in Chapter 1, military exigencies do not always dominate decision-making. On both sides of the English Channel, social and political pressures combined to reduce the level of preparation and joint planning. Even

Belgium, which depended on Great Britain to help maintain its neutrality in the face of German aggression, was so anxious to preserve the appearance of that neutrality that it forbade combined general staff talks with either Britain or France. Such isolation had the best of intentions, namely to demonstrate to France, Germany, and Britain that Belgium wanted no part of a war between the great powers. Nevertheless, the unfortunate geography of Belgium made it unlikely that the nation could avoid being swept up in a general war. Belgium's ability to stay neutral during the Wars of German Unification led to false hopes that it could do so again in 1914. Heavy Belgian investments in fortifications also held out hope that Belgium could defend itself. Still, Belgian failure to work consistently with any great power left them with few realistic choices when war broke out in 1914.

Even though some British generals such as Wilson and some French generals such as Ferdinand Foch argued forcefully for more formal and official military coordination between the two armies, politicians rightly understood that too close a relationship was not palatable to people in either nation. Each side wanted an alliance to help deter potential enemies such as Germany, but neither wanted that alliance to drag them reluctantly into war. Foch, a firm supporter of closer Entente relations, saw the British army as largely an adjunct of the French army in the event of a German invasion of France. The death of one British soldier on the continent, he believed, would rally British popular opinion and compel Britain to commit the full resources of the British Empire to the French cause.

British suspicions of French motives remained high, partially because of fears of being used just as Foch had intended. Alliance or not, the British were unwilling to go to war for events that they saw as exclusively to the benefit of the French. The reacquisition of Alsace and Lorraine may have been French goals in the event of war, but they were surely not goals for which the British were willing to send the British Expeditionary Force to the continent.

Alliance or not, British opinion demanded that the nation retain its freedom of action in the event of war. As British Prime Minister H. H. Asquith told an apprehensive House of Commons in 1913, "this country is not under any obligation not public and known to Parliament which compels it to take part in any war."[3] That desire to retain control of the timing of their own entry into the war led to considerable debate after Serbia's rejection of the Austrian ultimatum made a continental war look increasingly more likely. Even then, the British waited until the Germans actually invaded Belgium to enter the war.

Because British opinion forbade the imposition of conscription, the British army was comparatively small. While the German army could rely on 2,400,000 men at the outbreak of war and the French army 1,300,000 men, the BEF numbered only 100,000. Nevertheless, it was constituted by long-term volunteers and was therefore a high-quality force into which the British had invested heavily, especially after the humbling experience of the Boer War. Cognizant as well of their imperial responsibilities, British politicians were reluctant to commit the BEF unless vital British interests were at stake, especially since its deployment left the home islands with no protection except the Royal Navy. Widespread popular fears about a German amphibious landing made the overseas deployment of the British army a sensitive issue.

In short, sending the BEF overseas was not a decision to be taken lightly. British leaders had few doubts about the extremely high quality of the BEF. They confidently believed that it could defeat a force several times larger than itself. But even if it did deploy and defeat a German force, it might still suffer casualties that the empire could not afford. Replacing the highly-trained and experienced men that made the BEF such a lethal force would take months, perhaps years, to accomplish. Unlike their continental allies and rivals, Great Britain could not expect simply to raise another army via conscription or a call-up of another class of reservists. Even after the German invasion of Belgium these fears remained. The first deployment of the BEF involved only four of its six divisions. The remainder stayed in Britain until the emergency of the early months required it to follow.

Despite these concerns, the German invasion of Belgium compelled a British response for both military and moral reasons. Specially designed German artillery defeated the once-formidable Belgian fortifications. The professional German army steadily pushed the smaller Belgian army back toward the French border. The rapid German advance presented the real possibility of the Germans seizing not only the Belgian ports, but the northern French ones as well. Britain could not afford to give the Germans such an advantage.

Needing to keep to exacting timetables and fearful of a guerrilla war that might slow their progress, the Germans reacted ferociously to Belgian resistance. They deported some civilians, executed others, and burned entire towns. To cite one famous example, the Germans destroyed the priceless medieval university town of Louvain, complete with its library's irreplaceable Gothic and Renaissance manuscript collections. The "rape of Belgium" sullied the reputation of the German army (not for the last time in the twentieth century) and demonized the Kaiser.[4] British popular opinion reacted harshly to stories of German treatment of Belgium, causing many Britons to demand that their nation stand up for "poor little Belgium." Britain had now found not just a political *casus belli*, but a popular cause around which the nation could rally.

The BEF therefore went to the continent, but not without its own share of misgivings. The commander of the BEF, Sir John French, embodied all of Britain's concerns. In an odd counterpoint to his last name, French (hereinafter known as General French to avoid confusion) was not particularly fond of his allies. He did not speak French and was rightly suspicious that French generals largely envisioned using the BEF as an extension of the French army. When the British cabinet ordered him to take the BEF to France, he determined to operate with absolute independence from the French. He proved to be a stubborn and uncooperative ally.

The first major action that the British fought, the Battle of Mons (August 23, 1914), seemed to General French to confirm all of his fears. In accordance with the wishes of French army commander-in-chief General Joseph Joffre, General French reluctantly agreed to move the BEF into Belgium in cooperation with the French Fifth Army, under General Charles Lanzerac. At the town of Mons, the British ran into the German First Army, full of momentum and three times the size of the BEF. Superb British marksmanship held up the German advance (the Germans reported facing machine guns when in fact they were facing the expert rifle fire of the BEF's veteran marksmen), but Lanzerac retreated without informing General French or his staff. Furious with his French allies for leaving the BEF dangerously exposed, General French had to order a costly fighting retreat to the southwest. In just four days, the BEF had already lost more men than they had in any campaign since Waterloo a century earlier. As they continued to give ground and fight rear-guard actions, their relations with the French deteriorated even further.

The poor quality of Anglo-French relations put the entire Allied war effort in danger. General French considered moving his army to the north, to place it nearer to the ports on the English Channel in the event that the government ordered it to evacuate from the continent. At the same time, the movement of the German armies necessitated the deployment of the BEF closer to Paris, where a significant gap had opened between the French Fifth and Sixth Armies. General French's experiences with Lanrezac's Fifth Army at Mons did not incline him to move south and fill in that gap. He remained adamant about preserving his independence until British Secretary of State for War Lord Kitchener (the same man who had been the British commander at Fashoda in 1898) ordered him to obey Joffre's request, thus placing the BEF in a position to help France win the critical Battle of the Marne (September 5–10). That victory stopped the Germans just short of Paris and destroyed their plans to redeploy to the east.

It is, therefore, important to understand that the nationalism and attendant development of alliances impacted the way the sides went to war and fought. The early campaigns had done little to bring the British and the French together. If anything, relations were even worse after the First Battle of the Marne than they had been before. As a result, the British and French were essentially fighting two separate wars. Furthermore, their contacts with the Russians were tenuous, as they had to communicate across Germany via radio with primitive and unreliable codes.

Fortunately for the Entente, the Germans and the Austrians had fared little better in developing their own coalition. As noted in Chapter 1, each had assumed that the other would take primary responsibility for slowing down the advance of the Russians. In the event neither did so, with the Germans focused on France and the Austrians on Serbia. By August 17, the Russians were ready to invade East Prussia, the traditional seat of power for the German Junkers. Opposing them was only one German army, the Eighth Army under the command of General Max von Prittwitz, who owed his position less to his own abilities than to his popularity with the Kaiser. On August 20, the Russians won a victory at the Battle of Gumbinnen, causing great concern in Berlin and leading to Prittwitz's replacement by General Paul von Hindenburg, recently recalled from retirement. Hindenburg brought with him as his chief of staff one of Germany's heroes from the campaign in Belgium, General Erich Ludendorff.

Hindenburg and Ludendorff had to solve the problem of defeating a large Russian army without significant help from the Austrians. The latter's mobilization plan had resulted in great confusion. Staffel-A's thirty divisions did indeed advance into Poland as envisioned, but they soon suffered two major defeats, forcing them on a 100-mile retreat. They had also lost 350,000 total casualties (killed, wounded, and missing) and ceded two important fortress complexes that guarded the Carpathian mountain passes. The loss of Lemberg (taken on September 3 and soon given the Russian name of Lvov) and Przemysl (besieged from September 24 and finally taken on October 10) were shattering blows to Austria-Hungary's defensive plans. Conrad, the Austrian commander in chief, realized the emergency and tried to bring the twelve divisions of Staffel-B north to assist, but they arrived too slowly. As a result, Staffel-B did not play a significant role in either Poland or in Serbia.

This failure on the part of the Austrians placed Germany in an exposed position. The loss of the two Carpathian fortresses gave Russia an opportunity to advance on Krakow, the final fortress along Austria-Hungary's northern line and the key to control of Galicia. If the Russians could seize Krakow, they would have the option of using it as a base from which to approach Berlin from the southeast, a route that the Germans could not properly defend. Their deployments to France and East Prussia left precious few forces to guard against an advance from Krakow. Alternatively, the Russians could turn south and invade Hungary, thus placing the survival of the Austro-Hungarian Empire in doubt.

A successful German advance against the Russians thus became all the more important because it had both to protect East Prussia and to assist Germany's beleaguered ally. Not for the last time in the war, German operations were determined partly by the need to rescue their albatross, the ineffectual Austrians. Germany could count on only two advantages: the Russian First and Second Armies were too far apart to offer meaningful support to one another and their commanders, Generals Pavel Rennenkampf and Alexander Samsonov, respectively, distrusted one another so deeply that they barely spoke to one another.

The tensions between the two generals reflected long-standing fissures in Russian society. The Russian officer corps was divided into a dizzying array of factions and conflicting loyalties. Some Russian generals were Slavophiles who favored remaking the Russian army along traditional Russian lines in the hopes of gaining more popular support for the army. They were opposed by those who saw such reforms as hopelessly outdated and favored modernization along western models instead. This division had a long history in Russia, dating back as far as the westernization movement begun by Tsar Peter the Great in the eighteenth century. By the time of World War I, this debate had still not been settled. Neither had debates between those who favored a northern strategy (against Germany in East Prussia) versus a southern one (against Austria in the Carpathians); those who favored fortifications versus railroads; or those who favored artillery versus those who still favored cavalry as the shock arm of the Russian army.

These debates had important ramifications as two rival Russian promotion systems had developed. Rennenkampf had been promoted through the Russian General Staff system which had close ties to the Tsar and royal family. Samsonov, on the other hand, had been a protégé of the War Ministry under the command of General Vladimir Sukhomlinov, who was suspicious of the French and argued for more favorable relations with Germany. The rivalry between the two groups was so intense that it became a standard Russian practice to assign a second in command from the General Staff to an army commander from the War Ministry and vice versa. As a result, mistrust between army commanders and their immediate subordinates was commonplace.

Ludendorff, counting on Russian clumsiness, decided on a desperate gamble. He placed just one cavalry division opposite Rennenkampf's First Army and swung the remainder of his Eighth Army against the Russian Second Army. The result of this lightning operation was an encirclement of the Russians and one of the most lopsided victories of the war at the Battle of Tannenberg (August 26–31). The Russians lost 125,000 men, 500 heavy guns, and General Samsonov, who apparently committed suicide. The Germans then turned against Rennenkampf's First Army, inflicting an equally devastating blow at the Battle of the Masurian Lakes (September 9–14), a victory that partially compensated for their defeat at the Marne which occurred at roughly the same time.

With their plans on the western front in ruins, the Germans and the French began a series of flanking movements that became known as the "Race to the Sea." In effect, each side attempted to move around the other side's north flank in an effort to surround and "turn" their enemy. Neither side had the strength to do so as they were both exhausted and short of supplies. Upon reaching the English Channel, the Allies attempted to set up a genuine joint command under Ferdinand Foch, a French general with friends in high places in the British army. He took command of the exhausted and muddled French, British, and Belgian units, treated them as a whole and reorganized them into discrete national entities, each with responsibility for its own section of the line.

While rational and orderly, the system posed problems. Foch was a senior French general but technically he was lower in rank than either British commander John French, a field marshal, or King Albert I of Belgium. Neither General French nor King Albert wanted to take orders from a French general, but they did agree to follow Foch's overall strategy. The system worked well enough to allow the Allies to withstand two fierce German attacks: the Battle of Yser (October 17 to November 1) and the First Battle of Ypres (October 21 to November 12). Foch soon assumed the title of "Commander of Army Group North," but he lacked any formal authority to lead. Once again national sentiment forbade joint warfare as neither commander was willing to subordinate his units under a foreign general.[5]

Thus the campaigns on the western front largely ignored the lesson of joint command that the Ypres and Yser campaigns seemed to suggest. Throughout 1915 the British and French fought separate campaigns against a German opponent that had chosen high ground and heavily defended it with trenches, barbed wire, and machine guns. France's 1915 offensives in Champagne and Artois and Britain's offensives at Neuve Chapelle and Aubers Ridge failed. At their best, the two nations were able to time attacks to occur simultaneously in different sectors, but such coordination proved insufficient to oust the Germans from their strong defensive positions.

Outside of France, the allies tried two joint operations, both of which failed miserably. In October, 1915, the French and British sent a 45,000-man army to the Greek city of Salonika in the hopes of helping the struggling Serbs. The British quickly cooled to the operation, believing that it had more to do with French domestic politics than operational efficiency. The commander at Salonika, French general Maurice Sarrail, was a favorite of French parliamentarians because of his avowedly republican political sentiments, but his uniformed colleagues distrusted him and saw him as little more than a politician. The British came to believe that the Salonika operation was designed to give Sarrail an important command and ensure French influence in the Balkans after the war. The British were not interested in either goal, and as a result the Salonika operation accomplished little, soon earning the men the collective sobriquet, "the gardeners of Salonika."

The British had their own goals in Eastern Europe. In November, 1914, the Ottoman Empire had entered the war on the side of Austria-Hungary and Germany, hoping to regain some of the territory that they had lost during the Balkan Wars. Again, nationalism played an important role as most of the ethnically Turkish Ottoman ruling class was determined to restore the empire to its former greatness and, with it, return ethnic Turks to a position of dominance within the empire itself. The British responded by organizing their own joint operation. The brainchild of the young First Lord of the Admiralty, Winston Churchill, the plan aimed at seizing the Dardanelles straits, knocking the Ottomans out of the war, and opening up a warm-water communications link with the Russians.

The failure of British warships to do the job alone led to the landing of a force of 75,000 British and 18,000 French soldiers on the Gallipoli Peninsula and areas nearby. A heroic Turkish defense led by Mustapha Kemal (later the first president of the modern state of Turkey) stopped the British advance and led to the decision to land a much larger force, including thousands of Australians and

New Zealanders (known collectively as the ANZACS). The French and the Australians as well grew frustrated at British ineptitude and suspected that Britain supported the operation only in order to build an eastern Mediterranean empire after the war.

Thus the allied attempts at joint warfare in 1914 and 1915 amounted to little. The French and British could, however, take cold comfort in the knowledge that Austro-German relations were not improving either. The Austrians had lost nearly 1,000,000 men in the fighting of 1914, including 75 percent of their active-army captains and lieutenants. Austro-Hungarian ineffectiveness had led to a serious lack of German faith in Austrian ability. Moreover, in May, 1915, Italy finally declared war on Austria. That declaration left the Austrians with three fronts: a Serbian front, a Russian front, and an Italian front. Austrian pleas for German help in a planned offensive in the Carpathian Mountains fell on deaf ears with Kaiser Wilhelm II telling a senior Austrian general that "the Carpathians are not worth the bones of a single Pomeranian musketeer."[6] Relations hit a new low when the Germans unsuccessfully offered Italy parts of the Austrian Trentino in exchange for their neutrality.

Still, Germany could not stand by while its principal ally withered and died. The logic of alliance warfare demanded that the Germans assist the Austrians. In May, 1915, German armies struck the Russians in three places, decimating the Russians and forcing the general staff to order the "Great Retreat" out of Poland. Short of competent officers, heavy artillery, and motivated men, the Russian armies disintegrated in the face of efficient German staff work. In all, the so-called Gorlice–Tarnów Offensive cost the Russians 100 miles of territory and more than 1,000,000 total casualties.

For the Austrians, the success of Gorlice–Tarnów relieved the immediate Russian pressure, but the victory came at a great cost. At the last minute, the Germans forced the Austrians to accept the subordination of their own commanders under Germans. Effectively, the Austrian general staff ceased to function as an independent entity. Thereafter, the Austrians became almost completely subordinated to the Germans. The new German Chief of Staff, General Erich von Falkenhayn, did not even bother to inform his Austrian counterparts about the massive offensive he had planned for 1916 at the symbolic city of Verdun.

The allies spent the end of 1915 trying to create some synergy between their disparate forces. In December, 1915 senior generals of the French, British, Russian, and Italian armies met at Joffre's headquarters in the castle of Chantilly. They agreed to conduct simultaneous offensives on the western front, the Italian front, and the Russian front in the hopes of overwhelming the Germans and Austrians. The western front campaign would be a combined Franco-British attack along the Somme River. The Chantilly conference ended with the powers agreeing to launch their coordinated offensives in mid-summer, 1916. They never got the chance, as Germany seized the initiative with its own attack at Verdun in February.

## 1916: Fighting a people's war

As Helmuth von Moltke the elder had foreseen in 1890, a general European war soon became what he called a "people's war," dominated more by national fervor and deeply-held emotion than by military logic. The years 1914 and 1915 were periods of alliance warfare and "cabinet war," but 1916 became the year of people's war. The battles of 1916 largely took on lives of their own and moved well beyond the original designs and plans of the generals. The professional armies that began the war had taken enormous casualties. They, of necessity, had to be replaced by conscript and volunteer armies that produced much closer linkages between armies and societies. As a result, many of the battles of 1916 became national symbols for which nations committed all the resources they had, pushing some of them to the breaking point.

The battle that best typifies the struggles of 1916 occurred at the fortified French city of Verdun. In late 1915, Falkenhayn decided on a plan that he believed would take advantage of the tactical stalemate of the western front. Falkenhayn wanted to fight a battle at a place that had less military significance than national significance. He wanted to use the German army to threaten a place so sacred to French national pride that the French would feel compelled to send every last man to defend it. He did not want to capture this place because to do so might remove French motivation to fight for it. Instead, he wanted to create a "sausage grinder" into which the French would feed division after division while the German army systematically destroyed them and thereby "bled the French white."[7] With France thus defeated, he reasoned, Great Britain would have no choice but to seek peace terms, leaving Germany free to focus all of its efforts on the Russians.

Falkenhayn chose Verdun, a city on the Meuse River that held an unparalleled mythic status in French history. Verdun would demand just the kind of sacrifice Falkenhayn had envisioned. In 843 the Treaty of Verdun divided Charlemagne's empire into three parts, giving birth to the forerunners of the French and German nations as well as the disputed middle ground (including Alsace, Lorraine, and Verdun itself) that the two nations had fought over ever since. Verdun thus held a special significance for Germans as well as Frenchmen. In the tenth century, a German force violated the treaty and captured Verdun, keeping it until Henry II retook it for France in 1552. In 1792 and 1870 Verdun had heroically withstood German sieges before eventually falling. According to French national legend, the fort's commander in 1792 had committed suicide rather than surrender it to France's hereditary enemy. Painted on the door of one of the forts were the words "Better to be buried under the ruins of the fort than to surrender it" and "He who mocks the past does not deserve a future."

In the 1870s France invested in a new phase of construction that turned the entire valley around Verdun into a formidable citadel. By 1914, Verdun boasted 20 large and 40 small forts, most with steel guns and retractable turrets.

The major forts were concrete and steel giants with up to eight feet of earth on top to absorb the shock of enemy artillery shells. The largest, Fort Douaumont, covered three hectares and could protect a garrison of 500 to 800 men. Verdun had the reputation of housing the strongest forts in the world. The Germans understood and respected the strength of Verdun so much that their initial war plans envisaged going far to the north rather than testing Verdun's strength as German armies had attempted before.

In February, 1916 the Germans and Erich von Falkenhayn attacked Verdun again. Only this time, the goal was not to capture Verdun, but to create a gigantic killing cauldron in which Falkenhayn hoped to kill Frenchmen in greater numbers than the French could kill Germans. His plan was grim, diabolical, and certain to kill tens of thousands of men on each side. In order to maintain the morale of his young army, Falkenhayn shared few details of his plans with his subordinate commanders, instead leading them and their men to believe that the goal of this battle would be the capture of Verdun and opening of the road to Paris behind it.

Lt. Colonel Emile Driant, a member of the French Parliament who had returned to active duty in 1914, saw the attack coming. He was then commanding two battalions of French infantry in woods known as the Bois des Caures. From his position he had witnessed the German buildup and had guessed the meaning of the preparations ongoing in front of him. He had warned colleagues in the French Chamber of Deputies that higher headquarters had been removing many of Verdun's most important artillery pieces in order to use them in other sectors of the western front. Verdun, he believed, was too weak to protect itself from the attack he knew was coming. General Joffre reacted angrily to Driant's challenge to his authority, but sent his chief of staff, General Edouard Noël de Castelnau, to Verdun. After a quick assessment of the situation, Castelnau agreed with Driant and on January 20, 1916 ordered massive improvements to be made to the defenses around Verdun.

It was too late. On February 21, German artillery opened up a furious barrage all along the Verdun sector. More than 80,000 shells struck the area around Driant's position in the Bois des Caures alone. The bombardment resumed the next day as Driant prepared the 1,300 men under his command to fight a desperate battle against overwhelming odds. Despite being outnumbered nearly eight to one, he refused to surrender his position. His unit took more than 90 percent casualties, losing strongpoint after strongpoint, but never surrendering. On the afternoon of February 22, Driant burned his papers, stopped to give aid to a wounded comrade, then was struck by a German bullet. His heroic death had given France a national hero and yet another reason to fight for Verdun.

Verdun quickly produced more symbols for both sides. Three days after Driant's death, a handful of German soldiers sneaked into the lightly-defended Fort Douaumont and stunned the undersized garrison inside into surrendering without firing a shot. The victory seemed to German public opinion to symbolize a great turning point in the war. Churches rang their bells, schools gave children a special holiday, and it seemed to many Germans that the fall of France was just months, or even weeks, away.[8] But Douaumont became a symbol for France as well. The French fought for eight months to recapture it, losing, one French general estimated, 100,000 men in the effort to take it back.

Falkenhayn soon found that he could not control the monstrosity that the battle for Verdun had become. French counterattacks forced him to vastly expand his field of operations and commit greater and greater German resources to the campaign. He had not counted on Verdun becoming such an important symbol to the Germans that they would become caught in the same fervor as their French enemies. Verdun raged for ten months, with the desperation of both sides turning it into the worst killing zone the world had ever seen. France suffered 378,000 casualties and Germany 329,000. On average, almost 3,000 men were killed, wounded, or captured every day at Verdun. Yet the battle lines barely moved, even after ten months of systematic massacre.

Verdun destroyed the preparations that the allied high commanders had made at Chantilly. The original plan for the western front worked out by the British and French staffs involved a mid-summer offensive on both sides of the Somme River that would break through German lines. Once through the German defenses, the enemy's lateral lines of communications (those running generally parallel to the front) would be threatened, forcing a German withdrawal. The original plan envisioned the use of forty French divisions and twenty-five British divisions. The French front was to be the main operation, covering twenty-five miles. But the precarious nature of the French position at Verdun soon demanded that the Somme offensive be conducted as a primarily British operation. Consequently, the original forty French divisions were reduced to just sixteen and the French front from twenty-five miles to just eight.

These changes meant that the bulk of the Somme operation became the preserve of the British Army and its new commander, General Douglas Haig. Even though the original BEF had taken 90 percent casualties in 1914 and 1915, the British were still reluctant to impose conscription. Instead, throughout 1915 the British had turned to volunteerism, which meant that the government faced the challenge of motivating sufficient numbers of young men to sign up. The central government, overwhelmed by the exigencies of the war, turned to local authorities and gave them the power to promise men who signed up together that they would stay together during the course of the war. The strategy worked as men signed up "with their pals," creating 142 "Pals Battalions" with local names and close connections to a given town, district, or even a school.

This "New Army" was eager and patriotic, but woefully inexperienced. It lacked veteran officers and was untrained in most of the sophisticated arts of modern war. These shortcomings were supposed to have been balanced out by the experienced French reservists along whose side they were to fight. But most of those veterans moved south to help France survive the German onslaught at Verdun. Aware that his men lacked the abilities of the old BEF, Haig did not believe that he could expect much battlefield skill from his raw and untested army. He therefore hoped to compensate for their lack of tactical sophistication by protecting them with the most massive artillery bombardment to date. The artillery, he hoped, would clear the ground and allow his green troops literally to walk across no man's land and through the German lines. On June 24, the British started shelling with 1,537 heavy guns. In the course of one week they fired 1,627,824 shells along a sixteen-mile front.

Opposite the British, the German Second Army commander, Fritz von Below, had foreseen an Anglo-French operation in his sector and had heavily fortified his position. German soldiers dug deeply into the chalky soil around the Somme River and reinforced several bunkers with concrete. In places, German barbed wire belts were thirty yards deep. German soldiers and impressed civilians dug second, third, and fourth lines of defense that stretched the German position further and further back, diluting the power of the awesome British artillery. The Germans suffered badly from the shelling, but enough of them survived to ruin Haig's hopes for an easy victory.

Between 7:20 and 7:30 on the morning of July 1, 1916, the British guns fell silent. Then, the British detonated ten mines that they had tunneled underneath German lines. Seventy thousand British troops lined up, almost shoulder to shoulder, anxious to do their part. Nothing, they believed, could have survived under the weight of all those shells. Some men, young and innocent, even kicked soccer balls as they left their trenches. Believing that they were poised to conduct the war-winning breakthrough, the men carried with them almost sixty pounds of equipment, slowing their advance to a crawl.

The Germans quickly made it clear that the shelling had not destroyed their defenses. Eager to shoot back after suffering from the one-week artillery barrage, they sighted their machine guns and opened fire. The heavily-laden British "Tommies" were easy targets. Before the day was over, the British had lost nearly 20,000 dead and 40,000 wounded. Because of the Pals system, some small towns lost virtually all of their young men in a single hour. Britain's first day of the great offensive on the Somme had been a total disaster.

Despite the terrible losses (or perhaps because of them), the British could not call an end to the Somme campaign. Verdun was still threatened and most Britons believed that to stop so early would render meaningless the sacrifices of the men lost on July 1. There had also been some signs of success on the British south flank, where joint Franco-British attacks had captured significant ground and beaten back a violent German counterattack. Another great effort, many believed, and the British might achieve the desired breakthrough. Therefore, Allied generals violated an important military principle and reinforced failure.

They did so in part because they believed, correctly, that British artillery had inflicted enormous casualties on the Germans. The enemy, Haig and his staff hoped, might be on the verge of collapsing. German losses had been enormous. General Ludendorff said later that the Somme had "absolutely exhausted" the German army in the west. Nevertheless, the Germans found the strength to respond. In the first week of the offensive they moved twenty more battalions into the Somme sector while continuing their campaign farther south at Verdun.

The Somme campaign thus continued, with the British improvising their tactics and adapting the elastic, small-unit advances that the French had used with some limited success at Verdun and on their sector of the Somme battlefield. The British achieved some local triumphs, but nothing to justify the immense losses (150,000 casualties by the end of July alone) and nothing to indicate that a breakthrough into open country was imminent. In September, the British hastily introduced the first tanks into World War I in hopes of reenergizing their efforts on the Somme, but to little effect. That winter, the Germans began a retreat to a prepared set of powerful defenses known in the west as the Hindenburg Line, making any hopes of breaking German lines in 1917 seem even more unrealistic than in 1916.

The Somme, like Verdun, grew into a large, sprawling campaign that commanders found themselves unable fully to control. As Moltke had predicted twenty-six years earlier, nations could not be defeated in a single campaign because modern nations would admit defeat only as a last resort. Within weeks after the start of the battle, the British government produced and released a film called *The Battle of the Somme* that included both staged and actual combat footage. More than 20,000,000 people saw the film in just five months, bringing home the reality of the war to British civilians and, as the producers intended, closely connecting British society to the war effort. Efforts on the Somme would have to be renewed, even if its strategic justification had long since evaporated.

Thus, as Moltke had foreseen, the two battles continued to rage despite having lost their original purposes. Verdun had seriously weakened the French Army, but it had seriously weakened the German Army as well. In August, Falkenhayn was relieved as commander of German forces, largely because his Verdun plan had so badly backfired. The fighting on the Somme had further drained German resources, making the withdrawal to the Hindenburg Line a strategic necessity. The Somme campaign dragged on for 142 days and cost the British 419,000 casualties, the French 194,000, and the Germans 650,000. The lines had hardly moved and the allies were not in control of any strategically significant piece of ground on November 19 that they had not controlled on June 24.

Verdun and the Somme ruined all of the careful planning at Chantilly. The promised Italian offensive did little to help. General Luigi Cadorna had already attacked the Austrians along the narrow Isonzo River valley four times without positive result. Indeed, Italy's entry had proven to be the only unifying factor that Austria-Hungary could rally around. Virtually all of the empire's nationalities saw Italy as a perfidious foe, partly as a result of the Austro-Italian War of 1866, when Italy had taken advantage of Austria's loss to Prussia to declare war and seize Venetia. Even the minority groups inside the Austro-Hungarian Empire interpreted Italy's withdrawal from the Triple Alliance and their 1915 declaration of war as villainous Italian attempts to seize Austrian land while the empire was engaged on other fronts. Under the command of the able Croatian general Svetozar Boroević, the Austro-Hungarian forces seized and fortified high ground and repulsed four Italian charges throughout 1915, inflicting 235,000 Italian casualties.

At Chantilly, the Italians agreed to try again despite the losses they had already suffered for minimal gains. Urged on by France, Cadorna attacked on March 6, 1916, but rain and snow slowed the Italians considerably, leading to 50,000 more casualties. Nevertheless, as at Verdun and the Somme, the battles on the Isonzo took on lives of their own. They became symbols for the Italians, with heroic tales of their own including that of the composer Alberto Toscanini marching a band to the top of a recently captured hill and playing patriotic songs even while his unit was under shell fire. The battles were formative experiences for a young Italian journalist named Benito Mussolini. The Italians eventually launched eleven separate attacks on the Austrian positions in the Isonzo River. They achieved minimal success for enormous casualties in the steep and snowy foothills of the Julian Alps that overlook the river.

Elsewhere, the Austrians experienced less success. The only moderately successful offensive that came out of Chantilly was a Russian offensive planned and led by General Alexei Brusilov. Launched on June 4, the Russian army attacked the already faltering Austrians along a wide front without the prior use of heavy artillery to signal their intentions. They achieved near total surprise. In 72 hours, the Russians advanced 80 kilometers, took 200,000 prisoners, and seized 700 heavy guns. Before ammunition shortages forced Brusilov to call a halt in September, the Russians had captured 375,000 soldiers from an already weak Austrian army. The Germans rushed reinforcements from Verdun, saving the Austrians from a complete collapse (and greatly assisting the French effort by reducing the German contingent at Verdun), but the Germans took over nearly all phases of the Austrian war effort. In just two years of war, the Austro-Hungarian military had been reduced to a shell of its former self.

The Brusilov offensives also weakened the victorious Russians. Although they had pushed the Austrians back, the offensives did not lead to a Russian victory in the war more generally. Russia had also taken 1,000,000 more casualties, leading many Russians to question what all the sacrifice had been for. As a result, pressure continued to mount on the Tsar, who had taken over personal command of the Russian armies in the wake of the Gorlice–Tarnów disaster. As in 1905, Russian failure in the war undermined the logic of the Tsar as the "Great Father" of the Russian people. The Tsarist system, which had seemed secure, if not totally stable, in 1914, now seemed to be teetering on the verge of an abyss.

Monarchical systems were in a particularly difficult position as a result of the events of 1914–1916. Although the royals of Europe liked to wear military uniforms and attend dress parades, they had little real understanding of the intricate technicalities of modern war. Kaiser Wilhelm had commanded units in pre-war maneuvers, but the conclusion always had to be fixed so that his side won. Monarchs understood the complexities of modern industrial economics even less. When the shooting became real, the Kaiser, as well as the Austro-Hungarian Emperor (whose own military service dated to the 1848 revolution), the Tsar, and the Ottoman Sultan were revealed to be figureheads with no real role in the system. Even the Kaiser's own sycophantic staff came to understand his marginalization to grand strategic and operational decisions.

Legislatures also became increasingly irrelevant. British Prime Minister H. H. Asquith may have overstated the case when he told a friend that the only really effective government in wartime was a dictatorship. Nevertheless, the western democracies found it impossible to conduct war through the endless legislative committees that had characterized government before 1914. In Britain and France especially, legislatures had been particularly powerful as political thought in those nations argued for checks and controls on executive authority. During the war these controls broke down, leaving central executive authority much stronger. In France, Germany, and Britain the legislatures ceded much of their right to debate the war, only doing so behind closed doors or in exceptional circumstances. In Austria, the parliament went so far as to dissolve itself. The result was a tremendous growth in the power of executive authority.

Moreover, the war placed government officials into the lives of ordinary citizens in ways never before envisioned. Food rationing, price controls, propaganda campaigns, conscription, and government control over industry were only a few examples of the ways that the state regularly entered into the lives of Europeans. Enemy air raids by both Zeppelins and airplanes underscored the need to organize and centrally direct home defense. Those governments that could complete these tasks efficiently, including Great Britain, France, and (until 1918) Germany, could withstand the strains of war. Those that could not, including Russia, Austria-Hungary, and Italy, increased domestic tensions even further.

All across Europe people had begun to question what the war was about. The shooting of an archduke, an 1839 treaty guaranteeing Belgian neutrality, and esoteric commitments to poorly understood alliances all seemed to belong to a different world to the people of 1916. Motivating soldiers and civilians proved to be easiest in France, where German armies occupied most of the northeastern part of the country, and Germany, where victory always seemed to be close. The answers were harder to find in the increasingly archaic monarchies of the east.

As the assassination of the archduke and the spirit of 1914 faded, nations had to look for other reasons to keep fighting. Demonization of the enemy became a central theme. Allied propaganda focused on German targeting of civilians, including the trial and execution of Edith Cavell, an English nurse, for assisting wounded British soldiers in Belgium. The Germans appeared depraved when they rebuffed all diplomatic initiatives to spare her life. Germany's submarine warfare also killed civilians, including the 1,200 men, women, and children aboard the *Lusitania* when it was torpedoed off the coast of Ireland in 1915. The Germans not only refused to apologize for the sinking, they commemorated it with special medals and coins. The crew of the submarine that sank the *Lusitania* became instant German heroes.

Unlike Germany's submarine blockade, Great Britain's blockade of Germany with surface ships was legal by the laws of warfare, but it also affected civilians. As a result of the blockade, food shortages became commonplace in Germany. Wealthier families turned to the black market to supplement what they could not get otherwise, but poorer families suffered from hunger and malnutrition. The Germans defended their use of submarines as the only way to strike back at Britain; they dismissed the illegality of their blockade as an outdated distinction between surface ships and submarines. Still, in May, 1916, the anger of neutral nations, most notably the United States, forced the Germans to issue a pledge not to sink neutral ships without warning, temporarily limiting the effectiveness of their submarine campaign.

The pressures of war produced important and long-reaching outcomes, even in stable societies such as Great Britain. At long last, in 1916, Great Britain introduced a conscription bill. The extension of conscription to Ireland fueled long-simmering flames of Irish nationalism. The Germans fanned those flames by landing Irish nationalist Roger Casement (who had been living in Berlin) on the Irish coast by submarine. On April 24, the rebellion known as the Easter Rising broke out in Dublin, creating chaos throughout the Irish capital. The British tried and executed several ringleaders of the rebellion, including Casement, but a new generation of Irish leaders soon emerged, initiating the Anglo-Irish Civil War which lasted until 1921. The war eventually produced the separation of Ireland into an Irish Republic and a Northern Ireland still formally a part of Great Britain. One of the civil war's casualties was General Henry Wilson, an opponent of Irish statehood, who survived the First World War only to be assassinated on his doorstep by Irish nationalists in 1922.

The events of 1916 thus saw the war assume a character that no one had envisioned. Winston Churchill may have come the closest when he observed that "Victory was to be bought so dear as to be almost indistinguishable from defeat." Verdun and the Somme, to name just the two most famous campaigns of 1916, could not be called victories or defeat in the normal sense. Victory came instead to mean not losing. At Verdun, the French could claim that they had "won" only by virtue of still holding the city after ten months of the bloodiest combat in history. The Germans "won" at the Somme only by virtue of surviving the furious British artillery and not allowing their lines to be broken. At the end of 1916, the war appeared far from over; indeed, it seemed that the war itself was the only winner. As a German theology student, Friederich Georg Steinbrecher, observed in November, 1916, "The war which began as a fresh youth is ending up as a made-up, boring, antiquated actor. Death is the only conqueror." Like many young men of his generation, he survived 1916 only to be killed in 1917.[9]

## 1917: War, revolution, mutiny, and collapse

Steinbrecher shared the sentiment of many Europeans that the war had taken on a macabre life of its own. The pervasive belief in 1914 that the war would last just a few months contributed to the profound and deep sense of shock that spread through the continent as the war continued to kill uncontrollably. By 1917 the casualty lists had grown longer than anyone had imagined three years earlier; worse still, the war appeared no closer to a conclusion at the start of 1917 than it had one year earlier. The battles of 1917 increased the death toll dramatically without producing any noticeable gains on the western front. In the east, the war finally led to the collapse of one European society, Tsarist Russia, with another, the Austro-Hungarian Empire, not far behind.

Moreover, the short war illusion had led governments to delay the conversion of industry to wartime needs until the summer of 1915 or even later. As a result, few societies were fully prepared for the economic war that accompanied the military war. Critical resources such as food and fuel grew increasingly scarce, putting further pressure on the societies and home fronts that sustained war. The winter of 1916–1917 became known in Germany as the "turnip winter" due to the scarcity of most other comestibles. The British blockade squeezed the Germans more and more tightly, increasing the pressure on the German government to resume unrestricted submarine warfare, both as a way to try to win the war and as a way to strike back at England.

The war placed unprecedented pressure on the economies of the belligerents, further increasing the anguish of those at home. In Germany, inflation led to a trebling of the cost of living from 1914 to 1918, with wages unable to keep pace.[10] With people suffering, consumer goods unavailable, and inflation reducing what buying power money had, the results were predictable and included an increase in crime, material hardship, and increasing social and political tensions on the home front. Similar hardships affected Britain and France, although the entry of the United States into the war in April helped tremendously by increasing access to American credit and supplies.

The nationalist logic of the war fueled these tensions and created terrible hardships for some groups. People looking for scapegoats to explain their nation's inability to win the war often turned on reviled minority groups within their states. The worst example of this type of hyper-nationalism occurred in the Ottoman Empire, where accusations that the Armenians (a minority long despised by ethnic Turks) had aided and abetted the Russians led to a brutal campaign of repression that many scholars cite as the twentieth century's first systematic attempt at genocide. From 1915 to 1917, the Ottoman Empire forcefully relocated hundreds of thousands of Armenians from their native territories in eastern Anatolia to Mesopotamia and Syria.

The Ottomans did not create the industrial killing camps that the Nazis did in World War II, but they treated the Armenians with willful disregard for their health, safety, and welfare. The Armenians were systematically robbed of their property, forced on long marches through mountains and deserts without food or water, and viciously beaten. In the process, as many as 500,000 Armenians died, most from hunger and exposure. Foreign journalists and other witnesses recorded the deportations and attendant misery, but none of the great powers took action. The United States claimed that as a neutral it could do nothing and Germany refused to pressure its ally into stopping the torment. France did not officially recognize the genocide until 2001 and the United States, eager to maintain close links with Turkey, still has not done so. Adolf Hitler later took note of the unwillingness of European nations to express their outrage and decided that he had nothing to fear from them if he exterminated Europe's Jews.

Although World War I did not bring with it the unspeakable horrors of World War II for the Jewish community, Jews suffered terribly from 1914 to 1918. Although during World War I Jews volunteered to serve in their respective states' militaries disproportionately to their representation in the population more generally (including the only German Reichstag member to die in service), Jews had constantly to face the accusation that they belonged to the "Jewish nation," and were therefore not capable of being loyal to their resident nations. Ottomans, Germans, Poles, and Russians alike took advantage of the chaos of the war to loot Jewish shops, confiscate Jewish property, and destroy synagogues. The Ottomans deported thousands of Jews to Palestine, where many later joined a British unit. It was a small step from the anti-Semitism of the war years to the German army's desire to pass the blame for their defeat on a Jewish-Bolshevik "stab in the back" falsehood that was all too easy for many Germans to believe.

The pressures on Germany to win the war led to some extraordinary measures. Few of these steps were more cost-effective than the delivery into Russia of one of the veterans of the 1905 revolution, a forty-four year old revolutionary named Vladimir Ilyich Lenin. In April, the Germans took Lenin from Switzerland, where he had been living in exile, and delivered him in a sealed railway car to St. Petersburg. He arrived in the middle of a Russia in complete disarray, with workers on strike and soldiers no longer willing to fight for the Romanov dynastic system.

The Tsar's 1915 decision to leave St. Petersburg and lead from the general staff's headquarters in Mogilev meant that he was unable to help alleviate the suffering in the cities; by 1917 he had become an obvious target for frustrated Russians. As the new commander-in-chief he also shouldered much of the blame for military losses. The prestige and cachet that all monarchical systems depend upon therefore withered and the entire society began a descent into revolution. When a riot broke out in St. Petersburg in March, troops disobeyed orders to put it down. Many joined the rioters instead.

The rapid collapse of the Tsar's armies led to chaos. Many government officials fled St. Petersburg, leaving no formal institutions in place to maintain order. Rioters burned police stations, liberated prisons, seized arsenals, and organized the capital to prepare to defend it against a Tsarist counteroffensive. Stopped on his way back to St. Petersburg, the Tsar realized the hopelessness of the situation and abdicated. A new government soon formed under the leadership of a moderate politician, Aleksander Kerensky, who hoped to restore Russia's fortune with a successful counter-offensive that would rally the army and reinvigorate morale. The allies supported Kerensky because they saw in him the only realistic chance they had to maintain an eastern front.

The Germans hoped that Lenin could serve their own interests by fomenting revolution, undermining the remaining legitimacy of Kerensky's provisional Russian state, and forcing the Russian giant to abandon the war. Lenin was well-connected to Europe's communist leaders, most of whom saw the war as the opening shots of a worldwide worker's revolution. He pledged to get Russia out of the war, preaching the slogan "bread, peace, and land." The predictable failure of the Kerensky offensive in July led to the virtual dissolution of the Russian army as thousands of Russian soldiers simply deserted. The seizure of power by Lenin's Bolsheviks in November paid the Germans enormous dividends for the cost of Lenin's train trip.

German armies continued their march eastward until the Bolsheviks agreed to the Treaty of Brest-Litovsk, signed in March, 1918. The Bolsheviks got their peace, but not before signing an incredibly one-sided treaty. They surrendered the formerly Russian territories of Finland, the Ukraine, Bessarabia, the Baltic States, Galicia, and the Crimea. In all Russia lost 1,000,000 square miles of territory and 62,000,000 people. Russia also had to surrender to Germany vast stores of oil, grain, locomotives, heavy guns, and ammunition, which the Germans planned to use to compensate for the British blockade and to prepare for a 1918 offensive against France and Britain.

Seizing Russian resources represented one step in Germany's plan for 1917 and 1918. A second key element of that plan was the resumption of unrestricted submarine warfare. The Germans hoped that a submarine offensive against Britain might pressure the British to seek a separate peace. Such an offensive, they knew, carried with it the risk of bringing the United States into the war. The German high command calculated that Germany could use their submarines either to prevent the Americans from getting to Europe or to win the war before the Americans could make their power felt. Although the United States had enormous manpower and economic resources, its strict adherence to neutrality meant that it would take time to overcome inertia and organize its vast resources for war. President Woodrow Wilson had been so careful to retain the nation's neutrality that he had forbidden the Army's general staff even from planning for the dispatch of forces to Europe. The Americans had sent few observers to the war zones and had taken few steps to prepare their society for war. The German resumption of submarine warfare did provoke the United

States into declaring war in April, 1917, but it would take nearly a year for the Americans to develop a true fighting force.

The allies could not, therefore, count on much immediate help from the United States, although America's entry proved to be a tremendous boost to sagging Allied morale. Neither could they count any longer on the Russians. The Russian exit did, however, allow the allies to depict the war as a struggle between democracy and dictatorship. Furthermore, Brest-Litovsk (and an equally crushing treaty that Germany forced on Romania) signaled to Britain and France that any peace with Germany would be tremendously costly. They could not afford to lose now.

The Allies badly hurt their own cause in 1917 by launching two disastrous offensives. The first was a French operation designed to create a breakthrough in the Champagne region. Its architect was General Robert Nivelle, a slick and charismatic artillerist who had begun the war as a colonel, but had quickly risen through the senior ranks. He was best known for his innovative "rolling barrages" that had protected French infantry at Verdun and had helped France to recapture Fort Douaumont. He proposed to use similar tactics to achieve a major breakthrough of the German lines along the Chemin des Dames, a scenic and pastoral ridge that had attained its name ("the road of the ladies") because the women of the court of Louis XIV had enjoyed riding their horses there.

British generals were skeptical of the plan, but British politicians, especially Prime Minister David Lloyd George, were enamored of Nivelle. The general had an English mother, was charming, confident, and spoke perfect idiomatic English. He convinced Lloyd George to subordinate the British army under overall French command for the duration of the operation and also convinced Lloyd George to force Haig to agree to conduct a diversionary attack north of Champagne. Haig grew so incensed at being subordinated to the French that he almost threatened to resign; the King himself had to convince him not to do so.

Haig was, in this case at least, correct, because Nivelle's grand offensive turned into one of the great disasters of the war. A German trench raid seized a complete copy of the orders for the offensive, scheduled for April. In response, the German high command heavily fortified the Chemin des Dames and retired the bulk of their forces (which included 34 new divisions moved into the sector) back to the Hindenburg Line. French generals and politicians grew increasingly pessimistic about the offensive, but did not call Nivelle's bluff when he threatened to resign if the government ordered a postponement.

French morale had been surprisingly high, buoyed by the prospect of winning the war, the entry of the Americans, and the enormous artillery stocks Nivelle had assembled. Unfortunately, the German withdrawal meant that the artillery barrage largely struck undefended positions and chewed up the very ground over which the French soldiers were to advance. The French troops were easy targets as they advanced slowly through rain, snow, and fog uphill toward the Chemin des Dames. The French suffered 120,000 casualties in the offensive's first five days (April 17 to 21, 1917) without gaining any significant ground. The French medical corps, prepared to handle 15,000 casualties, was soon overwhelmed.

The Chemin des Dames catastrophe broke the soul and spirit of the French army. Men in half of the French divisions began to refuse orders to advance. Most of them were tough, battle-hardened veterans of Verdun who could not be accused of cowardice, but could not be coaxed into attacking either. For six weeks, the men of the French army effectively went on strike. The strikers' demands were partially material: they wanted better food, better pay, more frequent leave, and better medical care. But the demands were also political. They wanted a peace without annexations, but, tellingly, they urged the French government to insist upon the return of Alsace and Lorraine. The men could not, therefore, be accused of treason. The French army did not fraternize with the Germans, nor did they abandon their positions. Aware that they stood between the Germans and the eastern approaches to Paris, French soldiers were careful not to give the enemy a chance to achieve a breakthrough. Incredibly, the Germans did not find out about the strike until it was too late for them to take advantage of it.

To stem the crisis and return the French army to its fighting effectiveness, the government replaced the discredited Nivelle. The new commander, General Henri Philippe Pétain, soon took hold of the situation. Pétain had also been one of the heroes of Verdun, acquiring a reputation for concern for his men that was generally lacking among senior French officers. Pétain dismissed the allegations of many generals that the mutiny was the result of outside agitation. Rather, he understood that the men had expressed legitimate complaints and soon moved to improve their material conditions. As he had done at Verdun, he rotated units in and out of combat to give men longer periods of rest. He approved 49 executions, mostly of men who had committed serious crimes, but he commuted almost 500 death sentences, earning him a reputation for fairness that soon reinforced the adulation of his men.

If Haig had correctly predicted Nivelle's failure, his sense of triumph over the British politicians who had forced him to accept a joint command was short-lived. He soon directed and oversaw his own disaster in the Ypres sector of Belgium near the town of Passchendaele. One of the immediate goals of the offensive was the neutralization of the German submarine bases along the Belgian coastline. Germany's resumption of submarine warfare made such an operation seem critical if Britain were to take maximum economic advantage of America's entry into the war. Moreover, with the French army in tatters, the British would have to assume the responsibility for winning the war in 1917.

But Haig's staff work was inadequate to the task of removing the Germans from positions they had held, and fortified, since 1914. His grandiose plans (which included a cavalry charge that could not possibly have succeeded) counted on being able to conduct offensive warfare, a fallacy that the experiences of 1914 to 1917 should have exposed. Still, Haig remained supremely confident and ordered the offensive to begin in July, despite torrential rains that turned the Ypres salient into a sea of mud. From July to November the two sides fought a horrid slugging match in that mud, with each side losing 250,000 men; the lines barely moved. General Launcelot Kiggell, Haig's chief of staff, left his château headquarters long enough to see the mud for himself and allegedly exclaim, "Did we really send men to fight in this?"[11]

Passchendaele did not lead to the kind of wide-spread disorder and mutiny of the Chemin des Dames, but even in Britain morale showed signs of cracking. In September, a disturbance at the British training center of Etaples had to be put down by British troops. The breakdown of discipline at Etaples was a relatively minor incident but it underscored the precarious nature of military morale. Even in the Belgian army, most of whose nation was under direct German occupation, desertions rose from 1,203 in 1916 to 5,603 in 1917. Strikes also increased on several home fronts in 1917, often as a reflection of actions by men at the front. Female munitions workers in Paris, for example, went on strike after the Chemin des Dames disaster, in part to oppose the dangerous conditions of the factories and in part to support husbands and brothers at the front.

The situation was even more serious in Austria-Hungary, which entered its final death throes as various nationalities began to stake out territory after the death of Emperor Franz Joseph in November, 1916. His successor, Emperor Karl, took personal control of the army and saw no choice but to grant more autonomy to local minorities. It was too little too late as the empire continued to disband. In May, 1917, 50,000 workers at the critically important Skoda arms works went on strike, forcing Karl to order troops to put down the strike. Industrial production for civilian markets collapsed and the 1916 harvest was unusually poor, furthering the traumas of the empire. Conditions continued to worsen until by the end of 1917 Vienna was receiving less than 10 percent of the food deliveries it needed.

Nevertheless, the Austro-Hungarian Empire had one more success left, this time against the Italians at the Battle of Caporetto in October. Working under the overall authority of the Germans and using new "storm troop" tactics, the combined German–Austrian force smashed through the Italian lines and routed the Italian Second Army. Panicked, the Italians began a disorderly retreat that soon yielded 250,000 prisoners of war and untold thousands of deserters. The disorder did not end until the Italians reached the Piave River, just 20 miles from Venice. Italy replaced its ineffectual commander, Luigi Cadorna, with General Armando Diaz, who, like Pétain, had the confidence of his men. He offered deserters an amnesty that brought thousands of soldiers back to their units. Now seeing Italy in grave danger, Italian morale rebounded and prevented the loss of Venice.

The Caporetto fiasco led to the allies' first dedicated attempt at fighting a joint war. They rushed six French and five British divisions to the Piave River to reinforce the Italians, help stem the retreat, and establish a solid defensive line.

Several of the Allies' most respected and capable commanders, including Ferdinand Foch and Sir Herbert Plumer, went to Italy to supervise personally the reconstruction of the Italian army. The Allies then hurriedly called for a conference at the Italian city of Rapallo, near Genoa, on November 5 and 6 to decide how to proceed. The British generals, recalling the Chemin des Dames, remained adamantly opposed to a joint command structure. The compromise solution reached at Rapallo led to the creation of a Supreme War Council, consisting of one head of state, one cabinet member, and one senior military officer each from France, Britain, Italy, and the United States. The Council, which met in Paris, was a far cry from real unified command, but it provided a regular forum for discussion about issues of mutual importance.

No issue was more critical than the prospect of a massive German offensive in the Spring of 1918. With Germany able to spend much of the winter moving some of its resources from the Russian front to France, the Germans assembled an advantage of 199 divisions to 164 Allied divisions. The Americans were beginning to arrive, but they were inexperienced and short of most of the heavy equipment needed for modern warfare. Lacking a joint command, the Allies could not plan to defend the entire western front as a single theater. The British continued to focus on the area north of Amiens, the French on the area immediately around Paris, and the Americans on the relatively quiet sector opposite the St. Mihiel salient. No one on the Allied side doubted that the Germans would attack. But everyone had different ideas about exactly where and when the attack might come. Would the Supreme War Council be sufficiently effective to stop it? Would the Americans arrive in time to help? The year 1917 had been one of disaster for the Allies. If they could not stop the German offensive predicted for the spring, 1918 would be even worse.

## Further reading

Hew Strachan, *The First World War: To Arms!* (Oxford: Oxford University Press, 2001) covers only the start of the war, but will likely be one of the standard accounts of World War I for years to come. Two more volumes of this trilogy will follow. General introductions include Hew Strachan, ed., *World War I: A History* (Oxford: Oxford University Press, 1998); Michael Howard, *The First World War* (Oxford: Oxford University Press, 2002); James Stokesbury, *A Short History of World War I* (New York: William Morrow, 1981); Jay Winter and Blaine Baggett, *The Great War and the Shaping of the Twentieth Century* (New York: Penguin, 1996); Spencer Tucker, *The Great War, 1914–1918* (London: Routledge, 1998); and Martin Gilbert, *The First World War* (New York: Henry Holt, 1994). Norman Stone, *The Eastern Front, 1914–1917* (London: Penguin, 1975) remains the best survey of the east.

Other important works include Paul Fussell, *The Great War and Modern Memory* (Oxford: Oxford University Press, 1980); John Horne and Alan Kramer, *German Atrocities: A History of Denial* (New Haven: Yale University

Press, 2001); Alistair Horne, *The Price of Glory: Verdun 1916* (New York: St. Martin's, 1963); Dennis Showalter, *Tannenberg: Clash of Empires* (Hamden, CT: Archon Books, 1993); John Schindler, *Isonzo: The Forgotten Sacrifice of the Great War* (Westport, CT: Praeger Press, 2001); Denis Winter, *Death's Men: Soldiers of the Great War* (London: Penguin, 1979); Roger Chickering, *Imperial Germany and the Great War, 1914–1918* (Cambridge: Cambridge University Press, 1998); Holger Herwig, *The First World War: Germany and Austria-Hungary, 1914–1918* (London: Arnold Publishing, 1997); Leonard Smith, *Between Mutiny and Obedience* (Princeton: Princeton University Press, 1994) and Alan Moorhead, *Gallipoli* (New York: Harper Perennial, 2002).

# 3

# WORLD WAR I, 1917–1919

## The Yanks are coming

On April 2, 1917 American President Woodrow Wilson addressed the United States Senate with the purpose of asking its members to declare war on Germany. Just a year earlier, he had run for reelection on the slogan "He kept us out of war." He had won, but by the slimmest margin of victory of any American president since 1884. In fact, the Paris media had initially reported that his rival, Republican Charles Evans Hughes, had won. Despite his campaign pledge, Wilson now found himself asking the American people to support war with Germany.

The President understood the irony of his situation. Having so recently promised to keep the nation out of the bloody war in Europe, he was now asking America to accept the radical transformations necessary to become a belligerent in a global war. The United States, he therefore reassured the Senate, would fight not for profit or territorial gain, but for peace. The President made it clear that the United States could justify its entry in the war only if the nation fought for the highest of ideals. Foremost among those ideals was the destruction of Europe's last remaining autocracy, Germany:

> We are accepting this challenge of hostile purpose because we know that in such a government [as Germany's], following such methods, we can never have a friend; and that in the presence of its organized power, always lying in wait to accomplish we know not what purpose, there can be no assured security for the democratic governments of the world. We are now about to accept . . . battle with this natural foe to liberty and shall, if necessary, spend the whole force of the nation to check and nullify its pretensions and its power. We are glad, now that we see the facts with no veil of false pretense about them, to fight thus for the ultimate peace of the world and for the liberation of its peoples, the German peoples included: for the rights of nations great and small and the privilege of men everywhere to choose their way of life and of obedience. The world must be made safe for democracy. Its peace must

be planted upon the tested foundations of political liberty. We have no selfish ends to serve. We desire no conquest, no dominion. We seek no indemnities for ourselves, no material compensation for the sacrifices we shall freely make. We are but one of the champions of the rights of mankind. We shall be satisfied when those rights have been made as secure as the faith and the freedom of nations can make them.

Wilson's speech served its purpose, as the United States entered the war against Germany four days later (and against Austria-Hungary six days later) despite significant reservations on the part of many isolationist senators.

America's entry into the war promised to become both a blessing and a challenge for Britain and France. On the positive side, America's entry meant much greater access to that nation's vast economic resources. American banks, which had already been extending credit to cash-starved Britain and France at far greater rates than they offered to the Central Powers, could now do so without the fear that such credits would endanger America's neutrality. American credits to, and trade with, Germany and Austria-Hungary, naturally, would now stop. With the United States in the war, the allies could eventually count on hundreds of thousands of fresh, well-provisioned American troops. America's entry (combined with Russia's exit) also made it easier for the allies to depict the war as a struggle between democracy and autocracy.

America's entry was so important to the Allies that the French government sent Marshal Joffre on a tour of the United States to boost American support. His tour was a triumph, as he was greeted by cheering crowds everywhere he went. Shops and offices in Washington closed so that employees could join the admiring throngs. Joffre observed that the Americans were full of energy, enthusiasm, and a desire to fight. It would, of course, take time to husband the nation's vast resources, convert the economy from a peacetime basis to a wartime one, and train the millions of Americans who would either volunteer or be drafted. Building an officer corps would be an especially challenging task. Still, if the Allies could divine a way to organize, transport, and train the American army, it would prove to be a formidable weapon, and one that might well lead to an Allied victory.

But for all of these tremendous benefits, American entry came with some important drawbacks. Careful listeners to Wilson's speech would have noticed that the nation was not fighting for the same goals as the Europeans. Wilson, a supremely idealistic man, was fighting for principles that his European counterparts did not always support. On January 18, 1918, Wilson set out the goals of America's war effort in a famous speech known as the Fourteen Points. His points included an end to secret diplomacy, freedom of the seas, removal of trade barriers, readjustment of state borders based on nationalism, and the formation of an association of nations to resolve future disputes.

Some of these points, such as the demand that Germany return Alsace and Lorraine to France, fitted in perfectly with European goals, but several others directly conflicted with them. Wilson was adamantly anti-imperialist and many of his European allies saw in Wilson's arguments for national self-determination a scheme that might eventually undermine the logic of their own empires. To cite one example, the British and French had already concluded a secret agreement, known as the Sykes–Picot Agreement, that divided the Ottoman Empire's Arab territories between them. That agreement violated several of Wilson's points. Would the American president seek to invalidate such agreements? Would the president apply his guideline of national self-determination to Ireland or to India? If so, Britain might win the war only to find that an ally had given away its empire. The British, moreover, depended upon mastery of the seas and imperial preferences in trade, both of which violated Wilson's points.

Furthermore, American entry into European affairs came without precedent. No American president had ever visited Europe while in office. The omission, hard to imagine in contemporary circumstances, was due to more than the length of travel. Americans had made isolation from the affairs of Europe a point of special pride. George Washington himself had warned the nation of the dangers of alliances and most American politicians looked upon European diplomats as dangerous and corrupt. Association with European affairs, many Americans believed, sullied their own nation's virtue. Thus Wilson's sudden desire to remake Europe struck the Europeans as haughty, arrogant, and potentially perilous. French Prime Minister Georges Clemenceau, upon first reading the Fourteen Points, is said to have dismissively remarked, "God Himself only gave us ten."

Furthermore, the Americans were proving to be so uncooperative that they made Sir John French's behavior in 1914 look almost obliging by comparison. President Wilson refused to sign any formal alliances with Britain and France; he insisted on calling the United States an "associated power" rather than an ally. Wilson believed that America was fighting for different goals than the Europeans and he wanted to maintain absolute freedom of action for the United States. He wanted his country to make a distinct contribution to victory so that his voice would be the loudest at the post-war peace conference. To underscore America's separation from the Europeans Wilson did not send a high-level official to Europe to act as his emissary, instead sending to Europe a friend and political supporter named Edward House, who had the president's confidence, but did not have a formal appointment in the American government.

Wilson also gave the commander of the American Expeditionary Forces (AEF), General John Pershing, explicit instructions to avoid "amalgamating" the American army. Both the British and the French argued that the most effective way to use American troops was to integrate them into existing units on the western front. Such a scheme, they believed, would allow the inexperienced Americans to learn from the French and British. It would also alleviate supply problems and make the Americans almost immediately usable. The Europeans argued that it was folly to allow the Americans to build up their army in the United States while the Germans were preparing to attack on the western front. Much better, they contended, to ship the Americans to Europe at once, train them in France, then integrate them as quickly as possible into European units.

Like most Americans, Wilson was adamantly opposed to such a plan. To amalgamate the American army would be to seriously impair his ability to dictate the peace. It would also be a tremendous blow to American national prestige. American military commanders, mindful of the bloodletting at places like Passchendaele, the Somme, and Verdun, were horrified at the idea of French and British generals ordering Americans into battle. Pershing therefore went to France with a signed letter from President Wilson ordering him to resist any and all attempts to place American troops under European commanders.

These decisions accurately reflected common American assumptions. Despite significant opposition to American entry into the war before April, 1917, the American people responded to Wilson's call and his idealistic goals. Americans even accepted a draft, by which three in four American soldiers entered the army. Wilson and Pershing's principled opposition to having American soldiers fighting under European commanders also received broad support. Once engaged in the war, the Americans were anxious to prove themselves a great power in their own right.

The crisis that the Allies had anticipated arrived as discussions about how to use these new troops were ongoing. The Germans finally began their 1918 offensive on March 21 along a sixty-mile front. They had hoped to force the British to turn north toward the English Channel and the French toward Paris, thereby opening a gap and creating flanks that they could turn and expose. Their initial success was remarkable, gaining forty miles in just a few weeks. The Germans inflicted almost 240,000 casualties, although their own casualties were nearly as high. They had come close enough to Paris to compel the French government to evacuate to Bordeaux, as it had done in 1914. They also terrorized the population of the city with seven nine-inch guns capable of firing shells eighty miles into the heart of Paris. The so-called "Paris guns" had 117 foot-long barrels and fired their shells on a trajectory that carried them halfway to the edge of the earth's atmosphere. The guns were too inaccurate to be aimed at specific targets. The goal was to induce panic among the civilian populace. Although the shelling inflicted almost 900 casualties, it failed to achieve that aim.

The Allies responded to the crisis by finally creating a supreme command. On March 26 and April 3, the Allies signed two agreements that gave French general Ferdinand Foch the authority to determine overall Allied strategy. Foch pledged to maintain contact between the British and French lines, thus preventing a gap from opening between them. He cleverly and quickly shifted resources from a general reserve to cover emergencies as they developed. Most importantly, he inspired confidence in the Allied generals and began to speak of the "culminating point," or the moment that the German attacks would lose enough momentum to allow the Allies to counterattack.

The Americans were in an uncomfortable position. Their firm opposition to amalgamation meant that they were not formally a part of the system Foch had created. With the fate of Paris hanging in the balance, the Germans might win the war before the Americans could even make their presence felt. Pershing even told Foch at one point that he would rather see the Allied armies pushed back to the Loire River (which meant abandoning Paris) than amalgamate. Still, Pershing must have realized that he could not allow the spring offensives to culminate in a German victory. At the height of the crisis, therefore, Pershing made an extraordinary offer to Foch. In late March, in his imperfect French, Pershing told Foch: "the American people would consider it a great honor for our troops to be engaged in the present battle. . . . Infantry, artillery, aviation, all that we have is yours; use them as you wish."[1]

The offer, extraordinary as it was, did not solve the fundamental dilemma. With the Germans on the verge of a major breakthrough, Pershing knew that he would have to accept some compromises to his firm stance on the independence of the AEF. He agreed to operate within Foch's overall strategic guidance if Foch would agree that the Americans would fight only under American officers and under an American flag. Foch readily agreed; in fact, he had been one of the few Frenchmen who had argued that the Americans would fight better under their own commanders and therefore should be allowed to operate as a separate force.

The arrival of the Americans coincided with serious problems inside Germany itself. Privations on both the home front and, increasingly, in the army greatly reduced the fighting effectiveness of the German forces. In January, more than 500,000 workers went on strike in Berlin; an equal number struck throughout Germany's other cities. During 1918, Germany witnessed almost 500 separate strikes. The stresses of fighting a two-front war and the misery imposed by the British blockade were beginning to show. The initial successes of the Spring Offensives calmed these problems for a short while, but the general decline of German home front morale was becoming a serious issue.

Morale in the army sank as well as advancing German units saw how well-provisioned their enemies were. Hungry and thirsty German units often stopped fighting to loot Allied towns, supply depots, and trenches. Tired, underfed, and increasingly susceptible to disease and physical exhaustion, the German army became demoralized and increasingly less effective. The German assaults, moreover, were enormously costly for both attackers and defenders. Elite front-line formations tended to suffer the most, reducing the overall power of the German army. Second-line troops tended to be less well trained, provisioned, and motivated. Germany could not long sustain the enormous casualties that the offensives entailed.

In this environment, the arrival of the Americans contributed to an overall turning of the tide. The Americans made their first appearance on the battlefield in May and June at the battles of Catigny, Château Thierry, and Belleau Wood. Although obviously inexperienced, the Americans fought with an inspiring ardor and soon silenced many of their critics. Operating against veteran German troops in well-defended positions, three American divisions captured the town of Catigny, which sat at the extreme end of Germany's advances. They held the position despite six furious German counterattacks. American performance at Catigny impressed the French and "demonstrated clearly that they (the Americans) could plan and execute a successful operation."[2] The success at Catigny allowed Pershing to continue his opposition to amalgamation and demonstrated that the Americans, their inexperience notwithstanding, were a valuable battlefield ally.

Foch saw in the victories of May and June evidence that the culminating point was approaching. The Allies had learned how to adapt to the German Storm Troop tactics and had less difficulty in fighting lower-quality German reserves. More evidence of the weakening of the German army soon followed. A combined Franco-American counterattack at Noyon-Montdidier on June 11 stopped an advance by the German Eighteenth Army, inflicting heavy casualties. In mid-July, the American Third Division earned the nickname "the Rock of the Marne" for holding yet another German assault at bay. The Americans were more than holding their own. They were gaining the respect of their allies and enemies alike. As they continued to win on the battlefield and as more Americans arrived in France, Pershing's political position grew stronger and stronger. The Americans soon began arriving at the rate of 10,000 men per day, almost the equivalent of an entire European division. That mass, combined with the experience and confidence that the Americans were acquiring, gave the Allies another weapon in their defensive war and an enormous potential resource once defense turned to offense.

With Foch acting as a grand conductor, the various Allied efforts became something that resembled a coherent whole. The Allies stopped the German offensives and took advantage of an opportunity on the Marne River, as they had in 1914. The Second Battle of the Marne (July 18–August 5), like the first, was a major turning point in the war. The Allies assumed the offensive and never again yielded it. Troops from four nations (France, Britain, Italy, and the United States) fought together and, under Foch's leadership, created a unified command structure for the first time in the war. Eight American divisions fought at the Marne, with Pershing agreeing temporarily to place two of them under the overall command of French Tenth Army commander, General Charles Mangin. They performed brilliantly, capturing 6,800 German prisoners of war. Pershing's decision was not an easy one. The belligerent Mangin epitomized everything the Americans feared about European commanders. His aggressive style had earned him the nickname the "Butcher" and he had been one of the Nivelle Offensive's staunchest supporters.

The unified command system continued to yield important dividends. On August 8, a combined force of French, British, Canadians, and Anzacs scored an enormous victory at Amiens, capturing 30,000 Germans and inflicting a total of 100,000 casualties. The mounting numbers of POWs indicated that

German morale was cracking, as many troops were willing to give up rather than continue the fight. Amiens convinced German commander General Erich Ludendorff that the Germans could not win the war. It only remained to be seen how much of the German army's honor he could salvage and how favorable an armistice he could achieve.

Amiens had also demonstrated the improvements that the British and French had made since the disasters of 1917. The British in particular had made great strides in tactical artillery, targeting, and counter-battery fire. Allied logistics provided a steady line of supplies that enabled new technologies, including tanks and airplanes, to make spectacular impacts on the battlefield.[3] The effectiveness of Allied air and armor in 1918 underscored how dramatically the Allies had won the war of economics. Tanks, airplanes, gas, and artillery shells were arriving in ever growing numbers, providing the Allies with an advantage that the Germans simply could not match.

Aviation played a critical role at the battle of St. Mihiel from September 12 to 16. Under the command of an American airman, William "Billy" Mitchell, an Allied air armada of more than 1,400 airplanes from four air forces protected the skies and strafed German ground troops. The reduction of the St. Mihiel salient opened rail communications from Paris to Verdun and eastern France. More than 15,000 Germans surrendered, furthering Allied desires to press on.

Foch and Pershing worked together to plan the final operation of the war, the battle of the Meuse-Argonne (September 26–November 11), where 1,200,000 Americans attacked in conjunction with the French Fourth Army. The Germans proved less willing to surrender the Argonne Forest than they had the St. Mihiel salient. They had established three defensive belts there and fought hard for every inch of ground. Operating in terrain that made flanking and maneuver impossible, Pershing's open warfare tactics resembled those of 1914 and 1915. His frontal charges were costly, with more than half of America's casualties in the war occurring in this battle alone, but by the end of October, the Americans and the French had forced the Germans to surrender most of their positions.

Further to the north, the British, French, and Belgians renewed their assaults on the series of German fortifications known as the Hindenburg Line. The success of the Allied assaults demonstrated the widening gap between Allied and German fighting effectiveness. After successfully holding defensive lines throughout the war, the Germans found themselves able only to trade space for time. Although the Allies could not effect the total breakthrough Haig had sought, some Allied generals and politicians began to speak confidently of victory in 1918.

The September losses helped to convince the Germans that they must seek an armistice. Conditions at home were worsening by the day. In early October, Prince Max of Baden had asked Wilson for an armistice based on the principles of the Fourteen Points. Wilson replied that he would not deal with either the

Kaiser or the military dictatorship that Ludendorff had effectively created. France and Britain were furious at Wilson for negotiating with the Germans at all, creating important fissures among the Allies just as victory was coming into focus. Wilson had also ignored the position of Foch and others that an armistice was a purely military affair that had nothing to do with politicians.

In the hopes of persuading Wilson to rescue Germany from the vengeful French and British, Ludendorff resigned on October 27. Three days later, the German High Seas Fleet mutinied rather than fight a futile last battle with the Royal Navy. On the same day, the Ottoman Empire capitulated, signing the Armistice of Mudros. The Austrians soon followed suit, although it was a mere formality. Yugoslavia, Czechoslovakia, and Poland had already declared themselves independent states. The Kaiser convened a meeting of his senior generals at which he learned that he could not count on the loyalty of his army. Some of his advisors urged him to abdicate as strikes and riots became rampant.

A new German government, headed by Matthias Erzberger, arranged to meet with Foch to discuss armistice terms. In a railway siding in a forest clearing Foch icily informed the Germans that they could have an armistice subject to their total acceptance of the following terms: immediate evacuation of all occupied territory (understood to include Alsace and Lorraine) without damaging civilian and military equipment contained therein; surrender of 5,000 heavy guns, 30,000 machine guns, 5,000 locomotives, 150,000 railway cars, and 150 submarines; acceptance of three Allied bridgeheads across the Rhine River; and acceptance of the continuation of the British surface blockade until the conclusion of a final treaty.

Foch wanted to make absolutely certain that the Germans could not use the armistice as Ludendorff had intended, namely as an interlude and respite to be used for the reorganization of German forces during the winter of 1918–1919. The protests of the German delegation for leniency therefore fell on deaf ears. As a young man, Foch had volunteered to fight in the Franco-Prussian War and after the war he had studied for his entry exams into the French army while a German occupation army's band taunted the French with martial music. His political boss, Georges Clemenceau, was the last surviving member of the French government of 1871 that had signed the humiliating Treaty of Frankfurt. If the Germans expected generosity, they were looking for it in the wrong quarters. Foch gave Erzberger and his delegation three days to accept the terms. In the interim, the war would continue.

The armistice terms amounted to a surrender, but the German delegation had little choice. On November 10, the Kaiser abdicated and fled to Holland. The following day Erzberger signed the armistice, effective 11 a.m. on November 11, the eleventh hour of the eleventh day of the eleventh month. The war was over. The Americans had provided the difference of manpower that had enabled the Allies to win the war in 1918, not 1919 or even 1920 as many had feared. While it is impossible to say that the Allies would not have won without the Americans, it is fair to say that they owed the rapid conclusion of an armistice to the intervention of the Americans.

The British, the French, and the Americans had won by standing together, but the experience had not been altogether positive. National pride and conflicting ambitions had created important tensions. Moreover, the end of the war meant that the Europeans and the Americans would now have to work together to shape the peace. With the wildly divergent goals that the Old World and New World leaders had about that peace, that process would soon prove to be difficult. It was the start of an intense and ambivalent relationship between the Europeans and the Americans that has lasted ever since.

## Making peace

It is an old axiom that making peace is almost always harder than making war. That statement was never more true than in 1919. From January 18 to June 28 the leaders of France, Britain, and the United States attempted to remake the world at the Paris Peace Conference. The rulers of Italy and Japan played lesser roles. Delegates from smaller powers influenced events only through their access to "The Big Three": David Lloyd George, Georges Clemenceau, and Woodrow Wilson. Bolshevik Russia, Germany, Austria, and the Ottoman Empire were the most notable absences from the proceedings.

The failure of the Paris Peace Conference to establish the terms of a lasting peace in Europe has been the study of scores of books, articles, and dissertations. Most of these studies approach the problem from a strictly diplomatic point of view. Few understand, or attempt to understand, the social and cultural factors that limited the choices available to the Big Three. Nor do they understand that in trying to end World War I, the delegates effectively created a "cabinet peace," which, following a "people's war," could not have produced results amenable to the people of Europe.

The desires of the peoples of Europe and the United States to put the agonies and dislocations of the war behind them yielded important results at the polls. These results limited the bargaining ability of the national delegations. In the United States, the mid-term elections of 1918 returned a Republican majority. Whereas the 65th Congress of 1916–1918 had a Democratic advantage of six seats in the House of Representatives and nine in the Senate, the 66th Congress of 1918–1920 had a fifty-seat Republican advantage in the House and a two-seat Republican advantage in the Senate. The returns represented an obvious setback for Wilson, a Democrat. It was the first time in two decades that one party controlled the White House and the other both houses of Congress.

The loss of the Senate was particularly damaging to Wilson's agenda. According to the American Constitution, the President has the authority to negotiate treaties, but the Senate has the power to ratify them. Loss of Democratic control meant that the Republicans could easily negate any agreement that Wilson negotiated with his peers in Paris. By virtue of their victory, the

Republicans also obtained the right to choose the new chairman of the Foreign Relations Committee. They selected Massachusetts Senator Henry Cabot Lodge, who loathed Wilson personally and stridently opposed any treaty that might commit the United States to a long-term relationship with Europe. Several other Republican senators (the so-called irreconcilables) were opposed to the United States signing any treaty that left the nation with overseas commitments or threatened the Monroe Doctrine's claim to a unilateral American right to intervene in Latin America. President Wilson's decision to attend the Paris Peace Conference personally left him in a weakened position to negotiate regularly with Lodge's Senate opposition. He compounded the problem by not including any Republicans at all in the American delegation to the peace conference.

Shrewd Europeans understood the dilemma Wilson faced. President Wilson, the observant British diplomat Harold Nicolson knew, had "ceased to be a prophet among his own people."[4] The charismatic former President Theodore Roosevelt (who had run against Wilson for the presidency in 1912) undermined his old nemesis even further by announcing his belief that the election of 1918 meant that the American people had repudiated Wilson as their spokesman: "Our allies and enemies and Mr. Wilson himself should all understand that Mr. Wilson has no authority to speak for the American people at this time."[5] Wilson nevertheless acted as if the election of 1918 had never occurred. He assumed that when the treaty came up for ratification that he could win Senate passage by force of argument.

The British electorate spoke as well. In December, 1918, Britain held its first election since the start of the war. Lloyd George called for these elections in order to give him a mandate and thus assure his ability to represent the British people, but the timing proved to be unfortunate. The election, held so soon after the end of the war, existed within the context of abiding wartime hatred. Nicolson recalled that British distrust and anger at the Germans had reached a fever pitch. The German sinking of an Irish merchant ship in October had killed 450 men, women, and children. The British public, Nicolson believed, interpreted the sinking as a sign of German perfidy because the sinking occurred even as the Germans were seeking peace terms.

In that mood, even moderate politicians were clamoring for revenge against the Germans. The British media, especially those newspapers owned by the powerful British press baron Lord Northcliffe, screamed for Germany to pay dearly for the war they had started. The Northcliffe papers urged that the Kaiser be placed on trial for war crimes and demanded huge reparations from any post-war German government. As the conference was ongoing, one of Northcliffe's most popular newspapers, the *Daily Mail*, inserted a box on page 1 that read: "The Junkers will cheat you yet."[6] The result of all of these pressures was a British population, media, and Parliament that screamed for revenge and was guided more by hatred than a desire for a just peace.

Much the same could be said about the French, led as they were by their indomitable and iron-willed prime minister, Georges Clemenceau. Even an attempt on his life by a French anarchist in February could not slow down the seventy-seven-year-old Clemenceau. Although he took a bullet in his back, the French prime minister insisted upon discussing treaty matters the same day. He presided over the conference with an iron will that even his political foes had to respect.

Clemenceau's energy and patriotism symbolized France's goals and its fears. Germany and Austria, Clemenceau knew, may have been defeated, but they still had a combined 75,000,000 inhabitants against a combined 45,000,000 in France and Belgium. The German industrial infrastructure remained largely intact and, because of the Bolshevik revolution, Russia no longer served as an eastern ally and counterweight; thus Clemenceau and French generals took a keen interest in the creation of strong successor states to the Austro-Hungarian empire, especially Poland. The borders of those states, the French argued, needed to be strategically defensible even if those borders did not overlap perfectly with ethnic boundaries.

In France, too, the media reflected a general desire on the part of the population to have their political leaders guarantee their security. France had paid indemnities to their conquerors after defeats in 1815 and again in 1871. Why, they asked, should Germany not pay them now? Why, after the most destructive war in human history, should not the reparations be the highest in history? Even the French socialist newspaper *Humanité* called reparations a matter of "simple justice."[7]

The public, it seemed, had spoken. In their own ways, the citizens of the victorious powers spoke for security, peace, and a return to the life they had led before the war. But they also spoke for demobilization. Even Northcliffe, whose papers demanded an occupation of Germany, an invasion of Bolshevik Russia, and pressure on the Dutch to surrender the Kaiser, also called for demobilization of the British army. In France and America, too, the public wanted to disband the enormous and expensive armies they had built up over the previous four years. Soldiers wanted to go home and families wanted to be reunited with those fathers, sons, and brothers who were still alive. Few fully realized that demobilization was inconsistent with a muscular foreign policy. Inevitably, what the politicians agreed to in conference rooms in Paris could not be upheld because of a lack of troops and a lack of will among the winners to risk a repeat of the bloodletting so recently concluded.

Moreover, if the politicians and delegates expected to be able to conduct their affairs in the traditional diplomatic fashion out of the public eye, they soon learned otherwise. Diplomacy, by its very nature, is an activity that requires secrecy and discretion. But the people's war demanded a people's peace. The first of Wilson's Fourteen Points called for "open covenants of peace, openly arrived at." The great democracies and giant media empires therefore insisted on knowing what was happening in Paris. Citizens of the United States, Britain, and France wanted to learn how their leaders were advancing their national agendas and rendering meaningful their nation's sacrifices. The choice of Paris, itself a media center, as the host city for the conference only intensified the attention. "We felt," said Nicolson, "like surgeons operating in the ballroom with the aunts of the patient gathered all around."[8]

Furthermore, it seemed to many Europeans that Germany did not deserve a just peace. Their invasion of Belgium, their wanton destruction of enemy territory, and their callous prosecution of submarine warfare did little to diminish that view. Neither did the brutal peace settlements that Germany had imposed on Russia and Romania argue for a fair peace. Even moderates, for example Britain's foreign secretary, Arthur Balfour, had turned hard and vengeful. "Brutes they were," he said, "and brutes they remain."[9] The French hardly needed any encouragement to distrust the Germans. The German, Foch said, was "a trained bit of destructive machinery, ready to do the bidding, without question, of his masters."[10] If the tables had been turned, many asked, could the British and French have expected leniency from the Germans?

Indeed, German war aims would have resulted in a much harsher settlement than the Versailles Treaty, had Germany's gamble in 1918 resulted in victory. They planned to implement the September Program, agreed to by the German government in September, 1914. Its terms included the annexation of Luxembourg and the conversion of Belgium into a German vassal state, complete with German naval bases at Ostend and Zeebrugge. Germany would also have annexed the coal and iron fields of France's industrial northeast and imposed on France a heavy indemnity. Germany also had plans to annex France's Channel ports, most of France's Central African empire, and its North African seaports. Further territories would be added from Great Britain's colonies. The Germans planned to dominate the economies of eastern and central Europe through a customs union and a Mitteleuropa political structure.[11] Although the Allies did not know of the details of the September Program, the evidence from the Treaties of Bucharest and Brest-Litovsk suggested its broad outlines clearly enough.

Given this environment, it is virtually impossible to envision a conference that would have produced a generous peace because the people of Britain and France did not want one. The only chance for moderation came from the idealistic Wilson and his wish for a "peace without victors." Because he held out the hope of a lasting peace, he was greeted by enormous, adoring crowds when he arrived in Europe. Across the continent, even in Germany, the people of Europe looked to him to provide peace and security. In an effort not to lose his idealism, Wilson resisted all European attempts to take him to the battlefields, for fear that he would develop a hatred of the Germans inconsistent with his determination to remake Europe.

Although Lloyd George and Clemenceau suspected the President's motives, there was no denying the moral power he yielded when he arrived, almost like a *deus ex machina*, in France. Even seasoned diplomats like Nicolson fell under his spell:

Not only did I believe profoundly in [Wilson's] principles, I took it for granted that on them alone would the Treaties of Peace be based. Apart from their inherent moral compulsion, apart from the fact that they formed the sole basis of our negotiation, I knew that the President possessed unlimited physical power to enforce his views. We were all, at that date, dependent upon America, not only for the sinews of war, but for the sinews of peace. Our food supplies, our finances, were entirely subservient to the dictates of Washington.[12]

Nevertheless, as we have seen, Wilson had already lost much of his political authority in the United States. Whatever treaty he might have managed to negotiate would most likely not have received the required ratification from his own Senate. It also quickly became obvious, even to converts like Nicolson, that the President's idealism would not long survive the bitterness and hatred of the continent. Nor could it have, because the Fourteen Points were themselves contradictory, unenforceable, and not carefully considered. Wilson and his advisors were completely out of their league when considering the national boundaries and dizzying ethnic variety of Europe. Where, for example, did the "indisputably Polish" populations whom Wilson had guaranteed a state reside? How could the treaty create a state that was ethnically Polish without including thousands of non-Poles? How could such a state meet French requirements that it be both strategically and economically viable? The "Polish question" was just one of dozens of such irresolvable problems.

The Paris Peace Conference eventually produced four treaties, the most famous being the Treaty of Versailles that ended hostilities with Germany. It contained five major features. First, Germany lost one-seventh of its European territory and all of its overseas colonies; many of those in the Pacific Ocean went to Japan, from whom they would need to be wrested in the next world war. Among the European territories that Germany lost were Alsace and Lorraine and the coal-rich Saar region as well as the Pozen region to Poland. The Saar was indisputably German in ethnicity, raising fears on the part of Lloyd George that the treaty might have created an Alsace-Lorraine in reverse. He did not wish to create a source of anger in the Germans that might motivate them as "the lost provinces" had motivated the French after 1871. He therefore urged that a plebiscite take place in the Saar in 1935 and he successfully resisted a French military plan to create a separate Rhenish republic out of territories west of the Rhine River.

Second, Germany was effectively disarmed. Its army was limited to 100,000 men and it was forbidden from possessing a general staff to guide it. It could possess no airplanes, no submarines, no heavy artillery, and only 10,000 tons of surface ships. The Germans, for whom the army had served as a crucial domestic institution, resented these limits intensely. Most French generals were suspicious of the terms as well, believing that there was simply no way to enforce them without an Allied occupation. Demobilization made even the retention of the Allied bridgeheads on the Rhine, let alone a full occupation, seem tenuous at best.

Third, Germany was required to pay reparations to the victors. Reparations had been a common feature of European diplomacy for decades. There was nothing unusual in adding them to the Versailles Treaty. The controversy arose from the unwillingness of the diplomats to assign a specific monetary figure. Instead, a reparations committee was formed with the intention of fixing a number at a future date. In theory, the committee hoped to reduce the reparations bill as tempers cooled, thus enabling normal trade levels to resume. In practice, reductions proved to be inconsistent with domestic political pressures. The eventual figure was $56 billion, only slightly less than the cost of the war to Britain alone. John Maynard Keynes, Britain's chief economic advisor at the conference, calculated that Germany could pay no more than $10 billion. Exorbitant reparations, he believed, would destroy the economy of Europe.

Fourth, and perhaps most controversially, the treaty included the famous "Article 231," in which Germany admitted its guilt in starting the war. The measure was intended as a justification for reparations and as a substitute for a victor's march in Berlin. At the time, the Allies did not foresee the tremendous anger that Article 231 would create or how Hitler would use it to denounce the treaty and the western democracies that had imposed it. The war guilt clause instantly undermined the legitimacy of the very German government that replaced the Kaiser's, making post-war reconciliation even more difficult.

Understanding the harshness of the treaty *in toto*, the fifth main feature created a League of Nations. The diplomats hoped that the League would treat the Versailles settlement as a work in progress, to be modified as circumstances warranted. If the Germans proved cooperative, the League could reduce reparations or even remove certain clauses from the treaty. If they did not, the League could increase reparations or introduce further punishments. Clemenceau tried to turn the League into an anti-German military alliance, but Wilson, ever the idealist, held firm. The League, he hoped, would put right any injustices in the treaty itself.

Few people had any illusions about those injustices and other inadequacies of the treaty more generally. Lloyd George told a friend that the treaty was "all a great pity. We shall have to do the same thing all over again in twenty-five years at three times the cost."[13] Marshal Foch, who boycotted the signing ceremony out of a belief that the treaty was too lenient and therefore did not guarantee France's future security, prophetically remarked, "This is not peace. It is an armistice for twenty years." Nicolson, who had left for Paris with the hope of "doing great, permanent, and noble things" ended his conference diary with the words, "To bed, sick of life."[14]

The German reaction to the treaty was not hard to predict. The German fleet, moved to the British base at Scapa Flow in Scotland after the armistice, scuttled itself rather than turn its ships over to the British as demanded by the terms of Versailles. In a fit of anger, a Berlin mob burned French flags that had been captured in 1870. The flags were supposed to have been returned to France. In an effort to save the honor of the German army, German leaders like Ludendorff had already begun to propagate the myth that the army had not been defeated in the field, but stabbed in the back by Jews, socialists, and other domestic enemies. German Chancellor Fritz Ebert welcomed the German armies home by proclaiming that they were "unvanquished in the field."[15] Popular anger immediately called into question both the wisdom and the enforceability of the treaty.

The Italians, too, lashed out at the treaty, believing they were owed more than they had received. In protest at the Allies' abrogation of Italian claims stemming from the 1915 Treaty of London (these claims clearly violated national principles), they walked out of the conference in April only to sheepishly return the following month. The Italian poet and war hero Gabriele d'Annunzio began speaking of a "mutilated victory" and a Franco-British conspiracy to keep Italy from playing what he saw as its rightful role as a great power. Using the newspaper of fellow war veteran Benito Mussolini, he wrote of Italy's sacrifices at the Isonzo and the demand for "a Pax Romana, the sole peace that is fitting. If necessary we will meet the new plot . . . [with] a grenade in each hand and a knife between our teeth."[16] In September, 1919, d'Annunzio, without his government's approval, led a march of war veterans on the Yugoslav city of Fiume, the Allied denial of which had caused the Italians to leave the Paris Conference. He held the city until December 27, 1920, when an Italian force expelled and arrested him, although the Italians held onto the city. Within three years, Mussolini had built on popular anger to lead a Fascist coup and seize power in Rome.

The treaty therefore had massive repercussions unimaginable at the outset. As far away as China, spontaneous, popular reactions exploded against the treaty. At Beijing's Tiananmen Square a crowd of 3,000 students protested the provisions of the treaty that allowed the Japanese to retain the pre-war German colonies on the Shandong Peninsula. The demonstration turned into a riot as the crowd burned the house of a cabinet minister believed to be pro-Japanese, attacked China's minister to Japan, and led to a student strike. The movement inspired similar demonstrations in six other major cities and a year-long Chinese boycott of Japanese goods.

The other three treaties that resulted from the Paris Peace Conference reinforced the problems of the Treaty of Versailles and even extended these problems to the Middle East and eastern Europe. The Treaty of Sèvres (August 10, 1920), officially replaced the Ottoman Empire with the new state of Turkey. Most of the Arabic Middle East became "mandates" of the French and British under the supervision of the League of Nations. Palestine and Mesopotamia became British mandates, with a nominally independent Arabia falling under heavy British influence. Syria and Lebanon became French mandates.

The mandate system was supposed to guarantee peace in the region by leading to eventual independence, but Arab leaders saw the scheme as imperialism by another name. The British had made grandiose promises of independence during the war to Arab leaders in return for their pledge to rebel against the Ottoman Empire. The Treaty of Sèvres fell far short of those promises. Instead, it upheld the secret Sykes–Picot agreement of 1916 wherein Britain and France agreed to divide former Ottoman territories among themselves, though the treaty added the veneer of the mandate system. The treaty also ignored promises that the British had made to the Jews in the Balfour Declaration of 1916 which pledged Britain to support a Jewish homeland in Palestine. The conflicting aims of British policy set the Middle East on a long and tortuous twentieth century.

Greece, whose entry into the war had made the Salonica front possible, benefited as well from Sèvres. A nation with long-standing emotional and sentimental ties to Britain, Greece acquired all of European Turkey except the immediate area around Constantinople (which came under international control) as well as the city of Smyrna, several Aegean islands, and large parts of western Anatolia. The allies seem to have quickly appreciated, however, that demobilization left them in too weak a position actually to enforce these terms. The Greeks were already showing an appetite for more of Anatolia than the treaty permitted.

At the same time, Turkish nationalists were showing a determination to resist many of the terms laid out in the treaty. Brilliantly led by Mustapha Kemal Atatürk, the hero of Gallipoli, the nationalists planned to overturn the Treaty of Sèvres. They bristled at any ethnically Turkish lands falling under the hands of foreign control. Kemal determined to regain all Anatolian and Armenian lands for Turkey. Sèvres thus fell far short of bringing peace to the region.

The treaties of St. Germain (September 10, 1919) and Trianon (June 4, 1920) settled hostilities with Austria and Hungary, respectively. St. Germain reinforced the Versailles Treaty's prohibition on a union between Germany and Austria. It also gave the largely German South Tyrol region to Italy, but it avoided placing war guilt on Austria and its Emperor Karl and it did not demand that Austria pay reparations. Hungary, then wracked by a communist revolt led by Béla Kun, fared less well, losing two-thirds of its territory (mostly to Romania and Czechoslovakia), most of its raw materials, and was forced to pay reparations. Worse still, the territorial changes meant that after 1920 3,500,000 Hungarians lived under foreign rule.

The United States Senate, predictably, rejected the agreements made in Paris. America did not join the League of Nations nor did it make any long-term commitment to Europe. Clemenceau's hope of a firm post-war alliance between the wartime partners collapsed. Nor did the United States sign the Treaties of Sèvres, St. Germain, and Trianon. Displeased at what it saw as the furtherance of European imperialism in the region and never officially at war with the Ottoman Empire, the United States declined even to participate in treaty negotiations with Turkey. The Americans were incensed by a British proposal that they assume mandates in northern Turkey. The suggestion seemed to many Americans to prove the point that the Europeans had not learned anything from the war and were instead trying to implicate the Americans in their corrupt imperial system.

Some Europeans, like Keynes, were angered and disappointed by the American withdrawal from Europe. Others were relieved and content to see the meddlesome giant retreat back across the Atlantic. But the war and the peace process had created unbreakable links between the Old World and the New. Whatever desires for isolation some Americans might have harbored and whatever hopes some Europeans might have had to keep the Americans away, the two were now inextricably linked, for better or for worse.

## The impact of the war on European society

The consequences of World War I are so deep as to be almost unimaginable. More than 60,000,000 European men were mobilized for war and more than 8,000,000 died. The total number of wounded exceeded 20,000,000. Civilian casualties amounted to 6,500,000, the vast majority in Russia and Turkey. The rigidity of the front line in the west had the one advantage of stabilizing the positions of the armies and thus reducing the direct impact of the fighting on civilians. Only when the lines were fluid, as in Belgium in 1914, were civilian casualties common in the west. France, for example, suffered 40,000 civilian dead, but Serbia, where the lines frequently shifted, suffered 650,000 civilian dead.

The 52,000,000 surviving veterans formed a new and powerful social group that would make future financial, political, and social demands on the state. Caring for the veterans, their families, widows, and orphans soon amounted to an enormous state expenditure. Veterans' groups in Italy and Germany were important elements of the Fascist movements and in Britain and France they became powerful political constituencies as well. Lloyd George, always the consummate politician, understood the power of the veteran. He had campaigned in 1918 on the pledge that he would make Britain "a land fit for heroes to live in."

Partly due to Lloyd George's efforts in Paris, the political map of Europe and western Asia in 1920 looked so different from that of 1914 that it seemed to be another place entirely. Fourteen new states appeared on the map by 1921, although five of them (Armenia, Azerbaijan, Georgia, Ukraine, and White Russia) soon disappeared into the Soviet Union. Eastern Europe witnessed the creation of multi-ethnic states such as Yugoslavia and the reemergence of traditional states such as Poland. But these changes did not solve the continent's great national problems. National and state borders still did not overlap with any consistency or overarching logic.

The problem emerged from the difficulty of defining exact boundaries for the new states. These states had been created with three often mutually conflicting ideals in mind. First, the new areas were to be ethnically contiguous. Wilson believed that the war had been the result of the national frustrations of unrepresented groups. With independent nations each speaking for Europe's ethnic groups, he hoped, these frustrations would not lead to war as they had in 1914. With each state being represented at the League of Nations, each ethnic group would have a voice at a body that existed to mediate disputes.

Many areas, however, could not be so neatly divided, nor was the problem of nationalism solved by simply drawing new borders. Upper Silesia, for example, was 65 percent Polish-speaking. On the surface, the linguistic characteristics of the region should have argued for it to be placed within the new Polish state. Nevertheless, by ethnicity most Upper Silesians identified themselves as either German or Czech. The region had not been a part of any Polish political entity since 1163 and few of its inhabitants wanted to be incorporated into Poland. Even the official Polish position called only for the return of Poland to its 1772 borders.

The second ideal was economic self-sufficiency. Despite its official position, the Poles still pushed informally for the Allies to grant them Upper Silesia, in large part because the region had huge reserves of coal, zinc, and lead. Germany argued that for economic reasons, Upper Silesia should become German. The entire economy of the region had been built by German capital and was linked to German industry. Without Upper Silesia and with the removal of the Saar region in the west, the Germans argued, they would not be able to rebuild their economy and therefore would never be able to pay reparations. Unable to resolve the question, the region was placed under League of Nations guidance subject to a plebiscite.

A similar controversy raged about granting Poland access to the Baltic Sea port of Danzig (also known as Gdansk). The majority of ethnic Poles lived south of the coastline, but to create a Polish state without a port, many feared, would be to doom it to economic dependency on Germany. Nevertheless, Danzig was unquestionably more German in ethnicity than Polish. Lloyd George and Wilson compromised by creating a "Polish corridor" that formed a sleeve of Polish territory on the Baltic, but the corridor itself physically divided German East Prussia from the rest of Germany. Danzig became a "free city" under League of Nations guidance, a solution that pleased no one.

The third consideration was strategic. Even if a state could be created that was ethnically homogenous and economically viable, it would not long survive if it could not defend itself. To create a Czech state without the mountains of Bohemia to protect it would leave it open to a German invasion. But to grant the region to Czechoslovakia meant incorporating thousands of Sudeten Germans into a non-German state. Here again an uncomfortable compromise solved the question: the Sudetenland went to Czechoslovakia despite its obvious German ethnicity, but the Czechs agreed to allow the German minority to maintain its own schools, universities, and newspapers. The Sudeten Germans became a "lost cause" for Hitler and the Nazis in the 1930s, both for ethnic reasons and because they knew that Czechoslovakia without the Sudeten region was utterly unable to protect itself.

Compromises such as those at Danzig, the Sudetenland, and Upper Silesia all left one nation or another unsatisfied. Arguments that the Paris Peace settlement had been unfair created political and social grievances that opportunistic politicians could use to their advantage. Moreover, the demobilization of the Allied armies and the weakness of a League of Nations without American participation meant that no body existed to enforce the terms. Even d'Annunzio's comic opera seizure of Fiume, which had begun with just 200 disorganized volunteers, lasted fifteen months. France and Britain proved unwilling to intervene, agreeing only to set up an ineffective blockade of the port. In the end, d'Annunzio got what he wanted, though he personally had to surrender. In order to resolve the crisis, Yugoslavia agreed to allow Fiume to become a "free state" linked to Italy by economics and by a strip of Yugoslavian land ceded to Italy.

The weaknesses of the treaty were thus apparent from early on. Some scholars have argued that the Versailles Treaty made World War II inevitable, but it is more accurate to say that it made appeasement inevitable. Europeans and Americans alike understood that many of the territorial settlements reached at Paris could not withstand the reality of conditions on the ground. Perhaps more importantly, Britain and France would not be able to both demobilize and enforce the treaty indefinitely. With America's retreat into isolation, the nation abrogated any role in mediating these disputes, leaving no power except the enfeebled League of Nations to resolve the myriad quarrels of the continent.

Lloyd George, Wilson, and Clemenceau all hoped that the end of autocracy would help to soothe the problems created by Versailles. Four great monarchies, the Hohenzollern of Germany, the Hapsburg of Austria-Hungary, the Romanov of Russia, and the Sultanate of Turkey, all vanished. But if Wilson and others had hoped that the decline of monarchy in Europe would lead to democracy, they were overly sanguine. Democracy was just one model open to the peoples of Europe.

The success of Bolshevism in Russia proffered another model. Even as the treaty negotiations were ongoing, communist rebellions broke out in Germany and Hungary. In Germany, the Spartacist League, a pro-Bolshevist organization with moderate working-class support, attempted to seize power in January, 1919. The Allies at first disbelieved the stories of a Bolshevik revolt in Berlin, fearing that the Germans had concocted the story in order to be permitted a larger army.

To stop the Spartacists, German World War I veterans formed a quasi-professional military force known as the Freikorps. Building on the professional status of the German soldier, armed with modern weapons, and comprised of veterans of the western front, the Freikorps quickly attracted restless men who could not envision a return to civilian life. They formed a veteran, vengeful army of thugs that dedicated itself to destroying Bolshevism in their nation and returning honor and dignity to military service in Germany.

By January 15, the Freikorps had crushed the Spartacists and hunted down its leaders. More than 1,000 Spartacists lay dead, including most of its core leadership. The Freikorps, originally supported by the German government because it was the country's only organized military force, quickly grew out of control. It soon developed into a force that launched savage attacks on any presumably pro-Bolshevik group willing to try to replace the Spartacists. The German government soon found that it lacked the power to force the Freikorps to disband. Instead, the soldiers of the Freikorps lurked as a constant menace to the fledgling Weimar government as it developed the concept of a Führer (supreme leader to whom ultimate allegiance belongs), a virulent hatred of Jews, and introduced the swastika as its symbol. The men of the Freikorps soon became the core of the Nazi S. A. movement and enthusiastic followers of Hitler.

Reactionary forces like the Freikorps underscored the difficulties of introducing democracy to Germany, a nation that had never practiced it. The creation of the Weimar Republic did little to stem the violence. A wave of political assassinations, aimed mostly at Jews and socialists, ran through Germany. The government proved unwilling or unable to fully control it. The victims included Spartacists Karl Liebnecht and Rosa Luxemburg, Bavarian socialist Karl Eisner, and the conservative Jewish industrialist Walther Rathenau, who had been Germany's minister of finance during World War I. The German government conducted only the most cursory of investigations. The only man convicted in the Liebnecht and Luxemburg killings served two years in prison, but in 1933 he received a cash reward from Hitler.

To many western Europeans, Bolshevism was equally as horrifying as absolutism. Even before the end of World War I, the allies had supported a combined French–British–American intervention in Russia. The three nations' small contingents secured ports and protected railways, but failed to support the counter-revolutionary "Whites" enough to threaten the Bolshevik positions. Much of the subsequent political history of Europe to 1989 revolved around the struggle between the supporters of communism and its opponents. That pattern came as a direct consequence of World War I.

As Nicolson had noted, the financial relationship between the United States and Europe had changed dramatically in favor of the former. America emerged from the war as the world's wealthiest nation by far. The United States was no longer a debtor nation; it was now the world's largest creditor nation. By 1921, the European investments of American corporations had doubled compared to their pre-war levels. The Ford Motor Company built an enormous factory in Britain (it was then the largest ever built outside the United States) and even constructed a tractor plant in the communist environment of the Soviet Union.

The Americans realized that for full economic stability to return to Europe, a resolution had to be found to the reparations problem. Germany's failure to make a scheduled payment led to a French and Belgian occupation of the coal-rich Ruhr Valley in 1923, sparking fears that war might break out once again. Anxious to diffuse the crisis and ensure the continued growth of American investments in Europe, American banker Charles Dawes introduced a "triangular system" of payments. Through this system, the United States loaned $2.5 billion to the Germans. Germany, in turn, agreed to make scheduled payments of $2 billion to the Allies, who would then pay off $2.5 billion of their war debt to the United States. The plan seemed like an elaborate game of robbing Peter to pay Paul, but it did help to stabilize the German currency system until the great depression of 1929 undermined the world's currency controls. The Dawes Plan also visibly underscored how dependent the Europeans had become on the United States for their economic survival.

But close economic ties could not compensate for the obvious end of an American political and military presence. The United States demobilized as quickly as any continental power had and they showed no interest whatsoever in involving themselves directly into crises such as Fiume and the Ruhr. By 1923 the United States had abandoned its Coblenz bridgehead over the Rhine, leaving France and a reluctant Britain to "stand guard" alone. In 1920 the American people overwhelmingly elected a Republican, Warren Harding, to replace Wilson, and also returned even larger Republican majorities in the Senate and House of Representatives. The political mood was unquestionably opposed to direct American involvement in European affairs.

American foreign policy in the immediate post-war years was not the strict isolationism that some have posited, but certainly it did not involve further American commitments in European affairs. American policy in the 1920s rested on two self-interested principles: avoidance of entangling commitments and economic expansion. Secretary of State Charles Evans Hughes (the man who had narrowly lost to Wilson in 1916) also sought to reduce the size of the world's navies, both to promote peace and to reduce military expenditures. He hosted the Washington Conference of 1921–1922 at which the Americans convinced the great powers to scrap more than 2,000,000 tons of warships. It was, one observer noted, a greater accomplishment than all the world's admirals combined had realized in centuries. The powers also agreed to a ten-year ban on the construction of capital ships and created a ratio of shipbuilding that Hughes hoped would limit the size of the world's navies.

The Washington Conference represented America's largest contribution to European diplomacy in the 1920s. Otherwise, American views on Europe were decidedly negative. Seeing the abiding hatreds of the continent, Americans began to question the purposes of their own sacrifices. Intellectuals were soon calling into question the wisdom of America's entry into the war. On the political level, isolationist senators introduced legislation to ensure that the nation did not repeat what they interpreted as the mistake of 1917. In 1923, Senator William Borah proposed to outlaw war as an instrument of American policy and the following year his colleague Robert La Follette introduced a measure that would have required a national referendum before the United States could declare war.

Perhaps America's most important anti-European statements came in the area of immigration legislation. The war had temporarily slowed the massive migrations of Europeans to the United States, but in 1921 more than 805,000 Europeans crossed the Atlantic. Fearing the poverty, political radicalism, and potential disloyalty of immigrants, the United States Congress passed two laws. The first, passed in 1921, limited annual immigration by nationality to 3 percent of that group's population in the United States according to the 1910 census. Three years later the National Origins Act reduced that number to 2 percent of the 1890 census and banned all Asian immigration. The net effect was virtually to stop European migration, especially from eastern and southern Europe. The nation that had built itself on the "huddled masses" had shut itself off. The United States, which for decades had served as a safety valve for disaffected and impoverished Europeans, now turned against its traditions and, in the process, on Europeans as well.

World War I also impacted the European Powers' ability to govern their colonies at the same time that they were adding to their imperial responsibilities by assuming the mandates. Only a handful of prescient Europeans understood that the war had left Europe in a relatively much weaker position to control its far-flung colonial holdings. Germany, of course, was relieved of this responsibility when it lost its empire as a result of the Treaty of Versailles. Most Britons and Frenchmen sought to take advantage of the German and Ottoman collapses by extending their empires, both as a means of restoring national glory and as a means of returning romance to military and international operations.

But romance and glory proved to be hard to find. Closest to home, the Easter Rising in Ireland led to a civil war that lasted until 1921. The British dispatched troops and a constabulary force known as the "Black and Tans," but the violence continued. The Irish Republican Army (IRA) fought a guerrilla war against a British force that eventually numbered 100,000 men. Despite their efforts, the British could not contain the IRA and had to admit that they could not retain all of Ireland. In 1922, an agreement between the Irish and the British allowed the southern counties of Ireland to form the Irish Free State. The northern counties, known collectively as Ulster, remained with Britain but have been troubled by intermittent violence ever since.

Further from home, the war had also undermined Britain's relationship with its Dominions. Australia and New Zealand especially accused the British of having callously wasted the lives of imperial troops at Gallipoli and elsewhere. Australia's leaders, represented by their feisty prime minister William Hughes and his advisor Keith Murdoch, grew increasingly critical of the British and sought greater freedom for their own actions. The South African prime minister, Jan Smuts, argued for the creation of a separate South African empire, carved out of Germany's former African colonies, under his leadership.

In India as well, trouble was brewing. Britain had been forced to rely on Muslim troops from the Punjab to fight their co-religionists, the Turks. That army proved to be less reliable than the British had hoped. The British practice of dealing with deserters by execution only increased the tensions. Domestic protests quickly mounted, with the Indian National Congress rapidly developing into an important voice for independence. In 1919, a unit of Indian troops led by British officers fired into a crowd of unarmed Indian civilians, killing 379 and wounding 1,208. The incident was a major watershed in British relations with India.

The British and French mandate responsibilities in the Middle East further contributed to their growing imperial overstretch. The British army found itself fighting against anti-imperial forces in Mesopotamia, Kurdistan, Afghanistan, and Yemen. Similar problems existed in France, where, instead of reducing imperial operations, the French increased them. France deployed a 150,000-strong army to deal with a rebellion by the independence-minded Republic of the Riff rebels in Morocco. The Riffs had been fighting the Spanish since 1909 and were determined to expel all foreigners from Morocco. In 1921 they increased their attacks on French positions. Under the command of Abd el Krim, they captured fortified outpost after fortified outpost. The French and Spanish fought until 1926 before finally pacifying the Riffs. The French also had to fight the Druze in their new mandate of Syria.

It thus quickly became evident that World War I would fall well short of Wilson's desire that it should be the "war to end all wars." In 1920, British war correspondent Charles Repington published his book, *The First World War*. The title stood in stark contrast to the commonly accepted names "The Great War" and "The World War". Repington meant for his title to indicate that even though the First World War had only recently ended, he fully expected that the hatreds of the war and the inadequacies of the peace would make a second world war inevitable. Even as his book was going to press, wars were already brewing in Russia, Turkey, and Poland. As Chapter 4 will demonstrate, the 1920s avoided the general calamity that struck Europe in the 1910s, but it was far from a peaceful decade.

## Further reading

Start with the works cited in the endnotes. In addition, the American experience is well covered by David Kennedy, *Over Here: The First World War and American Society* (Oxford: Oxford University Press, 1980); Ronald Schaffer, *America in the Great War* (Oxford: Oxford University Press, 1991); John Whiteclay Chambers II, *To Raise an Army: The Draft Comes to Modern America* (New York: The Free Press, 1987); Paul Braim, *The Test of Battle: The American Expeditionary Forces in the Meuse-Argonne Campaign* (Newark: University of Delaware Press, 1987) and Jennifer D. Keene, *Doughboys, the Great War, and the Remaking of America* (Baltimore: Johns Hopkins University Press, 2001). Gregor Dallas, *1918: War and Peace* (New York: Overlook Press, 2001) covers the end of the war.

On the peace process, see the works cited in the endnotes, plus: Ruth Henig, *Versailles and After, 1919–1933* (London: Routledge, 1984); L. C. B. Seaman, *From Vienna to Versailles* (London: Routledge, 2002); David Fromkin, *A Peace to End All Peace: The Fall of the Ottoman Empire and the Creation of the Modern Middle East* (New York: Henry Holt, 1989); Arno J. Mayer, *Politics and Diplomacy of Peacemaking: Containment and Counterrevolution at Versailles, 1918–1919* (New York: Knopf, 1967); and Michael Howard, *The Invention of Peace* (New Haven: Yale University Press, 2001).

# 4

# THE INTERWAR YEARS, 1919–1939

## Warfare in Europe, 1919–1936

The end of World War I did not end the violence in Europe. While western Europe remained relatively stable in the immediate post-war period, eastern and southern Europe endured considerable turmoil. The Russian Revolution, itself a direct product of the war, continued its bloody course, producing a civil war inside Russia and a war between the Soviet Union and the newly created state of Poland. Further to the south, discontent with the post-war settlement ignited the ancient and passionate animosities between Greece and Turkey. These wars demonstrated not only that the Paris Peace Conference had fallen far short of its goals, but that the underlying causes of World War I, including nationalism, had not dissipated.

Driven by an ideological fervor not seen in Europe since the days of the French Revolution in the eighteenth century, Russia's "Reds" built a new army to defend the revolution against the anti-Bolshevik "Whites." This new army combined the spirit of revolutionaries, the experience of some veteran Tsarist officers (50,000 of whom joined the Reds, many under duress), and a political indoctrination process developed by "commissars" assigned to distribute propaganda in military units and keep a watch on presumably counterrevolutionary officers. The combination of these forces produced a unity of purpose that held the Red armies together in the face of their larger, but much more internally divided, foes.

The White forces were divided into several factions, including reform-minded liberals, reactionary Tsarists, and generals hoping to introduce a military-directed authoritarian regime. They were further divided into three main geographic areas: General Denikin's forces in the south, General Iudenich's forces based around the northern port of Archangel, and Admiral Kolchak's forces in Siberia. The Reds, although nearly surrounded, thus held the important military advantage of "interior lines," allowing them to rapidly move supplies and men between threatened fronts. The three separate White forces, on the other hand, could not effectively coordinate their efforts or share supplies.

The Whites benefited, however, from support from a variety of non-Russian national groups. Like the Whites themselves, each of these groups had different ambitions and goals. One of these forces was the so-called Czech legion, a 70,000-strong force made up of ethnic Czechs who had fought on both sides during World War I. Some of them were Bohemians who had served in the Austro-Hungarian army but had become Russian POWs during World War I. They were augmented by ethnic Czechs who had fought for the Russians against the Austro-Hungarians.

In the wake of the Russian Revolution, these troops, many of them armed, were combined into one force. In June, 1918 the allies agreed to transport this force out of Russia through the eastern port of Vladivostok if the Czechs would agree to fight on the western front. Once the Germans had been defeated, the Czech legion could then be transported to the new nation of Czechoslovakia to form the core of their nation's first army. On their way to Vladivostok via the Trans-Siberian Railroad, however, a Soviet force stopped them and demanded that they disarm. Rather than yield, the Czechs fought. They quickly augmented their resources with captured weapons, ammunition, and supplies and fought their way along the Trans-Siberian Railway.

The Allies saw in the Czech Legion a potentially powerful force that, if it could be properly supplied and united with the White armies, might serve as an important anti-Bolshevik ally. Failing that, the Allies could rescue the Czechs and get them out of Russia to be used in anti-German offensives in late 1918 or, if the war did not end, in offensives they were planning for 1919. Consequently, even as the combat on the western front was reaching its climax, the Allies decided to send troops to Russia via the Arctic Sea. From June to August, 1918, a small British, French, and American force seized the ports of Murmansk, Archangel, and Vladivostok with the ultimate goal of making contact with White forces and the Czech legion. The Allies also hoped to prevent the rapid transfer of German POWs from Russian camps into the German army.

The Allies soon found themselves in the middle of a chaotic civil war and embroiled in an impossible situation. The Americans, under strict orders to protect the Trans-Siberian Railroad but not to interfere with internal Russian affairs, refused to move inland alongside the British and the French. The Americans also had to contend with a 70,000-strong Japanese force whose own intervention into Siberia greatly concerned the western Allies. Despite their orders, the Americans inevitably found themselves engaged in light combat against Red forces. The deaths of 500 Americans in Russia increased domestic opposition to the American presence in Russia. Finally, in 1920, the chaos resolved itself when the Czechs at last reached Vladivostok. The Czech Legion's departure from Russia complete, the Americans left Russia in August with the British and French following suit that autumn.

The Czech Legion and the Allied (and Japanese) intervention allowed the Reds to appeal to Russian nationalism and claim that they were defending the motherland against foreign invasion. Throughout 1919 the Reds grew stronger as their military reforms became more effective and the divisions within the White forces intensified. By January, 1920 the Reds had taken the upper hand and defeated White forces on each of their fronts, driving the remaining Whites into the Crimean Peninsula and eastern Siberia.

Six years of near-constant warfare, plus the traumas of a domestic revolution, had created a desperate situation inside Russia. Hunger and disease reached epidemic proportions as communications, trade, and industry collapsed. Although exact figures are impossible to calculate, recent estimates suggest that as many as 10,000,000 Russians may have died. The dislocations in Russia also spread to the Baltic States and Finland, where a 10,000-strong German force fought alongside a former Russian cavalry officer, Carl Gustaf Mannerheim, against Finnish Communists. Mannerheim's leadership helped Finland achieve its independence from Russia in 1920. The Baltic republics of Latvia, Lithuania, and Estonia were successful in achieving their independence as well.

The Red forces also had to face a determined Polish nation under the command of the able General Joseph Piłsudski. The commander of the wartime Polish Legion, an anti-Russian force that fought as part of the Austro-Hungarian army in World War I, Piłsudski later grew dissatisfied with the Central Powers and increasingly pessimistic about Germany and Austria's ultimate chances of success. In July, 1917 the Germans arrested and detained him for the remainder of the war. Seen as a great Polish hero for his resistance to the Germans, the Austrians, and the Russians alike, Piłsudski became one of Poland's most compelling representatives at the Paris Peace Conference.

The Poles had a great deal of support from France, which feared that the Russian Revolution could have disastrous consequences for its own security. If Russia remained in Bolshevik hands, a Franco-Russian alliance would be politically impossible and France would not be able to recover the massive loans it had extended to Russia during the war. France therefore looked to Poland and Czechoslovakia to act as eastern counterweights to Germany as Russia had done before the war. Despite ardent French support for a large Poland, however, the United States and Britain refused to grant Poland the return to its 1772 borders that the Polish delegation had demanded. Piłsudski grew dissatisfied with the conference, leaving Paris in anger in April, 1919. A special commission headed by British diplomat Lord Curzon eventually set the eastern boundary of Poland west of its 1772 border. Despite their general dependence on the western Allies, the Poles refused to recognize the so-called Curzon Line.

Seeing Russia engulfed in civil war, Piłsudski decided to fight for the 1772 border that the Versailles Treaty had denied him. He appealed to Polish nationalism and built a new ethnically Polish army that he planned to lead personally. On April 25, 1920 Piłsudski attacked the Russians while anti-Soviet Ukrainians and the trapped White forces in the Crimea launched their own offensives. It seemed for a time that the combination might just overwhelm the Reds. The Poles pushed the Russians past the Curzon Line and eventually 125 miles east of it. In the Crimea, General Pyotr Wrangel's White army broke through into the Ukraine. The future of the Bolshevik Revolution seemed to be in doubt.

The Reds reacted with successful counteroffensives on all fronts. The Soviets mobilized 1,500,000 men and pushed Wrangel back into the Crimea. They then sent an army west under the command of a brilliant twenty-seven-year-old military strategist, General Mikhail Tukhachevski, to deal with the Poles. The Russians used a combination of old-fashioned Cossack cavalry charges and modern artillery to smash the right wing of Piłsudski's army. Tukhachevski captured the fortified cities of Lemberg, Vilna, and Grodno, then turned on Warsaw. Western and Polish generals alike feared that the Polish capital might fall by the end of the summer, leaving all of Poland in Bolshevik Russia's hands.

The western Allies especially feared that a successful Russian offensive at Warsaw might be the start of a general war against the Bolsheviks. With Germany in too weakened a condition to defend itself, the Allies urged Marshal Foch to assemble a large, multi-national force against the Bolsheviks and lead it personally from Poland. He refused, arguing that Bolshevism would die on its own as European economies recovered from the traumas of the war. Under French and British pressure to help the Poles, Foch sent his able chief of staff, Brigadier General Maxime Weygand, in his place. Weygand helped to reorganize Polish forces and the defenses around Warsaw, but Piłsudski resisted Weygand's attempts to assume command. Piłsudski rejected Weygand's recommendation of a counteroffensive on the Russian right, favoring instead a frontal attack at the overextended center of the Russian line. The fate of Poland, and perhaps all of central Europe, hung in the balance.

On August 16, 1920, Piłsudski personally led the Polish armies in a nine-day rout of the Russians. Tukhachevski's force found itself surrounded. Two Polish forces, acting like pincers, threatened to trap a much smaller Russian force. More than 66,000 of Tukhachevski's 200,000 Russians surrendered, along with 230 heavy guns, 1,000 machine guns, and 10,000 vehicles. Russian defeats at the Battles of Niemen and the Shchara in September ended any chance for the Soviets to capture Warsaw. In March, 1921, the Treaty of Riga gave Poland an eastern border 155 miles east of the Curzon Line. The defeat forced the Soviet Union to (temporarily) abandon its aim to reacquire Poland, but it also gave the Reds a chance to concentrate on, and soundly defeat, the Whites in Crimea.

At the time, westerners hailed the Polish victory at Warsaw as a monumental defeat of Bolshevism on par with Charles Martel's victory over the Moslems at Tours in 732. Although these comparisons were no doubt greatly exaggerated, Piłsudski's stature in Poland and in the west soared. In 1926, frustrated by what he saw as the weaknesses of Polish democracy, he led a coup and ruled Poland until his death in 1935. The defeat at Warsaw notwithstanding, Tukhachevski continued to rise through the ranks of the Soviet military, becoming chief of staff in 1926 at the young age of thirty-three. He advocated the construction of modern army units based around tanks and mobility. He therefore deserves much of the credit for the revival of the Soviet army in the 1920s and 1930s. Soviet leader Joseph Stalin, however, never trusted him. In 1937 Stalin ordered him arrested and executed as a part of the Great Purges that devastated the senior leadership of the Soviet army.

As a result of Piłsudski's efforts, Poland had not fallen to a communist government and had retained its independence, but the Soviet victory in the Russian Civil War had been an ominous sign to opponents of Bolshevism. German leaders especially feared the growing power of the mammoth Soviet state, which in 1919 created the Comintern (Communist International) aimed at spreading worldwide revolution. The Comintern's threat to private property and religion helped to rally conservatives in nations like Spain, France, Germany, and Italy. Fascists in all four countries later derived much of their popular appeal from promises to fight communism against all enemies foreign and domestic.

The Russian Civil War had many long-lasting impacts on Europe. Most importantly, the Bolshevik victory frightened conservatives and moderates across the continent. Radical leftists, on the other hand, saw the Soviet model as an attractive alternative to capitalism and parliamentary democracy. The crash of the New York stock market in 1929 and the ensuing global depression of the 1930s only confirmed that view. Hatred of Bolshevism proved to be a much more galvanizing force in Germany in the 1930s than hatred of Britain and France. Even as late as 1945 Hitler sustained real hopes that he could forge an alliance with the Americans and the British because, he assumed, they were more fearful of Bolshevism than they were of Nazism.

For Russia and Joseph Stalin, the Civil War confirmed fears that the western powers were part of a capitalist movement against the Soviet Union. American recognition of the Soviet Union in 1933 did not erase memories of the American intervention on the side of the Whites. Stalin remained intensely suspicious of western motives throughout the 1920s and 1930s. This suspicion helped to lead to the signing of several treaties and agreements between the Soviet Union and Germany, most fatefully the Nazi–Soviet non-aggression pact of 1939. Stalin so deeply mistrusted the west that he disregarded British intelligence warnings of an imminent German invasion in 1941.

Poland remained a source of great tension and controversy throughout the 1920s and 1930s. France, eager to place a strong nation on Germany's eastern border, was a firm supporter of Poland throughout the post-war years. Germany, fearing the spread of Bolshevism, almost immediately began to fortify its border with Poland in violation of the Versailles Treaty. The western Allies did not formally object to this violation because of their own fears of Russian advance. Both Germany and Russia objected to the presence of a large Poland on their borders, but France, and to a lesser extent, Britain, were determined that Poland should retain its independence. Poland's heroic victory at Warsaw engendered a great deal of sympathy in French and British government circles.

Moreover, after Piłsudski's death, the Polish government devolved into a melee of internecine struggles, with no leader emerging to unite the disparate warring factions. It is, therefore, no surprise that World War II in Europe began with a crisis in Poland.

World War I left simmering hatreds in the Balkans as well. The Greco-Turkish confrontation arising from both sides' discontent with the war's conclusion was one of the most serious post-war crises because of its potential to once again destabilize the volatile Balkan region. The traumas of the war created near anarchy in Turkey and soon called into question the viability of the new Turkish state. The Greeks, for their part, were anxious to capitalize on the chaos in Turkey to claim ethnically Greek territory in the Balkans and Asia Minor. The allied landing of a Greek force near Smyrna in 1919 enraged Turkish nationalists, who saw Greece as Turkey's most ancient and implacable foe. Atrocities committed by the Greeks against Turkish civilians further fanned these flames. Greek troops advanced on Turkish forces in Thrace as well, capturing the city of Adrianople.

It was amidst this environment of anti-foreign anger that the Allies imposed the Treaty of Sèvres on Turkey. The terms included a transfer of territory to Greece, western control over Turkish finances, and international (read: British, French, and Italian) control of Constantinople and the Dardanelles Straits. Under strong Allied pressure, the Sultan signed the treaty on August 10, 1920. Nine days later, the Sultan called the Turkish National Assembly into session to approve the treaty, but instead the Assembly rejected it and denounced as traitors those who had supported it. Sultan Mehmed VI thereupon dissolved Parliament, leading Turkey's hero from the Gallipoli campaign of 1915, Mustapha Kemal Atatürk, to proclaim a new nationalist government based in the interior Anatolian city of Ankara.

The Assembly's rejection of the treaty symbolized the effective end of the Sultan's influence. He attempted to resist his increasing loss of authority by working with the British, French, and Italian occupiers against Kemal's nationalists. As Kemal's forces grew stronger, however, it became evident that the Sultan no longer spoke for Turkey. The new government accused him and his ministers of treason for signing the Treaty of Sèvres and for collaborating with Turkey's occupiers and erstwhile enemies. In 1922, Mehmed VI fled the country, formally ending the Sultanate's control over Turkey.

The weakness of the Sultan contrasted dramatically with the dynamism of the nationalist government led by Kemal. Turkey's revitalized and reenergized army quickly moved to eject the despised Greeks and restore Asia Minor to Turkey. It rapidly concluded an agreement with the Soviet Union that resolved Turkish disputes with Russia and allowed the Soviets to focus on their own civil war. Turkey recognized Soviet incorporation of Azerbaijan, Georgia, and half of Armenia in exchange for purchases of surplus Soviet arms, Soviet recognition of Turkish control over the other half of Armenia, and Soviet diplomatic support for a revision of the Sèvres settlement.

Kemal used those Soviet arms to lead a campaign against the Greek occupation of Smyrna and its hinterland. The Greek army's 150,000 men in Anatolia soon moved to crush Kemal's nationalists. But events quickly began to conspire against them. In October, 1919 the Greek king, Alexander, died from blood poisoning following a bite from one of his pet monkeys. This rather odd death returned his father, Constantine, to the throne. Constantine had attended the German War Academy in Berlin, served in the Prussian army, and had married Kaiser Wilhelm II's sister, Sophia. As a result, he had shown pro-German sympathies and had been exiled under Allied pressure to Switzerland in 1917, leaving the throne in the hands of his son, Alexander. The Allies proved much less willing to support Constantine than Alexander, but Constantine decided to pursue the war in Turkey nevertheless.

Building on popular discontent with the treaty and the insult of the Greek invasion, Kemal led a brilliant military campaign from 1920 to 1922. In July, 1921 he defeated an offensive led personally by Constantine and then counterattacked, winning the battle of Sakkaria (August 24 to September 16). The victory allowed Kemal to consolidate his gains and reform his army. He recaptured Smyrna in September, 1922, with Turkish troops burning the Greek section of the city in order to avenge real and perceived Greek atrocities committed earlier in the war. Kemal's forces turned north to move on Constantinople, then under international control. The Italian, British, and French occupiers of the city had no desire to challenge Kemal and soon agreed voluntarily to withdraw. The Greco-Turkish War had been a tremendous victory for Kemal and Turkey.

Kemal looked to follow his success on the battlefield with success at the bargaining table. In November, 1922 eight nations co-sponsored a conference to consider revisions to the Treaty of Sèvres. The resulting Treaty of Lausanne invalidated the terms of the Treaty of Sèvres and resulted in Turkey attaining its modern borders. It included no provisions for the autonomy of either Armenia or Kurdistan, thus recognizing those minority regions' reincorporation into Turkey. Eastern Thrace and all of Anatolia also returned to Turkish control, settling border disputes with both Greece and Bulgaria. The military terms of the treaty were also favorable to Turkey. Greece agreed not to fortify its Aegean islands and also agreed not to fly military aircraft over Turkish airspace.

The treaty called upon Turkey to recognize British control of Cyprus and Italian authority in the Dodecanese Islands, but it freed Turkey from reparations payments that the Ottoman Empire had agreed to at Sèvres. Turkey did, however, agree to pay outstanding pre-war debts incurred by the Ottomans to the other signatories. The United States and the Soviet Union, though not signatories, lent their full support to the new treaty, signaling wide international acceptance both of the treaty itself and Turkey's new place in the community of nations.

The Greco-Turkish War and the Treaty of Lausanne established Turkey as the formal successor state to the Ottoman Empire, but the touchy problem of nationalism remained. Armenians, Kurds, and other minorities had no choice but to accept reunification with the Turks. For the Armenians, victims of the wartime genocide at the hands of the Turks, this provision was especially galling. Moreover, the new boundaries of Turkey and Greece placed many Orthodox Christians within Turkey and many Muslims within Greece. Many people, including Kemal, believed that peace would never flourish until state and ethnic borders coincided more perfectly. As a result, the post-war period witnessed one of the largest forced movements of populations in European history. Taking religion as the basis for defining ethnicity, Greek and Turkish authorities moved more than 1.2 million Eastern Orthodox Christians from Turkey to Greece. More than 150,000 Christians left Constantinople, leaving the city (soon to be renamed Istanbul) without many important members of its commercial and professional classes. Similarly, 380,000 Muslims moved from Greece to Turkey. The flood of refugees caused financial and social problems for both nations, but the region remained relatively stable for the remainder of this period.

The triumph of Kemal also meant the triumph of secular nationalism in Turkey. Kemal believed that Turkey's future would be more secure if it became identified more with Europe than the Arab-dominated Middle East. He therefore secularized Turkish society by abolishing the caliph, Islamic law, and many Islamic customs such as polygamy. He introduced a western calendar, western-style script for the Turkish language, western dress, and began to modernize Turkey around western technology. To bury old hatchets, he even constructed memorials to the heroism of the British and Australians who fought at Gallipoli. Unlike the Ottoman Empire, the new nation of Turkey was determined to open cooperative links to the west, eventually leading to Turkey's admission to NATO in 1952 and continuing debates about the propriety of Turkey's admission to the European Union.

## Disarmament, Locarno, and the rise of Fascism

The conclusion of wars in Turkey, Russia, and Poland left Europe relatively peaceful for the remainder of the 1920s. Germany remained the continent's most serious security problem. The immediate post-war German hostility to the Treaty of Versailles abated slightly, but did not disappear. The new German government, the Weimar Republic, faced an insurmountable crisis of legitimacy. Simply put, the government could not make its own citizens forget that it had signed the Versailles *Diktat*. It therefore had placed itself in the awkward position of distancing itself from the treaty at home while striving to show its good faith in respecting the treaty abroad.

German society refused to accept the principles upon which the treaty was based. In part, this refusal was a product of two Allied decisions made in 1918. First, they accepted an armistice rather than take the fight into Germany as some had recommended. They did so to end the bloodshed as early as possible, but, as a consequence, the German army could claim that it had ended the war on enemy soil and that it had therefore not lost. Second, the Allies did not undertake a visible victory march through Berlin. That decision was designed to spare Germans an intentional humiliation, but it further reinforced the notion that the German army had been unbeaten in the field.

Successive German governments therefore worked to undermine the treaty without directly challenging the stronger western powers that had charged themselves with enforcing it. In order to appease domestic constituencies and to begin the process of undercutting the treaty itself, the German government undertook a series of anti-Versailles programs. These programs used a variety of governmental and non-governmental vehicles to promote propaganda designed to undermine the fundamental tenets of the settlement. One of the most famous was the War Guilt Section of the German Foreign Ministry. These propaganda programs, for example, depicted French President Raymond Poincaré, a native of Lorraine, as an aggressive hawk who actively sought war with Germany in the years leading up to 1914.[1] Although historically inaccurate, these propaganda programs helped to promote the notion inside Germany that the nation had fought an essentially defensive war and therefore did not deserve the taint of war guilt and the host of punishments that the western powers imposed as a result.

This movement enlisted widespread support throughout German society. Prominent German academics, including Hans Delbrück and Max Weber, pleaded the case that Germany had fought a "defensive war against Tsarism."[2] The connection between the German government and some of its most prominent academics also yielded forty volumes of documents (more than 15,000 in all) in less than six years, all aimed at refuting the charge of German war guilt. These efforts did not meet with much support outside of Germany, but at home they reinforced the useful falsehood of the "stab in the back" and depicted Germany as the victim of a vengeful and malicious campaign by the western powers.

The venomous hatreds inside Germany led to a new German nationalist movement, led by the National Socialist Party, known by its acronym, Nazi. The Nazis had the support of military luminaries such as General Erich Ludendorff, who had been an early supporter of the stab in the back falsehood in order, he hoped, to preserve the honor of the German army. In 1923, Ludendorff marched with Hitler in the Beer Hall Putsch in Munich aimed at bringing down the Bavarian government. Hitler went to jail for a year (where he wrote *Mein Kampf*), but Ludendorff, a military hero in the eyes of most Germans, was exonerated. In 1925, Ludendorff's former superior, General Paul von Hindenburg, won election as Germany's president. Many in the west saw the election as symbolic of the German people's forgiveness of their military.

Germany sought allies, often using the continent's problems to create strange bedfellows. Despite popular German fears of Soviet Bolshevism, the Germans and Soviets negotiated a treaty of convenience. In 1922, the Treaty of Rapallo reestablished diplomatic relations between the two nations. The treaty included generous trade terms and annulled any claims by either side for war reparations. Both parties, pariahs in the eyes of the western powers, saw the agreement as mutually beneficial. Germany later secretly used it as a way to test weapons systems in Russia that were denied to them by the Treaty of Versailles. Although French and British politicians and generals were discomforted by the arrangement, its overt terms did not violate any clauses of the Versailles Treaty. It was, however, an ominous portent of what the west might face should Germany and Russia ally. That ghost continued to haunt the west throughout the 1920s and 1930s.

Germany also sought economic means, including intentionally inflating their currency, to subvert the terms of Versailles.[3] More directly, the German government willfully failed to make scheduled payments as promised in the Versailles settlement. Germany's 1923 failure to pay reparations led to the Ruhr crisis. The French government, under immense American pressure to repay war loans, and believing the Germans to be intentionally dragging their feet, decided on a show of force. In January, a French and Belgian force occupied the coal and iron rich Ruhr Valley and stayed for two and a half years. The occupation eventually resulted in a formal resolution that, with the introduction of the Dawes Plan, ended the immediate crisis, but the Ruhr crisis had dramatic impacts. The passive resistance of German miners to the French and Belgian occupation rallied German popular opinion in their support. French efforts to force the miners to return to work served only to further demonize the French in German eyes. Many Germans saw in the conclusion of the crisis a victory. German reparations were greatly reduced (in the end they paid far less than they had agreed to in the Versailles settlement) and the spirit of the miners indicated broad popular opposition to the French and British. The latter noticeably declined to support the Ruhr occupation, suggesting that Franco-British relations were souring.

The Ruhr crisis, a kind of "peace as war," also had unintended economic effects. The work stoppages in the Ruhr mines combined with an economy still in chaos from the war led to runaway inflation across the continent. Economic problems made German payment of their full reparations bill even more unlikely, further undermining the economic recovery plans of Britain, France, and, to a lesser extent, the United States. In France, the franc lost 46 percent of its value in the year following the Ruhr occupation. The economic crisis led to the election of a left-leaning *Cartel des Gauches* in 1924. The new French government, led by Aristide Briand, promoted a more moderate stance toward Germany, partly because the Ruhr crisis had shown the relative powerlessness of French policy.

Briand became France's foreign minister from 1925 to 1932 and, under his guidance, France adopted policies that he hoped would protect French interests by offering Germany reconciliation. His most important diplomatic achievement was the Locarno Pact of 1925. Britain, France, and Germany agreed to accept as inviolable the boundaries of western Europe. Germany was unwilling to accept the same terms in the east, although they did agree to consult with France and Britain before seeking any territorial adjustments there. The symbolism of the treaty was important as well. The treaty was a true negotiation, with much of the initiative coming from German foreign minister Gustav Stresemann. As an agreement among equals, its signature in the neutral venue of Locarno, Switzerland held an important symbolic value as well.

Locarno seemed to initiate a new era of peace in European history. Briand and Stresemann shared the 1926 Nobel Prize for Peace. In the same year, Germany entered the League of Nations as a permanent member of the Council. Briand seemed to many to be "the pilgrim of peace" in Europe, declaring "Make way, rifles, machine-guns, cannon! Make place for conciliation, arbitration, and peace!"[4] Although French conservatives criticized him for being too idealistic and too conciliatory to the Germans, Briand continued to work with Stresemann and British foreign secretary Austen Chamberlain on ways to advance peace on the European continent.

Briand also worked with American secretary of state F. B. Kellogg to extend his vision of peace worldwide. In 1928 he and Kellogg negotiated a treaty that has forever been linked to their names. The Pact of Paris, more popularly known then and now as the Kellogg–Briand Pact, outlawed war as an instrument of national policy unless used in self-defense. Eventually 65 nations signed the pact, including Germany and the Soviet Union, leading many Europeans to hope that eastern problems could be resolved as Locarno had resolved western problems.

Some contemporaries criticized the pact for having no enforcement mechanisms and depending upon the dubious peaceful intentions of nations. Ferdinand Foch disparaged France's adherence to the Locarno and Kellogg–Briand Pacts as a strategy of grand illusion. Still, these agreements did lead to improvements in economic relations, including an International Steel Agreement that gave Germany the largest share of the European steel market, and also led to increased cultural exchanges across the continent.

The vexing problem of German reparations remained and the Europeans turned once more to the Americans to help solve the problem. Stresemann, now seen as a great statesman both at home and abroad, helped to negotiate a new economic plan known as the Young Plan, named for its American sponsor, Owen D. Young. The plan reduced Germany's overall reparations by two-thirds and extended the period for making those payments to 1988. The Young Plan was scheduled to go into effect in May, 1930. With America again acting as creditor, the financial future of Europe appeared sound. Stresemann's death on October 3, 1929 cast a slight cloud of sadness over the continent, but the mood remained generally optimistic.

Europe, it seemed, could look forward to a peaceful and prosperous future. German reparations had been significantly reduced and the allied occupation of the Rhine River bridgeheads ended much earlier than the Versailles Treaty had proposed. The Allies did not press the Germans to turn over war crimes suspects, allowing the Germans to conduct those trials themselves. The results were entirely predictable. The Germans did not inflict punishments on any of its war leaders and did not press Holland to surrender the exiled Kaiser. Britain, too, soon let the matter of trying the Kaiser drop, leaving him to live quietly in Holland until his death in 1941.

Moreover, it seemed that the harsh spirit of the Versailles settlement had abated. The Allies had demonstrated their willingness to amend significant portions of the treaty and not hold the Germans to the letter of the agreements they had signed. They had accepted significantly less money than had been due them and had largely retreated back into domestic affairs. They had consistently reelected men such as Briand who sought peace and repudiated hawks such as Georges Clemenceau, who lost the 1920 French presidential election and thereafter disappeared from politics. The psychology of post-war hatred, many hoped, had been broken. The conditions for peace seemed better than at any point in the century.

Nevertheless, despite the general absence of war on the continent and the moderate successes of treaties such as Locarno, a dangerous mix of hatred, recrimination, and fear existed below the surface in Europe. Most disturbing was the rise of a new and ultra-nationalistic ideology, Fascism. Because of its virulent nationalism, Fascism differed in all of the European societies where it took root. Nevertheless, Fascists tended to have four factors in common: a focus on race as the definition of national identity; an increased role for the state; single party rule; and a joint public–private approach to economics.

Fascists defined the nation as a racial unit with a special historical mission. This definition necessitated a return to the irredentism of the years before World War I and demanded that all areas containing members of the national race be placed under one state. Thus German Fascists argued for the annexation of ethnically German areas including the Sudetenland, Danzig, and portions of the Baltic States. Fascists reviled "inferior" racial minorities for the supposedly negative effects that these groups had on the majority population. Most famous, of course, was Germany's persecution of Jews, which, in the early phases, involved a clear and distinct separation of Jews from Aryan Germans. Other groups, such as the Roma Gypsies, suffered terribly as well.

Second, Fascism reduced the role of the individual in favor of state-directed mass participation. The rights, desires, and interests of individuals mattered less to Fascists than the perceived needs of the race and the nation. Thus in many states, even procreation came under government regulation, as Fascists pressed women to bear as many children as possible (with other members of the same race) in order to extend and continue the race. This stress on conformism and membership to a racial group led to an intense fear and hatred of outsiders and dissent. It also produced desires to weed out the weak, later leading to a German program to murder and sterilize the physically and mentally handicapped (including many World War I veterans).

Third, Fascists gave virtually unchallenged power to a single party or single ruler. This party controlled communications and propaganda as well as access to government resources. Fascism combined left-wing popular mobilization with right-wing appeals to confrontation and a glorification of the war experience. Significantly, two of the earliest and most forceful Fascists, Italy's Benito Mussolini and Germany's Adolph Hitler, were both war veterans who looked back positively at their military experiences. Disaffected World War I veterans were key elements of Fascism's grassroots support because they were wooed by the Fascists' deification of the soldier.

Fourth, Fascists were virulently anti-Bolshevik and consequently they respected private property. Most Fascists favored a "corporatist" economic strategy wherein the state directed the overall economy while permitting individuals to retain property and generate wealth. In this way, they hoped to avoid both the ideological excesses of communism and the material excesses of capitalism. For this reason, Fascism appealed to many members of Europe's middle classes, many of whom had lost their fortunes as a result of the continental inflation that generally characterized the period after 1923.

Perhaps Fascism's most popular appeal was its facile scapegoating. Disaffected soldiers, impoverished members of the bourgeoisie, and people without hope could turn their problems on others. Fascists told members of the chosen race that their poverty, their hopelessness, and their despair were the fault of others. The scapegoats tended to be groups that were traditional lightning rods, such as Jews, or common foes such as Britain and France. Fascists assured disaffected people that their membership in a superior race entitled them to a special role in human history and called on them to give their total allegiance to the party in order that the party could lead the race to greatness. Fascism therefore gave people both a calling and an excuse for their misery. Many dismissed its dark and sinister sides, with enormous consequences for the future.

Before 1929, Fascism was a minority movement, with only the Italian Fascist party, under Mussolini, controlling a state. German Fascists, led by Hitler and Ludendorff, had gained support, but were not close to controlling Germany. In 1924, the German Fascists, represented by the National Socialist Party, won 6.4 percent of the seats in the Reichstag, but later that proportion fell to just 3 percent. Nazi attempts to support Ludendorff (a Nazi Party Reichstag delegate from 1924 to 1928) for the presidency failed in 1925 when his former superior, Hindenburg, won instead. Ludendorff received just 211,000 of the 27,000,000 votes cast. As late as 1928, the Nazis were still a fringe party, with just 2.5 percent of the seats in the Reichstag.

Moreover, Fascism could not develop as a unified European movement because so many significant differences remained. Spanish Fascism, for example, was much more closely identified with the Catholic Church than either German or Italian Fascism. Some German Fascists, for example Ludendorff, supported a movement to abolish all formal religion and replace it with a modern German version based on Norse mythology. The hyper-nationalism of Fascists also tended to reduce their ability to work together. Still, the coincidental rising of so many such movements suggested a common popular response to the underlying traumas of the immediate post-war years as well as the sluggishness of Europe's economy.

Other weaknesses existed in the European structure as well. The major treaties of this period had been concluded without the assistance of the League of Nations, a body that was quickly showing itself to be impotent. Several important states, most notably the United States, were not members. Germany and the USSR did not join until 1926 and 1934, respectively. Control of the League rested in the Council (Britain, France, Italy, Japan and, later, Germany) with smaller nations able to observe the Council's proceedings, but unable to have a direct influence on Council decisions. In theory, the Council could impose moral, economic, or military sanctions, but to do so required a unanimous vote. Moral sanctions carried little weight and no nation was willing to use military sanctions.

All of these problems came to the surface when the New York Stock Exchange crashed in late October. By mid-November, the world's wealthiest stock market had lost one-third of its September value. With Europe fully dependent, both directly and indirectly, upon the American economy, the crash hit Europe quickly and ferociously. Although it took economists almost two years to realize that a depression of unprecedented intensity had in fact begun (John Maynard Keynes and others at first welcomed the stock market devaluation as the first steps of a positive redirection of the world economy) the economic downturn had massive ramifications. In 1930, as stocks were making a modest recovery, the American government passed its highest protective tariff in history, indicating American desires to solve the economic crisis by insulating itself as much as possible from foreign trade.

This economic protectionism emerged from America's interpretation of the crisis. Many Americans blamed the economic downturn on the instability of European affairs, thus the desire to shield the nation from continental chaos by passing a prohibitive tariff. That tariff effectively cut the American economy off from those of its largest trading partners and sent the signal that America would involve itself less often in European diplomatic affairs as well. Although many Americans saw that the tariff would produce similar tariffs in Europe and contribute to an intensification of nationalism, the mood of protection won the day.

By 1931 the depression was plain for all to see. All across Europe unemployment rose, construction dwindled, and businesses failed. The political results were not hard to predict. The Fascist movements, which assigned blame for the crisis to foreigners and minorities, grew enormously in popularity. The Nazi representation in the Reichstag grew from 2.5 percent in 1928 to 18 percent in 1930, 34 percent in 1932 and 45 percent in 1933. In 1932 Hitler received 13,700,000 votes for the German presidency. In January, 1933 a new political crisis inside Germany led President Hindenburg to name Hitler the new chancellor. Less than a month later, Hitler took advantage of a fire inside the German Reichstag to implement sweeping new powers. Hitler quickly accused communists of arson, declared Berlin under siege, and arrested 100 communist Reichstag deputies. Evidence that the Nazis had started the fire themselves did little to contain the fury.

Seeing the fire as a "sign from heaven," Hitler seized upon the (most likely self-created) crisis to make himself the dictator of Germany. He ended the Weimar government, arrested hundreds of political suspects, and introduced a totalitarian police state that controlled nearly all communications. Despite Hitler's seizure of virtually all individual rights in Germany, a plebiscite showed that 89 percent of Germans approved of his new powers. Nazism had been democratically elected.

The weakness of German democratic institutions produced significant openings for Nazism, but even states where democracy was more firmly established, as in France, were susceptible. Several ultra-nationalist groups such as *Action française* and the veterans' group *Croix de Feu* showed Fascist tendencies and emulated many of Hitler's and Mussolini's styles. They blamed France's problems on Jews and foreigners and looked to overturn France's troubled Third Republic. A financial scandal in 1934 led to the resignation of the prime minister; the power vacuum gave the right its chance. On February 6, a group of right-wing protesters rushed the police line protecting the Chamber of Deputies. An aggressive police response left fifteen members of the extreme right dead and more than 2,000 people injured.

Fearful that the incident presaged a descent into Fascism, left-leaning parties joined together to form the Popular Front. Its members also feared that the army, long opposed to communism and tempted by Fascism, might join in opposition to the government. France's middle classes were already showing signs of supporting a Fascist movement. "The best minds," noted France's financial paper *Le Capital*, "envision the experiment of an authoritarian government on the lines of those in Italy and Germany." Another middle-class newspaper argued "The country is nauseated and disgusted, and ready for fury and acts of violence."[5]

Much of France's subsequent history in the 1930s and early 1940s was characterized by the struggle between the Popular Front and the pro-Fascist elements anxious to tear down the Third Republic and build a regime fashioned along lines similar to those in Nazi Germany. France became further and further polarized, with the Popular Front and its opponents often seeing each other as a greater threat than any foreign power. Often these clashes turned violent. In 1936 *Action française* thugs beat the Jewish and socialist Popular Front leader Léon Blum so badly that he had to be hospitalized. In the midst of this chaos, protests and strikes mounted, including strikes in 1936 and 1937 that crippled the French aviation industry at a critical moment in France's rearming process.

The political chaos in democratic France contrasted with the stability of the brutal dictatorship in Germany. From 1932 to 1939 France had nineteen different governments and eight ministers of war. The Popular Front resisted spending money to improve the army for fear of enhancing a weapon that might later be used by Fascists against the republic. Thus as Germany was rebuilding and rearming, France was so wracked by domestic disorder that it could not even develop a coherent plan for rearming let alone carry one out to a successful conclusion. French military strategy thus focused purely on defensive operations and only belatedly reacted to the threat from Germany.

France was also threatened by a crisis to its south. In July, 1936 much of the Spanish military, led by General Francisco Franco, revolted against the Spanish government. That government bore many resemblances to France's own Popular Front. Although France initially reacted by declaring a policy of non-intervention, it struck many as unlikely that France could remain aloof from the civil war in Spain. It seemed much more likely that the war in Spain would spill over into France, perhaps sparking a civil war there as well. French reactions to a Fascist challenge to democracy on its southern border would prove to be both a litmus test and a harbinger of their inability to deal with it on their eastern border. In both cases, France failed miserably, leading the nation into an abyss more horrifying than either the Popular Front or the *Croix de Feu* could have imagined.

## Spain, Munich, and the road to Warsaw

Although Spain had remained neutral in World War I, the nation was not immune to many of the problems that struck Europe in the interwar period. Economic dislocation, political polarization, and a rising level of violence struck Spain in the 1930s. In at least one important sense, however, Spain differed; its definition of nationalism was uniquely Spanish. In part because Spain did not fight in the war and was only peripherally involved in the pre-war tensions between the competing alliances, Spain did not nationalize by 1918 or even 1936 to the same extent that France and Italy did. Without a common crisis to face, Spain's regional identities continued to supercede its national identities. World War I had placed Frenchmen, Italians, and Germans from various parts of the nation together under the same flag and in the same uniforms. Spain lacked such a unifying experience. The nation was therefore much more regionally fragmented than most other European nations. Strong nationalist and separatist movements existed, most powerfully in Catalonia and the Basque country.

Economically, the absence of a wartime experience inhibited Spain's transition from a rural economy to an urban one. As a result, Spain remained less developed economically than many of the World War I belligerents and was therefore in an especially exposed position when the New York stock market crashed in 1929. With the markets for its agricultural exports shrinking, the Great Depression devastated an essentially pre-modern Spanish economy.

Economic dislocations produced social and political tensions in Spain as they had in Italy, Germany, and France. Even before the depression struck, Spain's government had showed tendencies toward centralization. General Miguel Primo de Rivera established an authoritarian government, loosely based upon Italian Fascist models, that ran Spain from 1923 to 1930. Some members of Spain's right wing, for example the future defense minister José María Gil Robles, more closely linked reactionary politics and the Catholic Church, assuring the support of that crucial institution and many of its followers.

The polarization of the 1930s produced a native Spanish Fascist movement, known as the Falange, that received occasional support from Mussolini. Its founder and leader was General Primo de Rivera's son, José Antonio Primo de Rivera. The Falange based its doctrine around a virulent hatred and fear of communism, justifying its power plays as preventative measures against a "Red coup." It blamed Spain's problems on foreign ideologies such as Marxism and parliamentary democracy. Most leaders of the Falange sought to use centralized authority to restore real and contrived past glories of Spain. They were thus opposed to the extension of regional autonomy to Catalonia and the Basque region because they argued that regionalism weakened the essential strengths of Spanish traditions. Although the Falange was a relatively small movement (it had no seats in the Spanish Parliament, the Cortes, in 1936), its militancy and dedication to violently challenging Spain's republican government created tremendous instability.

The rise of the Falange and other movements led to a Popular Front in Spain similar in broad outline to that in France. As in France, the principal characteristic unifying the members of the Popular Front was their opposition to Fascism. As a result, in both nations the Popular Front was an uneasy marriage of convenience. In Spain, it encompassed a volatile and divisive mix that included local separatists, communists, republicans, anti-clericals, and socialists. After a failed attempt by Gil Robles to seize power for the CEDA, a coalition of right-wing Catholic parties, the Popular Front held together to narrowly defeat CEDA in the 1936 elections. Through a technicality of the Spanish constitution, the Popular Front, although it gained just 48 percent of the vote, was able to control 55 percent of the Cortes and thus could govern almost without consultation with the right, which had gained 46 percent of the vote. Gil Robles and others of the Spanish right began to call for a union of the Falange, the CEDA, and the Spanish military in order to dissolve the republic, form a new government and "save civilization" from Bolshevism, revolution, and national division.[6]

The early days of the Popular Front government were wracked with turmoil. The new Prime Minister, Manuel Azaña, declared the Falange illegal and arrested José Antonio Primo de Rivera. The Cortes then deposed the Catholic and Monarchist President, Niceto Alcalá Zamora. Political disorder soon devolved into street violence, most notably in the assassination of a leftist army officer, José Castillo. In retaliation, the leader of the parliamentary opposition, the monarchist politician Calvo Sotelo, was himself assassinated. General strikes, more street violence, and acts of vandalism against churches underscored the precarious nature of Spanish democracy. Despite Azaña's declaration outlawing the Falange, it continued to grow in popularity and soon had many sympathizers in the army.

In July, the portions of the Spanish army stationed in Morocco defied the Popular Front and rebelled against the government. The generals of the "African Army" established a national defense junta and, with the help of German and Italian airlift support, soon transferred its forces from Morocco to Seville. The intervention of the Germans and Italians underscored the sensitivity of the conflict. Spain, long on the periphery of European military affairs, was now engaged in a civil war that threatened to spread across the continent. Just as a crisis in the Balkans had caused a general war in 1914, so in 1936 a crisis in Spain threatened to do the same.

Seeing the possibility of the war in Spain erupting in more general hostilities, the French and British largely tried to stay neutral. They hoped that by containing the war to Spain, they could prevent a spread of the fighting to their own borders. For France, intervention in Spain seemed to be a no-win situation. Prime Minister Léon Blum at first supported the idea of assisting the government against the army rebels, but to do so meant walking a precarious tightrope. The Spanish Republic that Blum wanted to aid contained many of the elements that the French right most loathed, including anti-clericals, communists, and regional separatists. Blum therefore knew that if he supported the Spanish government, he might put his own government in jeopardy. "Spain could not have been saved," Blum later recalled in explaining his decision not to sell arms to the republic, "but France would have gone Fascist."[7]

The British and French therefore established the Non-Intervention Committee, based in London, to assure that their nations did not get involved and consequently spread the conflict. The British warned France that if it helped the Spanish republicans and thereby brought on a war with Italy or Germany, France could not count on British support. The legal government of Spain could not, therefore, purchase arms from Britain or from France. France went so far as to close its border with Spain in 1936, thus eliminating any sustained level of support from sympathetic Frenchmen to the Spanish republicans. Only the Soviet Union, anxious to aid fellow communists, supplied arms, but most of these weapons were outdated World War I and Civil War surplus arms. These supplies, paradoxically enough, made intervention by France and Britain even more difficult because neither government wanted to appear to be fighting on the same side as the Soviets.

Official British and French unwillingness to aid the republicans opened the door for the Italians and the Germans. Although both nations formally adhered to a non-intervention agreement, they supplied the Spanish rebels (also known as the nationalists) anyway. The Spanish rebels' leader, former army chief of staff General Francisco Franco, showed Fascist tendencies that appealed to Hitler and Mussolini. The Germans, anxious to combat-test weapons developed since the Nazi seizure of power in 1933, proved especially willing to help Franco. German naval cruisers bombarded republican positions in Ibiza and Almeria and the Germans supplied more than £32 million worth of arms to Franco. Italy sent 47,000 ground troops, 700 airplanes, light tanks, and artillery pieces.

The most notorious use of foreign weapons occurred on April 26, 1937 when the German Condor Legion bombed the Basque town of Guernica. The Germans used incendiary weapons to attack on a market day, killing 1,000 unarmed civilians. The town, a traditional symbol of Basque independence, was destroyed, a grim foreshadowing of German air attacks on Rotterdam and Warsaw in the opening days of World War II. Not to be outdone, the Italian air force bombed Barcelona in 1938, inflicting what was then the heaviest casualties ever via an air campaign. Both incidents horrified the world; Pablo Picasso's famous work commemorating the destruction of Guernica served as a symbol of Fascist perfidy. Still, the incidents failed to translate into any tangible foreign support to the Spanish republic.

Like Picasso's masterpiece, the war in Spain became a global symbol of the war between Fascism and its many opponents. Despite the official neutrality of France, Great Britain, the United States, and others, men and women came from all over the world to fight. Some, like the International Brigades, were supported by the Soviet Union and the Comintern. They brought together communists (many of them unemployed factory workers) from Germany, France, Belgium, and eastern Europe. American volunteers, including Ernest Hemingway, came as well; many joined a volunteer unit known as the Abraham Lincoln Brigade. The British writer George Orwell first came to Spain to report on the war, but "had joined the militia almost immediately, because at that time and in that atmosphere it seemed the only conceivable thing to do."[8] He explained why:

> Since 1930 the Fascists had won all the victories; it was time they got a beating, it hardly mattered from whom. If we could drive Franco and his foreign mercenaries into the sea it might make an immense improvement in the world situation, even if Spain itself emerged with a stifling dictatorship and all its best men in jail. For that alone the war would have been worth winning.[9]

These militias were motivated by a common hatred of Fascism, but were woefully short of military expertise and modern equipment. The same could be said of the loosely trained militiamen who joined the nationalists. Orwell wryly noted the lack of skill among these soldiers when he recalled "goodness knows how many times the Spanish standard of marksmanship has saved my life."[10]

The issue for many non-Spaniards, like Orwell, was therefore much less about the future of Spain than the future of Europe. A Fascist triumph there would add to Fascist triumphs in Germany, Portugal, and Italy and provide momentum for Fascists in France and elsewhere. Still, the republicans faced nearly insurmountable odds. The internecine struggles between various members of the anti-Fascist coalition created insoluble problems. Orwell referred to the republicans as "an alliance of enemies."[11] Often they spent more time fighting one another than the Fascists. Just as the White armies of the Russian Civil War, they were unable to put aside their differences long enough to mount an effective resistance.

Even had they been able to ally, they simply did not have the weapons. The failure of the western democracies to aid the anti-Fascist forces left the latter hopelessly outgunned. Only the Soviet Union and Mexico recognized the right and need of the republicans to purchase arms. Mexico simply could not provide these arms in large quantity and the Soviet Union supplied them primarily to Spanish communists. They, in turn, often impeded the flow of arms to non-communist members of the anti-Fascist coalition for fear that such groups might later turn those arms against fellow communists.

The superior equipment, training, and leadership of the nationalist forces overwhelmed the gritty determination of the republicans. By summer, 1938, the nationalists were in control of most of Castile, Aragon, and the Basque country. The republican positions were divided into two regions: one centered upon Barcelona and the other upon the southeast of the country near Valencia. In the autumn, nationalist offensives reduced both areas significantly. The French decision to keep their border with Catalonia closed further prevented arms from reaching the beleaguered republican forces. In January, 1939 Barcelona fell, sealing the republicans' fate. In February, France and Britain reluctantly recognized Franco's government. The Spanish Civil War was over.

Many historians subsequently analyzed the war in Spain for the military lessons it offered, but equally important was the war's impact on civilians. In this manner, more so than in the military similarities, the war in Spain foreshadowed the ferocity of World War II. Being both a civil war and a war often fought by untrained militias, civilians suffered terribly. The massacre at Guernica was only the most dramatic example of warfare intentionally perpetrated upon non-combatants. Being a war of ideologies, both sides significantly blurred the lines between civilian and soldier with murderous results. This pattern was soon to repeat itself across Europe.

It was exactly the fears of such horrors spreading that led France and Britain to adopt a policy of appeasement. Simply put, the western democracies hoped that by making reasonable accommodations to German desires they could avoid a war that they did not want and for which they were not prepared. The war in Spain had demonstrated the impotence of Britain and France to deal with a major crisis. Their best policy, many believed, was to accommodate Germany rather than to fight.

Although critics such as Winston Churchill likened appeasement to feeding a tiger raw steak and hoping he will one day become a vegetarian, the policy was more popular than many people realize today. The general absence of the United States from European affairs after the onset of the Great Depression reinforced the notion among many Europeans that they did not have the strength to fight the Germans. The American president, Franklin Roosevelt, sympathized with France and Britain, but had been elected to solve the country's domestic problems. He had repeatedly campaigned (à la Woodrow Wilson) that he would not send American boys to die in a foreign war.

Consequently, the American military had been pared down to minimal levels and the American people showed little interest in European affairs. The Congress continued to assume that American involvement in Europe was a distraction at best, a disaster waiting to happen at worst. From 1935 to 1939 the Congress passed four Neutrality Acts that banned munitions exports and loans to belligerents, restricted American travel on vessels belonging to belligerent nations, and banned American ships from carrying war goods to belligerent ports. With the United States firmly committed to staying on their side of the Atlantic, the French and British governments thought it best not to confront Germany.

Furthermore, the French and British made two fundamental errors. First, they assumed that Hitler and Germany wanted peace as much as they did. They hoped that Hitler's rhetoric was just that, rhetoric. In this assumption they were very much mistaken. Unbeknownst to the west (and to the Soviet Union) Hitler had announced to his generals and his foreign minister in November, 1937 that he intended to annex Austria and Czechoslovakia and seize Poland and Russia. Slavic and Jewish residents of the latter two were to be forcibly moved or killed in order to create *Lebensraum*, or living space, for Germans.

Second, the British and the French assumed that their own armed forces would suffice to hold off the Germans, if not defeat them. While the professional forces held the Germans at bay, the full economic, social, and military efforts of the nation could be mobilized as they had been in 1914–1918. French and British doctrine and weapons development in the interwar years therefore tended to focus much more on defense than that of Germany, especially after Hitler's rise to power in 1933.

Focusing weapons development on defense had the additional virtue of being consistent with foreign and domestic policy. A defensive posture, many French officers believed, would send the message to France's neighbors that the nation had no offensive intentions. France did not invest heavily in an offensive air force or navy because to do so might send hostile signals to Britain as well as to Germany. France needed good relations with the British, but colonial rivalries and abiding suspicions combined to keep Franco-British relations cool.

On the domestic front, a defensive posture allowed France to invest in military systems that fit in with the tensions between the Popular Front and its right-wing rivals. Each side feared that constructing a large offensive force could be a mistake because of the possibility of it being later used by the government to suppress domestic dissent. Popular Front leaders were especially concerned because so many army officers had Fascist sympathies. Heavy investments in the army, they feared, might create the very instrument that could be used by the Fascists against the Popular Front. The war in Spain, which began with the army rebelling against a legally elected government, served as a frightening harbinger.

France therefore constructed a series of defensive works known collectively as the Maginot Line. Although much maligned after 1940 as a hopelessly out-dated expression of the defensive, the Maginot Line must be placed in a wider societal context. The construction of defensive works sent a message to the Germans that France was ready to defend itself, but that it was not interested in investing heavily in an army capable of threatening its neighbors. It also sent a message to fellow Frenchmen that the army's main role was to guard the frontier, not to engage in foreign adventures or play politics at home. The tragedy of the Maginot Line was less its failure to bring France safety in 1940 than that the Germans had no interest in listening to the message that it sent. Although Germany had constructed its own line of fortifications opposite the Maginot Line (known as the West Wall), by the end of the 1930s, German military planning, in sharp contrast to that of the French, was entirely offensive.

French and British defensive planning reflected a popular attitude that generally opposed involvement in war unless the homeland were attacked. As Brian Bond has perceptively noted, French thinking reflected more the Verdun spirit of "They Shall Not Pass" than the "On to Berlin" spirit of 1914.[12] German thinking, on the other hand, changed dramatically throughout the 1930s. At the time, a defensive posture seemed to many in Britain and France to make sense; it was only later that the British and French realized how much of the initiative for military operations they had ceded to the Germans. They had erred in believing that the Germans, having suffered as badly in World War I as they had themselves, would react in the same manner. They badly underestimated the genuine desire on the part of many Germans to expunge the memory of World War I not by resorting to peace, but by prosecuting a new war.

Because French (and to a lesser extent, British) military planning and social attitudes focused so heavily on defense, the western democracies were poorly positioned to react to German aggression. The western democracies therefore did not respond to the German remilitarization of the Rhineland in 1936, even though the action was a clear and provocative violation of the Treaty of Versailles. Neither did they respond to the *Anschluß* of 1938 that unified Germany and Austria, another violation of the Treaty. The two actions placed German military forces directly on the French and Belgian borders, added 6,000,000 eager and enthusiastic Austrians to the German empire, and created a dire situation for Hitler's next target, Czechoslovakia.

The Czechs understood all too well the crisis they were facing. The *Anschluß* meant that Germany now outflanked Czechoslovakia on both its northern and southern borders. Hitler soon demanded German annexation of the

Sudetenland, the extreme western part of the nation, which included 3,000,000 ethnic Germans. Forming a "C" at the western end of Czechoslovakia, the Sudetenland also contained most of the Czech frontier defenses and a large proportion of Czech industry. Annexation to Germany would doom the rest of Czechoslovakia. Hitler expected France and Britain to reject his demands and declare war. Instead, they yielded to practically all of his demands, granting Germany the Sudetenland in return for a German promise to respect the new Czech border. While British Prime Minister Neville Chamberlain announced "Peace in Our Time," Hitler fumed at having been robbed of his chance to start a general war.

Determined to provoke the west, Hitler violated the terms of the Munich Agreement in March, 1939 by annexing Bohemia, Moravia, and Memel. Still, Britain and France did nothing. The Russians looked uneasily upon German growth but the French had not matched Soviet support for Czechoslovakia the previous year and the Russians, feeling themselves increasingly isolated, were not willing to act on their own. Believing the western powers and Russia hopelessly weak, Hitler demanded Danzig and the Polish corridor.

These demands placed Britain and France in a precarious position. Although most people in the west were still unenthusiastic about "dying for Danzig," German aggression had shown the futility of continued negotiations with Hitler. On September 1, 1939 Hitler invaded Poland after concluding a non-aggression pact with the Soviet Union (see Chapter 5). France and Britain replied with declarations of war, but even this gesture proved to be more symbolic than real. The western armies were in no position to effect the only real assistance to Poland that they could have offered, an invasion of Germany from the west. Instead, they remained in defensive positions and engaged in what has become known as the "Phony War." Poland was left to suffer a twin invasion from Germany to the west and the Soviet Union to the east. World War II in Europe had begun, even if war in the west was barely discernible from peace.

## Further reading

On Germany, see Holger Herwig, "Clio Deceived: Patriotic Self-Censorship in Germany after the Great War," *International Security* 12 (Autumn, 1987), 5–44 and Richard Bessel, *Germany After the First World War* (Oxford: Clarendon Press, 1993). Among the best single-volume works on the Russian Civil War are W. Bruce Lincoln, *Red Victory: A History of the Russian Civil War* (New York: Simon and Schuster, 1989) and Marion Aten, *Last Train Over Rostov Bridge* (New York: Julian Messner, 1961).

On France, see Alistair Horne, *To Lose a Battle: France, 1940* (London: Penguin, reprint edition, 1990); Paul Marie de la Gorce, *The French Army: A Military-Political History* (New York: George Braziller, 1963); Eugenia Kiesling, *Arming Against Hitler: France and the Limits of Military Planning* (Lawrence: University Press of Kansas, 1996); and Robert Doughty, *The Seeds of Disaster:*

*The Development of French Army Doctrine, 1919–1939* (Hampden, CT: Archon Books, 1986).

There are several fine books on the Spanish Civil War including: Antony Beevor, *The Spanish Civil War* (London: Orbis, 1982); Raymond Carr, *The Spanish Tragedy* (London: Phoenix, 2000); and George Orwell's masterful account of his service in the Republican army, *Homage to Catalonia* (New York: Harcourt Brace Jovanovich, 1952). Gerald Howson, *Arms for Spain: The Untold Story of the Spanish Civil War* (New York: St. Martin's Press, 1999) details the failure of the western democracies to aid the republic.

# WORLD WAR II,
# 1939–1942

## Germany's war: Conquest and collaboration
## in the west

In order to understand Germany's war, one must understand two concepts that were central to German social assumptions and, therefore, to German military policy as well. The first, the "stab in the back," or *Dolchstoß*, we have already examined. Originally designed to deflect the blame of German military defeat in World War I onto Jews, communists, and other perceived domestic enemies of the Second Reich, it developed a life of its own and became a seminal construct of Third Reich thinking. When combined with German notions of their own racial and military superiority, the *Dolchstoß* had important military ramifications. It implied that German defeat could not come on the battlefield. If Germany were to be defeated again, it would be at the hands of domestic enemies, as the believers in the *Dolchstoß* understood the defeat of 1918. German military officers and special police therefore became obsessed with rooting out enemies and suspected enemies. This manic fixation led the Nazi regime to criminalize and demonize many sections of German society and to commit all manner of crimes. It also significantly detracted from Germany's ability to prosecute the war effectively.

The second major concept, *Lebensraum*, argued that "living space" must be created for Germans in the east, specifically in Poland and Russia. The Nazis generally disliked cities, viewing them as centers of industrial unrest and Bolshevik agitation. The German people would therefore need space. Poland and Russia would provide the majority of that space for the growing German population that Nazi family policy would create. Since Nazi racial ideology denigrated the Poles and Slavs as sub-human and Nazi political ideology reviled Bolshevism, eastern Europe became an obvious and popular target. The Poles, Jews, Russians, and other Slavs, who in Nazi eyes were sub-human anyway, would be enslaved, forcibly relocated, or murdered.

These two concepts explain Germany's devotion of so many of its resources to its war with Russia after 1941 and the descent of German society (and thus also its war effort) into mass murder, slavery, and genocide. Those societies that did not collaborate with Germany in turning over their Jews, subordinating their economy to German war needs, and providing military bases would be coerced or occupied. Because Germany understood its enemies to be internal as well as external, Germany's war was a war of unprecedented cruelty and fury. Resistance movements, political opposition, and any other suspect groups all faced German wrath. There could be no mercy for Germany's enemies.

Before the Germans could reshape eastern Europe in their own image, the democracies of the west would need to be neutralized. In the early stages of the war, Hitler imagined that Great Britain could be cajoled or convinced into remaining neutral. The policy of appeasement pursued by the government of Prime Minister Neville Chamberlain gave him little reason to think that Britain had much desire to fight. Britain's declaration of war against Germany in response to the latter's invasion of Poland did not produce any popular sentiment for war comparable to that of 1914. In Hitler's mind, the Anglo-Saxon British race would perforce come to understand its close racial ties to Aryan Germany and its common anti-Bolshevik politics. A war with Britain therefore might not be necessary and, if it was, few German senior officers expected Great Britain to be able to exercise much muscle on the continent if France could be effectively neutralized. As it turned out, both assumptions were wrong.

France, on the other hand, was a different matter. The domestic problems of the 1930s notwithstanding, most German generals feared the French army, then the largest in western Europe and (on paper, at least) a formidable foe. Few Germans expected to defeat France as easily as they had defeated Poland. But France was a part of much larger German ambitions. Gerhard Weinberg has recently argued that the German plan for war against France must be seen in a much wider context. It was, Weinberg contends, a plan to deal with France, Britain, *and* Russia. Striking through the Ardennes Forest, German armor and infantry would head not for Paris as in 1914 but north toward the English Channel. If the French army and the British Expeditionary Force were caught in the pocket thus created, they would be destroyed. If not, the Germans could establish a solid defensive line as they had done in World War I. From that line they could hold French and British attacks at bay while they attacked Allied shipping from air and sea bases on the Belgian and French Channel coastlines. This kind of favorable stalemate in the west would permit the Germans to turn their forces against the Russians in the east.[1]

To ensure a more favorable sea and air war against Britain, Hitler turned his sights on Norway. The seizure of the country with Europe's longest coastline would dramatically extend the base of operations that the German navy could use for submarine warfare and give the Germans direct access to the North Sea. Thus the German navy could avoid being bottled up as it had been in 1914–1918. Northern English cities would also be within range of bombers based at Norwegian airfields. Finally, control of Norway would facilitate the control and transport of Scandinavia's iron ore deposits, especially those of Sweden.

Norway, a small and impecunious nation, had virtually disarmed in the 1920s and 1930s. Although the Norwegians had a conscription law, its terms required just 84 days of mandatory service. The army's peacetime strength was authorized to be at 30,000 men but rarely exceeded 7,000. The navy was intentionally kept small so as not to appear to threaten Britain, which saw itself as Norway's protector. Upon full mobilization, Norway could depend on just 106,000 men (the vast majority of them lightly-trained reservists) and only about 40 serviceable aircraft.

Germany's willingness (indeed eagerness) to attack virtually defenseless neutrals provided it with tremendous strategic advantages in the early stages of the war. To compound the problem, many British politicians refused to see the attack coming. In April, 1940 Neville Chamberlain revealed the insoluble psychological contradictions in Allied thinking when he said "The accumulation of evidence that an attack [in the west] is imminent is formidable . . . and yet I cannot convince myself that it is coming."[2] Shortly after Chamberlain's statement, German forces invaded both Norway and neutral Denmark. Both countries, unprepared for the unprovoked attacks, were easy prey.

Seeing the threat to their North Sea communications, the British and French organized a hasty and ill-coordinated operation to aid the Norwegians, but the poor execution of the plan only served to underscore the lack of Allied preparations and the enormous chasm that separated British and French thinking. The speed of German operations and Allied inability to establish secure communications with the Norwegians added greatly to the confusion in London and Paris. Norway had been so long on the periphery of European military and diplomatic affairs that in 1940 British Foreign Secretary Lord Halifax mistook the Norwegian–Swedish border on his map for a railroad line.[3]

Winston Churchill, returned to the government as First Lord of the Admiralty in September, 1939, supported an operation to eject the Germans from the ice-free port of Narvik. The British navy had laid mines in the fjord near Narvik, but that operation failed to stop ten German destroyers and 2,000 German troops from occupying the port. The Germans took heavy naval losses, but prevented the Allies from conducting effective operations in Narvik and elsewhere in Norway. German forces completed their victory and occupied all of Norway with a speed and a relative ease that boosted German confidence and led to the collapse of the Chamberlain government.

Norway is also significant for studying both resistance to, and collaboration with, the Nazi regime. The Germans benefited from the agitation of Norwegian Fascists, led by a man whose very name became a global synonym for traitor, Vidkun Quisling. A gifted mathematician, he had graduated from the Norwegian Military Academy with the highest marks ever earned. In 1931 he became Norway's Minister of Defense. Two years later he left the government, formed his own political party, and began to warn Norwegians of the imminence of a Soviet or British invasion. Quisling's ill-chosen method for dealing with this perceived crisis was to adopt Fascism, see enemies lurking everywhere, and develop links with Germany "in order to forestall occupation by the British, a civil war . . . and Bolshevization of the whole country."[4]

While German paratroopers landed in Oslo on April 9, Quisling, with Hitler's blessing, attempted a coup d'état, broadcasting to the Norwegian people an appeal to collaborate with, and not resist, the Germans. He also gave German Admiral Erich Raeder critical defense information (which, as a former minister of defense, he was well positioned to give) and urged the Germans to act as quickly as possible. He moved to consolidate his control of the Norwegian government's bureaucracy and urged the Narvik garrison commander, a Quisling supporter, not to resist the German landings.

The Germans benefited from such support in almost all of the nations of western Europe. The collaborators' motivations were diverse. Some hoped for financial gains, some were openly sympathetic to Nazi ideology, some believed that Fascism was preferable to Bolshevism, and many shared Germany's anti-Semitism. In some cases, collaborationist groups believed that as long as the Germans were winning the war it was more prudent to make peace with them than to fight them.

Britain, which had a relatively small Fascist movement, moved quickly to avoid the problems that could potentially be created by domestic subversion. In May, 1940 the British government interned Sir Oswald Mosley, founder in 1932 of the British Union of Fascists, finally releasing him near the end of 1943, by which time the risk of a domestic Fascist movement disrupting the British war machine had virtually disappeared. The British also dispatched the Duke of Windsor (the former Edward VIII who had abdicated the throne in 1936 in order to marry an American divorcée, Wallis Simpson), believed by some to have pro-Fascist tendencies, to the distant Bahamas, where he spent the war as the islands' governor. The Duke's 1937 friendly visit to Hitler had alarmed some government officials, although there is no evidence that he had contact with Nazi officials after 1939 and he remained on friendly terms with Churchill. Nevertheless, the Bahamas seemed a safe, distant place for the Duke to spend the war.[5]

Collaborators aided the Germans in many ways, usually assisting in the rapid seizure of Jewish property and the abduction of Jews to be murdered in German camps. Several nations sent men to Germany to work in factories or even to fight in the German army. Non-Germans even served in the Waffen SS (Schutzstaffeln or "protection squads"), contributing large shares of the troops for 22 of the 38 SS divisions. These units, independent of the larger German army, soon became intimately linked to the harshest features of the Nazi regime, including mass executions of civilians and the economic and social exploitation of occupied areas.

In areas where the Germans deemed the occupied peoples to be close in race to the occupiers, the imposition of Nazi rule was intended to be light. A light occupation would also keep the size of the occupying German army low, thus freeing troops for other operations. Norwegian, Dutch, Danish, and Belgian prisoners of war were quickly released and for many people life returned to a reasonable semblance of the pre-war years. The Germans initially permitted the Norwegians, Dutch, Danes, and Belgians to keep their government officials in place, as long as they collaborated in economic policy and in implementing anti-Semitic policies. When government officials did protest Nazi policy, they were removed in favor of more ideologically sympathetic or more pliable officials. German occupation officials, known as *Gauleiters*, oversaw local politicians and ensured that they carried out Nazi policy.

For Jews and other perceived enemies of the Reich, the occupation meant discrimination and, eventually, death. Jews in Holland, for example, were first dismissed from public offices and banned from social intercourse with non-Jews. The Germans began anti-Semitic propaganda, including showing the notorious film, *The Eternal Jew*. Starting in 1942, Dutch Jews were forced to wear Stars of David and by the autumn the deportation and murder of 105,000 Dutch Jews had begun. They were joined by many other western European Jews including 24,000 from Belgium and more than 83,000 from France. In Denmark, courageous Danes risked their lives to help Jews cross into neutral Sweden, thus saving the nation's small Jewish population from the German death camps. Denmark, however, proved to be the lone nation in northwestern Europe willing to take such risks.

Collaborationist elements existed in France as well, although it is probably more accurate to depict the mood in that country in the spring of 1940 as defeatist rather than collaborationist. On May 10, 1940 while fighting in Norway continued, Hitler's armies attacked France, enacting Fall Gelb (Operation Yellow). Explanations of France's astonishing six-week collapse generally revolve around two sets of arguments. One set involves an analysis of the many operational, strategic, and tactical mistakes that the French army high command made in the critical days of the campaign. These include, but are surely not limited to, a failure to establish a full reserve that might have met German advances, a confused command structure rife with personal and political intrigue, and the placement of 500,000 French soldiers (half of its army) inside the static defenses of the Maginot Line. These men largely sat motionless while the German army crashed through the supposedly impregnable Ardennes Forest.

Scholars of this school also focus on the failure of the French war plan, the Dyle Plan. As in the years before World War I, there had been far too little coordination between the French, Belgian, and British staffs. Holland, whose neutrality in World War I the Germans had respected, and Belgium, the violation of whose neutrality had brought Britain into the war, had again refused cooperation with the French general staff. They hoped that in the coming war the Germans might follow the Holland model of World War I and respect the rights of neutrals. As we have seen, however, neutrality meant even less to the Germans of 1940 than it had to the Germans of 1914. Given these parameters, the French and British decided that upon hostilities they would advance into Belgium in the hopes of denting a German advance and (as the Belgians surely realized) to avoid having the devastations of war hit northern France again. As a result, the French and British forces that had advanced in 1940 had been trapped by the German drive from the Ardennes to the English Channel.

The second school of thought argues that French collapse was a result of the essential defeatism that the memories of World War I and the tensions of the 1930s had instilled. With so many Frenchmen seeing their fellow country-men as the real enemies, it was impossible for the nation to focus sufficient energy on Germany. This internal paralysis made any sustained military response to Germany's invasion of Poland socially and politically impractical. The inactivity of the Phoney War period further sapped French fighting morale. The shock of the German advance led many in France to presume that they had been betrayed by Fifth Columnists and spies at home. The belated decision to recall General Maxime Weygand (Ferdinand Foch's chief of staff from World War I) from Syria proved to be futile. "If I had known how bad the situation was," Weygand is said to have remarked upon arriving in France on May 19, "I never would have come back."

France then turned to another of its heroes of World War I, Henri Philippe Pétain. The 84-year-old Pétain had saved French positions at Verdun in 1916, brought the French army back from the abyss of mutiny in 1917, and was ultimately named Marshal of France. Despite his mythic status in France and his reputation as the soldier's favorite general, his close associates from World War I had always mistrusted his tendency toward despondency. This trait had cost him the chance to be the supreme Allied commander in 1918 in lieu of the more aggressive and confident Foch. Although Pétain had served as minister of war in an interwar government, he largely remained out of politics, refusing several entreaties to run for the presidency. His politics, however, were always intensely conservative; symbolically, he became France's first ambassador to Franco's Spain.

It was from this post that he observed the collapse of the French military and came to believe that no latter-day "Miracle of the Marne" would save France. Finally, on May 18, he was recalled to Paris by Prime Minister Paul Reynaud in an effort to boost public confidence in the government. Unable to bring himself to sign a surrender, Reynaud stepped aside on June 16 in favor of Pétain, who quickly began armistice negotiations. Hoping to spare France the horrors that Poland had suffered, Pétain actively began to collaborate with the Germans (the term "collaboration" comes from a Pétain radio broadcast in October, 1940) and soon installed into government like-minded collaborationists such as Pierre Laval, who openly cheered German battlefield victories and did all he could to hand to the Nazis France's Jewish population.

The surrender agreement signed in June divided France into nine zones. Alsace and Lorraine returned to Germany and parts of the southeast were annexed to Italy, which cravenly entered the war only after German victory appeared certain. Other areas were demilitarized or reserved for future German expansion. Effectively, Germany controlled Paris, Bordeaux, the entire Atlantic, English Channel and Biscayan coastlines, and the industrial northeast. The remainder of France (the largely agricultural south-central region) was reborn as Vichy France and headed by Pétain. Vichy also controlled the French overseas empire. Hitler was willing to allow the arrangement because it reduced the number of German troops required to occupy France and because he believed that the Pétain regime would be sufficiently pliant.

To underscore the reversal of fortune since 1918, the surrender was signed in the same railway car in which Foch and Weygand had presented armistice terms to the defeated Germans twenty-two years earlier. The German army then marched through Paris along the identical route taken by the French army in their 1918 victory parade. The surrender of France held enormous political, military, and symbolic value, but, once defeated, France was not an issue of central concern to the German high command. It was in the east, not the west, that Hitler had set his sights. He visited Paris only once (not even staying long enough to eat a meal there) and for most of the war France was mainly garrisoned by second-line troops. From the invasion of Russia until early 1944, France largely became a place for exhausted units from the eastern front to go for resting and refitting. Such a cavalier attitude was possible because, as Hitler had guessed, the cooperation of Pétain kept the southern half of France placid and quiescent.

The Vichy regime soon developed into an authoritarian and punitive state that would have made any Nazi proud. The cult of personality around the aged Pétain was the cornerstone of a National Revolution that aimed to eradicate republican impulses. Vichy replaced France's traditional Republican motto of "Liberté, Fraternité, Egalité" with "Travail, Famille, Patrie" ("Work, Family, and Fatherland") and ended Bastille Day as a national holiday. Vichy began to introduce anti-Semitic laws and establish internment camps for Jews long before they were pressed by the Germans to do so. Vichy forces in the French empire were encouraged to work with the Germans and resist any British or (later) American attempts to "invade" French soil. Most Vichy leaders were vehemently anti-British, sentiments that only intensified after the British sank the Vichy French fleet at Mers-el-Kébir in North Africa in July (killing 1,297 French sailors), out of fear that the fleet would be used as an adjunct arm of the German navy.

Of course, not all Europeans were collaborators, but in the early stages of the war there was little that resistance groups could accomplish. German infiltration of the groups led to a dispersed system of organization; savage German reprisals often demoralized or eliminated enemies of the Third Reich. British intelligence officials established a Special Operations Executive in July, 1940 to assist resistance groups, but in the early years of the SOE's existence, Britain was too concerned with home defense to provide the arms and other resources that resistance groups needed. Until the German invasion of Russia in June, 1941,

Moscow actively discouraged communist cells from operating against the Germans. The real possibility of help from the western Allies did not materialize until 1944, leading many people to lie in wait.

Still, many brave men and women did what they could. Led by France's greatest resistance hero, Jean Moulin, the French resistance formed an umbrella group known as the MUR (Mouvements Unis de la Résistance; "mur" means "wall" in French) and, later, the Conseil National de la Résistance, made up of groups from all ideological perspectives, including the mutually antagonistic communists and supporters of Charles de Gaulle. Resistance groups rescued downed Allied fliers, provided intelligence, hid Jews, and recruited new members. They also began to organize and prepare to assist the Allied invasion, whenever it might come.

Others resisted the Germans passively, most commonly by organizing work slowdowns and strikes. In Holland there were three mass strikes, including one in 1941 to protest the deportation of Dutch Jews. In tiny Luxembourg, the citizens courageously took part in a plebiscite (organized by the Germans in the hopes of validating their regime) that voted 97 percent against the occupation. Resistance groups grew in strength as the war dragged on and as the Germans began to exploit more ruthlessly the economies of occupied areas. The forced movement of men from occupied countries to German factories especially aroused the ire of resistance groups and added to their rolls as many men preferred the resistance to life inside Germany. The French resistance group known as the *maquis* attracted many of its recruits from men who escaped to the mountains and forests to avoid compulsory labor laws.

De Gaulle, Norwegian King Haakon VII, and Dutch Queen Wilhelmina were among the leaders who established governments in exile to provide inspiration and keep the flame of freedom alive. The Free French military eventually produced a number of skilled senior officers including Marie Pierre Koenig, who gave Free France its first military victory of the war against the Afrika Corps at Bir Hakeim in June, 1942; Jean-Marie de Lattre de Tassigny, who escaped from a Vichy prison cell and went on to lead a Free French army of 137,000 men across Africa and Europe; and Philippe Leclerc, who fought in west Africa and the Normandy campaign. He was commander of the first Allied unit to enter Paris.

But these accomplishments were made possible only by the stout resistance of Great Britain which, from the fall of France to the German invasion of Russia, stood alone against Germany. If Hitler had truly believed that the fall of France would quickly lead to a British surrender, he was very much mistaken. Shortly after France's surrender, a London newspaper vendor's sign read "France signs peace treaty; we're in the finals!" The humor may have been a bit misplaced, but it reflected the determination of the British people and its leadership not to become another of Nazi Germany's victims.

## Britain's finest hour

Great Britain's war quickly became connected to its charismatic, controversial, and intensely bellicose new prime minister, Winston Churchill. The Chamberlain government was too closely connected to the discredited policy of appeasement. The fiasco in Norway had underscored the strategic bankruptcy of that policy and had led to the collapse of the government. Consequently, King George VI asked Churchill to form a new government of national unity on May 10, 1940, the same day that Germany invaded France. In many ways, Churchill was an odd choice to lead a government, especially one of national unity. He was unpopular with many influential members of the British establishment, including many in his own party. Most people of influence, including the King, would have much preferred to see the less impulsive Lord Halifax assume the prime ministry. Moreover, the very Norway disaster that had led to the fall of Chamberlain had been largely Churchill's idea. Now he stood to gain from it politically by being named prime minister. Many in the government and in the military remembered another Churchill brainchild turned humiliation, the failed British operation at Gallipoli in 1915. Could this man now lead Britain in its hour of greatest need?

As time would soon tell, Churchill had many positive qualities that offset his shortcomings. Unlike Halifax, Churchill had a long and varied experience with the military and warfare more generally. As a young man, he had served in the Sudan, fighting in the battle of Omdurman in 1898. He also served in the Boer War and, after the 1915 Gallipoli debacle cost him his job as First Lord of the Admiralty, he served in a battalion in the trenches of Flanders. He therefore had familiarity with both the army and the navy, as well as both the civilian and military defense establishments. Moreover, he had composed histories of the Boer War and an acclaimed six-volume history of World War I (*The World Crisis*), merging a scholarly appreciation with his own first-hand experiences. He was also familiar with the Americans, and was distantly related to President Franklin Roosevelt, although few realized just how important his personal relationship with Roosevelt would become.

Most immediately, Churchill had to deal with the disaster in France, and the attendant threat to the ten British divisions on the continent. The new prime minister flew to France on May 22 to meet with the French commander Maurice Gamelin and the BEF commander, the World War I hero and former Chief of the Imperial General Staff, Lord Gort. Churchill had supported the BEF's participation in Weygand's new plan to attack southward, perhaps in emulation of Sir John French's southward turn in 1914. Gort, however, could see that the supporting French attacks northward from the Somme River valley were not going to materialize as promised. He therefore disobeyed Churchill's directive and headed north.

That action made possible one of the truly astonishing events of the war: the evacuation of more than 330,000 men from the northern French port of Dunkirk. Had Gort moved to the south, his units would have been too far away from the coast to have been rescued and the BEF would likely have been destroyed. As it was, the BEF was able to regroup and establish a defensive perimeter around Dunkirk on May 26 only because Hitler (probably encouraged by General Gerd von Runstedt) had ordered the Germans to halt for 48 hours. At the time of the order, lead German armored units were just ten miles away from the Dunkirk pocket and might well have destroyed the BEF if given the chance. Hitler's exact motivations for ordering the halt are still debated, but the most likely explanation is that the German army wanted time to resupply their armored units and bring supporting infantry units forward. Some scholars speculate that Luftwaffe commander (and, until April, 1945, Hitler's chosen successor) Hermann Göring had convinced Hitler that the air force could destroy the British forces in the Dunkirk pocket, thus sparing further German casualties and bringing glory to the air force, the most Nazified of the German military arms.

Whatever the motives, the delay allowed Great Britain to execute Operation Dynamo, the evacuation of the British (and some French) troops from the Dunkirk pocket. Admiral Sir Bertram Ramsey coordinated 900 Royal Navy vessels and private craft that headed for the French coast. They included everything from custom-designed military transports to a fifteen-foot fishing boat, the *Tamzine*, that evacuated two soldiers and is now on display at London's Imperial War Museum. Dunkirk was close enough to English air bases to provide air cover, although Fighter Command lost 100 planes and the Luftwaffe still managed to sink 200 British ships. The calm weather in the English Channel proved a great boon to small vessels that would not have been able to operate safely in marginal weather. The Royal Navy, close to home ports, was able to provide some protection from submarines and German surface vessels.

French military officials were furious when they realized that the British were using Dunkirk as a stage for evacuation, not as a base for regrouping. At first, British ships refused to evacuate French troops, although eventually almost 53,000 Frenchmen joined the 338,226 British soldiers evacuated between May 26 and June 3. "Bloody Marvellous!" read the headline in the *Daily Mirror* celebrating the success at Dunkirk, but Dynamo was not all good news. The soldiers of the British army had left France with literally nothing but the clothes on their backs and maybe a rifle. All of the BEF's heavy equipment had to be left behind in France. Still, the men had been saved the fate of death or internment in a German POW camp.

Churchill was at his rhetorical best when he appeared before Parliament on June 4, but he realized that Dunkirk was, in his words, a deliverance, not a victory. "Wars," he told Parliament, "are not won by evacuation." He concluded with one of his most prophetic and stirring speeches:

> We shall defend our island, whatever the cost may be. We shall fight
> on the beaches, we shall fight on the landing grounds, we shall fight in

the fields and in the streets, we shall fight in the hills; we shall never surrender; and even if, which I do not for a moment believe, this island or a large part of it were subjugated and starving, then our Empire beyond the seas, armed and guarded by the British Fleet, would carry on the struggle until, in God's good time, the New World, with all its power and might, steps forward to the rescue and liberation of the Old.[6]

Churchill's speech was a defiant and rousing performance, but it did not change the serious situation Britain faced. With no other foe for the Germans to face, many Britons feared that the war might next come to England itself. No serious attempt to land a foreign force on English soil had been contemplated since Napoleon and none had succeeded since William the Conqueror. Still, the world of 1940 bore little resemblance to 1066. The military situation was not reassuring. The army had lost most of its heavy equipment in France, the RAF had lost half of its fighters in the campaign for France, and the Royal Navy was stretched literally all over the world. It had to protect shipping lanes from India through the Suez Canal and across the Mediterranean. It also had to deal with a German U-boat threat in the North Atlantic and Japanese fleets that menaced British bases in Hong Kong and Singapore. Even Churchill's mood was somber: "Twice in two months [Norway and France]," he later wrote, "we had been taken completely by surprise. . . . What else had they got ready – prepared and organized to the last inch?"[7]

With the home islands thus threatened, British society mobilized as never before. Many parents living in the southeast sent their children to relatives living far from potential landing sites, scrap metal drives provided the raw materials for a reinvigorated arms industry (and, perhaps more importantly, gave Britons something productive to do), and the British rapidly mobilized a 1,000,000-strong home guard. Most of its men were only rudimentarily trained and many were World War I veterans. The Home Guard would not be much of a match for the Wehrmacht, but it provided some protection. To prepare for the worst, the British removed street signs in order to confuse the first wave of German forces, mined beaches, and moved sixteen infantry divisions to the coastline. Churchill rallied the spirit of the British people and became the very symbol of action and energy. A famous photograph from July, 1940 shows the then-66 year-old Churchill in a pinstripe suit, bow tie, white pocket handkerchief, and bowler. A cigar dangles from the corner of his mouth. The ordinariness of the prime minister's attire contrasts with the Thompson submachine gun he is holding. The image is quintessentially Churchill. It is obviously an act of self-promotion, but it is equally an act of defiance, energy, and combativeness.

The Germans did not expect the British to show such determination. They had, moreover, not devoted adequate energies to planning an invasion. The military problems of landing a force on the British Isles were indeed formidable. German weapons were designed to win ground wars on their borders against nations such as Poland, Czechoslovakia, and France. Germany did not possess large numbers of strategic bombers (the Stuka dive bomber, so feared in Poland and France, had a limited range and a very small bomb load) nor did the navy have sufficient amphibious landing craft. As a result, German plans for an invasion (code-named Sea Lion) were confused, with the army, navy, and air force each developing their own (often mutually exclusive) plans.

As a result, Hitler authorized German bombers to strike at British air fields and cities in the hopes of forcing the British to sue for peace. From August, 1940 until May, 1941 the Luftwaffe concentrated its main striking forces against Britain, with less intense raids continuing throughout the war. The German raids were aimed at strategic targets, population centers, and cultural sites. From April to June, 1942 the Luftwaffe attempted to destroy all English buildings marked with three stars in the Baedeker travel guides. Massive air attacks were exactly what the RAF had feared. RAF leaders doubted that the English working classes would be able to sustain their morale in the face of an aerial onslaught. The key, they believed, was to break German morale through bombing before the German bombing broke British morale.[8]

But in the Battle of Britain aerial bombardment did not break civilian morale as quickly as many had feared. Although 40,000 Britons died in the bombing and thousands more lost their homes, British morale stiffened. Factories continued to operate and the RAF soon learned how to take maximum advantages of radar in order to concentrate their resources. A German decision in September, 1940 to shift targeting from RAF fields to London placed the capital under tremendous strain, but the shift allowed the RAF to regroup. Britain thus suffered, but survived. The RAF's "Finest Hour" and the stout determination of the British people delivered Germany's first defeat.

The Battle of Britain had two other important ramifications. First, it led to a massive campaign by the British Royal Air Force Bomber Command to attack Germany. Without British or Allied forces on the continent, bombing was the only way for Britain to strike back directly at Germany. Despite heavy casualties, British bombers brought the war home to Germans. In February, 1942 Arthur "Bomber" Harris took over Bomber Command and brought with him a fierce determination to attack German population centers. In part, his strategy was a recognition of the inability of British bombers to hit precise targets. A British report from September, 1941 showed that less than 20 percent of air crews raids were able to put a bomb within five miles of their targets. Harris thus decided on a strategy of area bombing, often using incendiary bombs to terrorize and "dehouse" the German population.

Driven by a determination to make Germany "reap the whirlwind," Harris harnessed the awesome power of the bomber and concentrated it on German civilian targets. The RAF assembled 1,000 bombers to attack Cologne, Essen, and Bremen in May and June, 1942. The raid on Cologne destroyed one-third of the city and convinced Harris that with enough resources bombing could win the war by itself, as interwar air enthusiasts including the Italian Guilio Douhet and the American Billy Mitchell had prophesied.

Harris's army and navy colleagues were less certain and were, moreover, uneasy about the intentional targeting of civilians. Bombing might be a way to strike at Germany, but it also meant that the RAF was using the same horrifying tactics that the Luftwaffe was using against British civilians. This attitude reflected a general British discomfort with air strikes intentionally aimed at non-combatants. Despite the effectiveness of his bombing campaign, Harris was left off the Victory Honours list of 1946 and his Bomber Command never received its own campaign medal. Area bombing might have been effective, but the damage it inflicted upon non-combatants clearly left many people uneasy. Bombing thus placed military effectiveness at odds with commonly held social values.

The second major impact of the Battle of Britain was the creation of links between the United States and Great Britain. The shocking fall of France awakened many Americans to the reality that the eventual defeat of Germany depended upon the survival of Britain. American journalist Edward R. Murrow's emotional broadcasts from London (with explosions and sirens often audible in the background) drew the nation's attention to British suffering. As the Lafayette Escadrille had done for France in World War I, three American volunteer "Eagle Squadrons" flew for the RAF despite the risk that their American citizenship might be revoked as a consequence. America was still far from willing to enter into the war, but it was becoming increasingly clear that American sympathies lay with Britain. These sympathies translated into tangible assistance. Thus in the summer of 1940, often in violation of the Neutrality Acts, American firms provided Britain with 500,000 rifles and 80,000 machine guns.

President Roosevelt searched for a way to help Britain even further without directly involving the United States in the war. He eventually found it in the programs that became known as Lend-Lease, an elaborate, though improvised, arrangement that permitted the American government to provide direct material assistance to nations considered vital to American national security. The enabling legislation, patriotically (though ironically considering the program's intended recipient), numbered House Resolution 1776, was crafted to give Roosevelt maximum flexibility. For example, one of the restrictions imposed by the Neutrality Acts required that trade be conducted on the basis of "cash and carry," meaning that American firms could neither extend credit nor transport materials across the U-boat infested Atlantic Ocean. The goal had been to avoid the loans and questions regarding the rights of neutrals that isolationists had believed had led the United States to war in 1917.

Between the passing of these acts in the late 1930s and the Battle of Britain, however, the global situation had deteriorated considerably. With Britain nearly out of hard currency, trade under the cash and carry provisions became virtually impossible. Lend-Lease therefore allowed the United States to "lend" Britain any goods deemed by the president to be in the interests of national defense (thirty-seven nations were later added to the list). As intended, this authorization gave Roosevelt tremendous authority, which he used to provide Britain with fire-fighting equipment, foodstuffs, industrial goods, and almost anything else the British requested. There was neither provision for repayment of goods nor even a procedure for tracking British debts. A grateful Winston Churchill told Parliament that Lend-Lease was "the most unsordid act in the history of any nation."[9]

Lend-Lease mixed altruism with pragmatism. Roosevelt and Churchill both understood that, in the President's words, "the best immediate defense of the United States is the success of Great Britain defending itself."[10] Accordingly, another agreement, the destroyer-for-bases agreement of May, 1940, provided the British with 50 (admittedly antiquated) American destroyers in exchange for leases on some British naval bases in the Western Hemisphere. Only nine of the destroyers ever contributed to British naval strength, but the agreement had several important subtle outcomes. The leases allowed the United States to assume the defense of the British West Indies, Newfoundland, and Bermuda, thereby allowing the British to shift military assets from those bases to home waters. It allowed the United States to assume the responsibility for protecting convoys over a larger area and gave Roosevelt the justification he needed to ask Congress for a larger navy. In April, 1941 the United States assumed the defense of the west coast of Greenland, giving the Americans an even larger presence in the North Atlantic. The British reciprocated with "reverse Lend-Lease" that included technology transfers and intelligence sharing.

On a more symbolic level, Churchill and Roosevelt met in August, 1941 at Placentia Bay, off the coast of Newfoundland. There they announced the conclusion of a common statement of aims known as the Atlantic Charter. It proclaimed the rights of all peoples to self-government and the two leaders pledged to return self-government to those people forcibly deprived of it. The Charter specifically referred to the period "after the destruction of the Nazi tyranny," thus connecting American policy to British war efforts. The United States was still far from belligerent, but the Charter was a dramatic step in linking the aims of the two nations.

The Americans were providing material and moral support, but it was up to Britain to do the fighting. From May, 1940 to June, 1941 the British found themselves facing the Axis powers alone. Britain fought U-boats in the Atlantic, faced aerial bombardment of the home islands, conducted raids against the Italian fleet, and engaged in active combat in North Africa and Greece. The British also had to face the threat that Japan posed to British interests in Singapore, Hong Kong, India, Burma, and Australia. Some of Britain's operations were dramatically successful. In November, 1940, twenty-one antiquated British Swordfish biplanes attacked the Italian fleet anchored at Taranto in the Italian heel. For the loss of just two planes, the British destroyed or damaged three battleships and a cruiser and also destroyed most of the facilities at Taranto's dockyards. As a result, the Italians transferred the fleet to other bases, thus greatly easing the pressure on British convoys through the Mediterranean.

Operations in North Africa also provided early victories. Italian forces under the command of Rodolfo Graziani had invaded Egypt from Libya. Graziani thought the decision unwise, but Mussolini had determined that Germany should not have all the glory. "I only need a few thousand dead so that I can sit at the peace conference as a man who fought" he confided to his Army Chief of Staff.[11] In the end, he got his few thousand dead and much more. The Italians were ill-prepared for the campaign despite a large numerical advantage and the complication of poor relations between the British and the Egyptians. But the success of the Taranto raid had greatly complicated Italian supply efforts. The early advances of Graziani's units into western Egypt only extended his already drawn-out supply lines across miles of desert.

Britain won its first major land victory of the war in December, 1940 when a British and Indian force attacked the Italians at Sidi Barrani, capturing 39,000 Italian prisoners. By the time the Italian retreat across Libya ended ten weeks later, British and Commonwealth forces had captured 130,000 prisoners and had seized the critical ports of Tobruk and Benghazi. They had advanced 500 miles and virtually annihilated the Axis presence in North Africa. Free French units in Chad and Niger had joined in the fighting, suggesting that other French units in Africa might do the same, thus placing pressure on the set of contradictions and conflicting loyalties that Vichy France was based upon. With Britain surviving the bombing, the future began to look less grim.

But after the capture of Benghazi British fortunes wavered. On February 12, 1941 the Germans sent one of their heroes from the campaign in France, Erwin Rommel, to take command of Axis forces in Africa. His Panzer forces' audacious charges quickly changed the balance in North Africa, inducing the British to leave Benghazi in April without firing a shot in its defense. Rommel's Afrika Corps then pushed British forces back to Tobruk, capturing three British generals along the way. In just two weeks, all of Britain's important North African gains had been lost to Rommel. Moreover, 35,000 Commonwealth forces were besieged in Tobruk, unable to break out and causing the British war effort considerable agony.

Events on the continent were even more desperate. Churchill had hastily ordered a British response to Germany's invasion of Greece. Although unwilling to allow such naked aggression to go unchallenged, the British had no war plan for operating in Greece. Churchill soon realized the mistake he had made. Troops sent to Greece depleted British reserves destined for Africa and divided the Royal Navy's efforts even further. Germany completed its conquest of Greece, forcing another British evacuation, on April 21. Although his military advisors wanted to relocate the veterans of the Greek campaign to Alexandria, where they might help efforts in North Africa, Churchill ordered them sent instead to Crete, perhaps in the hopes that they might be able to return to Greece.

Although British intelligence had learned of the German plan to attack Crete with airborne troops, that information did not reach the local commanders in time. Using the Luftwaffe to inflict heavy damage on the Royal Navy, the Germans sank three cruisers and six destroyers, thus isolating the 35,000-strong British garrison on Crete. A daring, and highly costly, German airborne attack seized the Cretan airfields and demoralized the exhausted British troops. The British lost 1,742 men killed and 11,370 captured. British forces had been thrown out of Europe for the fourth time in less than two years.

By the summer of 1941, the British were looking for deliverance once again. British society had supported far-flung operations on three continents and survived a vicious German air assault. Nevertheless, Commonwealth forces were fighting without allies and with the increasing likelihood of hostilities with Japan. Churchill's defiance and confidence had seen Britain through some of its worst days, but without help, it might all be for naught. A respite, if not deliverance, came on June 22, 1941 when Germany attacked the Soviet Union.

## Russia's Great Fatherland war

Because of British intelligence decodings, Churchill had known about German plans to attack the Soviet Union in advance. He had tried to warn Soviet leader Joseph Stalin about the impending invasion, but Stalin did not believe him. Suspicious that the British warnings were a ploy to induce him into a declaration of war, he preferred to view the German military buildups in Poland as posturing for improvements to the terms of the Nazi–Soviet Pact signed less than two years earlier. A Soviet spy in Germany's Tokyo embassy confirmed the British estimates and even provided Stalin with the exact date of the invasion. Still, Stalin refused to take measures necessary to defend Soviet territory; shipments of grain to Germany continued up until the very morning of the invasion.

Consequently, warnings notwithstanding, Stalin was caught entirely by surprise by the massive German invasion of June 22, 1941. The attack involved 3,000,000 German troops and 1,000,000 more soldiers from German allies that included Romania, Hungary, and Italy. Together, the Axis had 3,350 tanks, 7,000 field guns, 2,000 airplanes, and more than 600,000 horses for transporting goods across the primitive Russian steppes. The war in Russia was the war Hitler had intended to fight for nearly two decades. His *Rassenkampf* (or "race war") would achieve his aims of murdering the Slavs and Jews of the Soviet Union, destroying Bolshevism, and clearing eastern Europe for *Lebensraum* and resettlement by Aryan Germans.

The Red Army, taken completely by surprise, was entirely ill-prepared to meet this massive force. Part of Russia's problems was self-inflicted. Their principal weaknesses were a function of the development of Soviet society since the great Revolution of 1917. The Russian Civil War had shown to Stalin and his Bolshevik party's senior leaders that not all Russian officers had been completely converted to the revolutionary cause. Scores of officers, including one of the commanders at Tannenberg, Pavel Rennenkampf, had been imprisoned or executed for their loyalty to the Tsar or their presumed opposition to the new regime. Stalin continued to suspect the trustworthiness of many of the most senior officers, often misreading their professionalism and commitment to the army for a lack of loyalty to the Soviet system. In the new revolutionary society, the army had to serve as a political instrument above all else. Stalin was thus willing to sacrifice a certain amount of military capability in favor of political reliability.

The result of Stalin's mistrust was a massive and ruthless purge of the Soviet officer corps in the 1930s that eventually affected 36,671 officers, including 403 of 706 brigade commanders and 3 of 5 marshals. The Red Air Force was particularly hard hit. Stalin and the young and revolutionary Soviet system (the Bolshevik state was just twenty years old when the most widespread purges began in 1937) feared that the "reactionary" elements of its own officer corps were as much a threat to the revolution as any foreign enemy. Suspect officers, therefore, had to be removed lest they destroy the revolution from within. The lucky ones, like future Marshal of the Soviet Union Konstantin Rokossovsky, spent time in a Soviet prison before being reinstated to command. The unlucky ones, like Mikhail Tukhachevsky, commander of the drive on Warsaw in 1920, were tortured and executed. Those officers not purged often felt so afraid for their careers and their lives that they refused to do anything that might call attention to themselves. Such a state of affairs did little to encourage initiative or aggressive behavior in the Soviet officer corps.

These problems became evident when Stalin decided to invade Finland in the fall of 1939. Finland had long been a part of the Russian empire, but had achieved its independence in 1917 as a result of the same revolution that eventually brought Stalin to power. According to the terms of the Nazi–Soviet Pact, Finland fell within the Soviet sphere and thus Stalin knew that Soviet aggression there would not meet with German resistance. With the British and French at war with Germany, moreover, Russia was unlikely to face serious resistance from the western democracies. He expected that his much larger and more modern military would make short work of the Finns, much as the Germans had done to the Poles.

Much to Stalin's surprise, however, the Finns proved to be tough adversaries and determined fighters on their own soil. The Soviet invasion in November, 1939 rallied Finns of all political and ethnic persuasions against a common foe. Finland's outmanned army fought well and gave ground slowly, but the Finns had woefully inadequate weapons and virtually no modern mobile artillery pieces. Like Norway, Finland was not a wealthy nation and had suffered badly from the global economic depression. Their defense spending, therefore, was largely concentrated on a formidable series of frontier defenses, known collectively as the Mannerheim Line. Named for an ex-Tsarist officer who now commanded the Finnish Army, the line held the Soviets at bay for most of the winter of 1939–1940.

Lacking a talented officer corps, Soviet tactics were crude, often resembling the fighting of 1914 and 1915 more than the Blitzkrieg tactics the Germans had shown in Poland in 1939. Slow and cumbersome Soviet infantry columns provided easy targets for rapid Finnish troops, some of them made more mobile by the use of skis and snowshoes. The Finnish campaign cost the Soviets more than 200,000 casualties and the Finns just 25,000. Still, the Finns could not match Soviet material and manpower superiority. Despite high morale, the Finnish high command saw no choice but to sue for peace in March, 1940. The resulting Treaty of Moscow forced Finland to cede one-tenth of its territory, but the nation avoided the concession of a complete reunification with Russia.

The enormous cost of the minor Soviet victory did little to convince the world of the value of Soviet military might. Instead, the sight of Soviet ineptitude in Finland served only to boost the confidence of the German army and Hitler personally. The German General Staff believed that an army that had such trouble defeating Finland would not stand a chance against the mighty Germans. Stalin's blatant aggression against an unprovoked neighbor diminished his stature even further in western eyes. The British and French all but assumed that Stalin and Hitler were allies, a fearful possibility. They considered sending a relief expedition to Finland and perhaps even trying to open a Scandinavian front against Germany and Russia. Even Hitler's ally, Mussolini, tried to send help to the Finns, but Hitler convinced him otherwise.

The growth of German power and the seeming frailty of the Soviet military led many Balkan states to ally with Nazi Germany. Hungary, its pride still smarting from the humiliation of the Treaty of Trianon after World War I, had sought an alliance with Germany as early as 1933. One of the lesser provisions of the Munich Agreement of 1938 ceded parts of southern Slovakia and Ruthenia to Hungary as a reward for their support of the Germans. The Hungarians became signatories to the Tripartite Pact (Italy, Germany, and Japan) in late 1940. Hungary proved to be a more than willing ally to Germany in the invasions of Yugoslavia and the Soviet Union, but, to their eternal credit, the Hungarians resisted turning over their Jewish population to the Nazi killing machines until 1944. In that year, with German forces retreating all across Eastern Europe, the Nazis replaced the Hungarian government with a more pliable one led by Ferenc Szálasi and his Hungarian Fascist party, the Arrow Cross. Little more than a gang of thugs, the Arrow Cross proved to be more than willing to give the Germans the last large group of Jews in their zone of control. As a result, 200,000 Jews who had theretofore been protected were shipped to death camps.

Romania, too, joined the Axis cause, partly for economic reasons and partly out of the fear that if they did not join the Axis the Germans might support Hungarian claims to Romanian lands. The Romanians sought territory at the expense of the Soviet Union and therefore promised the Germans massive Romanian support for any German invasion of Slavic lands. Germany's leading position in the Bulgarian economy also led that country (a German ally in World War I) to throw in its lot with the Axis. The Bulgarian army and government, however, were far more concerned with their traditional territorial claims in Macedonia and Serbia than in the Soviet Union and thus did not contribute large numbers of forces to the German war in Russia.

All of these nations later suffered greatly from their decisions to fight alongside the Germans. But no Balkan nation suffered so badly from the war as did Yugoslavia. A hodge-podge of mutually antagonistic ethnic and political groups, Yugoslavia became a target for the Germans so that they might secure their southern flank and provide a staging area for further offensives in the Balkans and into Greece. On Sunday April 6, 1941 the Luftwaffe unleashed a massive aerial bombardment on Belgrade that killed 17,000 people, then the bloodiest single day of the war. The Serbian majority in Yugoslavia had hoped for Soviet or Allied assistance (as in 1914) but none was forthcoming. An extreme Croatian nationalist group, the Ustasha, united with the Nazis and took advantage of the war to slaughter thousands of Serbs and Muslims.

For the remainder of the war, Yugoslavia endured both an Axis occupation and a series of civil wars between rival ethnic and political groups. A charismatic communist leader, Josip Broz, better know as Tito, managed to unite some of these groups out of their common hatred for the brutality of the Ustasha. His partisans proved to be one of the most effective resistance groups of the war, but he had to fight against both the Axis and a rival resistance group known as the Četniks, led by the Serbian Colonel Dragoljub Mihailović. Both groups were quite effective, but Tito's partisans were more successful in attracting both Soviet and British support. Mihailović survived the war only to be arrested by communist forces in 1946 and then executed. Tito went on to lead Yugoslavia in the post-war period and, despite his communist ideology, managed to keep his country reasonably free of both Soviet hegemony and ethnic warfare.

By the end of April, 1941, the Axis had forced a British withdrawal from Greece, secured the direct aid of Hungary, Romania, and Bulgaria and partially pacified Yugoslavia. The Germans were then free to step up their planning for the invasion of Russia, code-named Barbarossa. Delays in beginning the operation threatened to extend operations into the fierce Russian winter but most German planners were not worried. They viewed the Soviet system as hopelessly corrupt and racially inferior. One massive assault, they believed, would cause its collapse, as in 1917. The Germans would thereby quickly accomplish what Napoleon could not. The Germans were so enamored of their own military and so disdainful of the Soviets that they arrogantly predicted that they could win the war in four weeks. They made no plans to supply the German army with winter weight motor oils, antifreeze, or cold-weather clothing.

German racial assumptions were central to this campaign and the way the German army fought it. The war in Russia was to be a war of the Aryan race against the Slavic race. Even the operation's code name was designed to underscore the racial nature of this war. Holy Roman Emperor Frederick I, better known as Frederick Barbarossa, was famous in Nazi lore as a Teutonic knight who had fought several successful battles against the Slavs in the twelfth century. The targets in this war were to be both soldiers and civilians. German orders included a call for a "ruthless Germanization" of the new territories. German units were ordered to execute all Red Army commissars and German soldiers were exempted from prosecution for crimes committed against civilians. Mobile killing squads called *Einsatzgruppen* accompanied the Wehrmacht into Russia with the mission of killing Jews and Slavs. In a little over a year, these units killed 600,000 Jews, but their inability to kill even faster and more efficiently led the Nazis to construct a vast network of death camps to do the job. Senior officers were entirely complicit in this mass murder. Field Marshal Erich von Manstein told his soldiers:

> The Jewish-Bolshevik system must be eradicated once and for all. Never again may it interfere in our European living space. The German soldier is therefore not only charged with the task of destroying the power instrument of this system. He marches forth also as a carrier of a racial conception and as an avenger of all the atrocities which have been committed against him and the German people.[12]

Antony Beevor, Omer Bartov, and other historians have argued that years of Nazi propaganda and centuries of German enmity for Slavs had dehumanized eastern Europeans in German eyes to such an extent that on the eve of the invasion German soldiers were "morally anaesthetized" to killing civilians.[13]

The effectiveness of the German killing machine was partly the result of the nearly complete collapse of the Soviet military. Having failed adequately to prepare for its own defense, the Red Air Force lost 2,000 planes in two days, most of them on the ground. In the first three weeks of fighting, the Soviets lost 3,500 tanks, 6,000 planes, and 2,000,000 men. Before the end of July another 300,000 men, 3,000 tanks, and 3,000 guns were lost after encirclement near Smolensk just outside Moscow. In the south the Russians lost another 100,000 POWs. On September 21 the Battle of Kiev ended with 665,000 more Russian POWs. The magnitude of Soviet losses had no parallel in the history of warfare.

The Soviet ability to recover from this incredible tragedy is one of the most amazing stories of the twentieth century. Military historians have long focused on the weather (one joke posited that Russia's two best officers were General Winter and Colonel Mud) and the ever-extending supply lines caused by the rapid German advance. While these factors undoubtedly played key roles, social factors were critical as well. Foremost among them was Nazi ideology, which, with its manic obsession with race war, disrupted the focus of German military operations and steeled the resolve of the Soviet people. Because of Germany's racism, even domestic opponents of the Stalinist regime made common cause with the Soviet system.

This pattern emerged most obviously in Ukraine. Anti-Russian sentiment in this Soviet republic ran deep, especially after the politically-motivated famine there in the early 1930s. Stalin's policy of compulsory agricultural collectivization and the forced transfer of food from Ukrainian farms to ever-growing Soviet cities may have caused the deaths of as many as 7,000,000 Ukrainians. Had Nazi ideology not been so determined on oppressing the Ukrainians, the Germans might have been able to tap into the dominant hatred that Ukrainians and other non-Russians felt for Stalin and his regime.

Indeed, ethnicity and social composition posed a major problem for the Red Army. In 1941 nearly half of the Red Army was composed of non-ethnic Russians. In World War I, the lukewarm loyalty of many ethnic minorities to the Russians had played a key role in the decline of Russian fighting power. Unwilling to see the Ukrainians and other non-Russians as potential allies, however, the Nazis insisted on a brutal occupation. Hundreds of thousands of Ukrainians were killed or forcibly moved to Germany to serve as slave laborers. As a result, a native resistance group, the UPA, emerged in 1942. The UPA was determined to fight both the Nazis and any attempt by the Soviets to reoccupy the region after the war. Their presence in the German rear seriously disrupted German operations.

Popular opposition to the Nazis led to a reawakening of genuine Russian nationalism. One of the most remarkable achievements of this new patriotism was the removal of the vast majority of the Soviet industrial infrastructure to locations east of the Ural Mountains and therefore safe from German reach. Soviet workers, many of them female, dismantled entire factories and reassembled them hundreds, or even thousands, of miles away. An estimated 1,360 factories were spared in this manner. This economic miracle allowed Soviet industry to produce tanks, artillery pieces, and small arms at levels that stunned German intelligence officials. Within just ten weeks of being relocated, the Kharkov Tank Factory produced its first tanks. Although the war had reduced the Soviet labor pool by 8,000,000 workers, the Soviets nevertheless outproduced Germany in almost every category. In 1942 the Soviets produced 25,436 airplanes to Germany's 15,409. Two years later Soviet industry produced 29,000 tanks while Germany produced 17,800.

The Soviets benefited tremendously from American and British economic assistance. The United States extended Lend-Lease aid to the Soviets in November, 1941 despite the enabling legislation's specification that American aid could be sent only to democracies. Supplying the Soviet Union proved to be a major logistical challenge, necessitating air routes over Africa, sea routes across the Arctic, and land routes through Persia. The Americans and British provided the USSR with 34,000,000 sets of uniforms, 15,000,000 pairs of boots, 350,000 tons of explosives, 3,000,000 tons of gasoline, many millions of tons of food, 12,000 railroad cars, 375,000 trucks, and 50,000 jeeps. The Soviets received so many American trucks that for years the word "Studebaker" was a common Soviet term for a truck. British and American aluminum, manganese, and coal made good most of the Soviet supplies of critical raw materials that the Germans had seized early in the war. Thus was the Soviet industrial system able to continue operating.

Whether motivated by patriotism or coerced by the brutal Stalinist system, men (and many women) joined the army and compensated for early losses. German intelligence in early 1942 had estimated that the Russians could produce at most 200 divisions. Instead, the Russians had 360. The Soviets motivated their people by restoring the Orthodox Church in 1943 and terrified them with merciless discipline. The People's Commissariat for Internal Affairs (better known by its Russian acronym, NKVD) shot or imprisoned an estimated 422,000 of their own men for cowardice or desertion.

The Soviet war effort was therefore every bit as harsh to civilians as was their Germany enemy's. The Luftwaffe killed 40,000 people in one week of air attacks preceding their assault on Stalingrad. Still, Stalin refused to allow civilians to leave the city he had named for himself and the gateway to Soviet oil fields. During the mammoth battle for the city, the Russians executed 13,500 of their own people for failure to meet the high standards of the Soviet regime. The Germans deported 60,000 more civilians to serve as coerced laborers. Only 10,000 civilians survived the seven-month-long battle for the city and, when it was over, just nine children were reunited with both of their biological parents.

To break the siege, Soviet Marshal Georgi Zhukov decided to strike at the demoralized Romanians that guarded the flanks of the German Sixth Army. Romanian hopes for territorial gain at the expense of the Russians had been buried in the deep snows and mud of Russia. With no victory in sight they had continued to fight, but with decreasing effectiveness. German commanders routinely rerouted supplies destined for the Romanian flanks and gave them instead to German units fighting for their survival in the city itself. The Germans assured their allies that the Soviets were out of reserves and close to capitulation. In November, 1942 the supposedly feeble Russians sliced through Romanian positions north and south of Stalingrad, linked up, and thereby encircled the Germans.

Hitler and the German high command were astonished. Unable to believe that the Soviets were capable of such an offensive, Hitler fumed at the Romanian leader, Marshal Ian Antonescu, accusing his troops of cowardice. He also refused Sixth Army commander General Friedrich Paulus the permission he had sought to execute a withdrawal to more defensible positions. Instead, he promoted Paulus to Field Marshal, reminding him that no German Field Marshal had ever surrendered. Theatrics, however, were no substitute for supplies. Göring had promised that his air force could supply the Sixth Army via an "air bridge," but the Luftwaffe could provide only one-third of the minimum number of sorties needed to keep the Germans alive. In the process of trying to fly airlift missions in the Russian winter, moreover, the Germans lost 400 planes and 1,000 valuable aircrew members.

In January, 1943 Paulus surrendered along with 91,000 men and 22 generals. Stalingrad had held and provided Germany with its most important defeat of the war. A stunned German public, theretofore kept largely ignorant of the downturn in German fortunes in Russia, received a shattering blow to morale. German generals, some of them furious with Hitler's sacrifice of the Sixth Army, began to see the war in a new light. The fighting at Stalingrad coincided with two other critical events. In October, 1942 British armored units, under the command of General Bernard Montgomery, defeated Axis forces at the battle of El Alamein in Egypt. The following month an Anglo-American invasion force landed in three separate places in North Africa. It was America's first taste of the European war.

The entrance of the United States into the war had enormous ramifications for the Soviets. Richard Sorge, the same spy who had warned Stalin about Barbarossa, informed the Soviets in September, 1941 that the Japanese had decided against invading Siberia as Hitler had been begging them to do. Instead, Sorge relayed, the Japanese intended to turn south against the Pacific colonies of the western powers. The Soviets would not, he assured, have to fight a two-front war. For Stalin, this intelligence meant that he could silently transfer forces from Siberia and bring them west to help in the defense of Moscow. On December 5, with temperatures approaching −40°C, the Soviets launched a massive counterattack that broke the siege of Moscow. Two days later, the Japanese indeed moved against the western powers by striking the American naval base at Pearl Harbor, Hawaii. With that act, and Hitler's brash declaration of war against the United States four days later, America had entered the war. The Grand Alliance, perhaps more accurately described as the Grand Marriage of Convenience, was born. In London, Winston Churchill placed a call to President Roosevelt to confirm that the attack had indeed happened. "It's quite true," the President told Churchill, "They have attacked us at Pearl Harbor. We are all in the same boat now."[14]

## Further reading

World War II has been the subject of many excellent books. Winston Churchill's six-volume history is valuable as a history written by a major participant. "History will be kind to me," Churchill is reputed to have said, "for I intend to write it." See his *The Second World War* (London: Folio Society, 2000). Good general histories include Gerhard Weinberg, *A World at Arms: A Global History of World War II* (Cambridge: Cambridge University Press, 1994); Richard Overy, *Why the Allies Won* (New York: Norton, 1995); Williamson Murray and Allan R. Millett, *A War to be Won: Fighting the Second World War* (Cambridge: Harvard University Press, 2000); and Jeremy Black, *World War Two* (London: Routledge, 2003).

Studies of the German army include Omer Bartov, *Hitler's Army: Soldiers, Nazis, and War in the Third Reich* (Oxford: Oxford University Press, 1992) and his *The Eastern Front 1941–1945: German Troops and the Barbarization of Warfare* (London: Palgrave Macmillan, 2001). See also Stephen Fritz, *Frontsoldaten: The German Soldier in World War II* (Lexington: The University Press of Kentucky, 1995). The fall of France is covered by Marc Bloch, *Strange Defeat* (New York: Norton, 1999); Alistair Horne *To Lose a Battle: France 1940* (London: Penguin, 1940); and William Shirer, *The Collapse of the Third Republic: An Inquiry into the Fall of France* (New York: Simon and Schuster, 1971).

Among the excellent works on the German war in Russia are: Antony Beevor, *Stalingrad: The Fateful Siege, 1942–1943* (New York: Penguin, 1998); John Erickson, *The Road to Stalingrad* (New Haven, Yale University Press, 1999); David Glantz and Jonathon House, *When Titans Clashed: How the Red Army Stopped Hitler* (Lawrence: University Press of Kansas, 1998); and Richard Overy, *Russia's War* (London: Penguin, 1998). There is less on Italy, but MacGregor Knox's *Hitler's Italian Allies* (Cambridge: Cambridge University Press, 2000) is a good place to start.

# 6

# WORLD WAR II, 1942–1945

## America's war in Europe

The events of December 7, 1941 did indeed bring the United States into World War II but there was no necessary connection between Japan's attack on Pearl Harbor and the war in Europe. With America's military resources limited, it remained far from clear that the United States could (or should) conduct a two-front war. Much of American popular opinion screamed for the early war effort to be directed at Japan in order to avenge the Pearl Harbor attack. Most members of the United States Navy, seething for the chance to take revenge, agreed; they argued vehemently against shifting significant naval resources to the Atlantic. The nation's most senior admiral, the irascible Chief of Naval Operations Ernest King, held a passionate and often childish enmity for his Royal Navy counterparts.[1] He argued strongly for a full and immediate devotion of American resources to the Pacific Theater, even if such a movement placed Great Britain and Russia in peril. The politically influential General Douglas MacArthur, ignominiously forced out of the Philippines by a Japanese attack soon after Pearl Harbor, agreed.

Germany's and Italy's declarations of war on the United States on December 11 did little to change that sentiment. While Roosevelt and his staff were busily developing the case for war against all of the Axis nations, Hitler made their jobs easier by issuing a declaration of war. His exact reasons remain subject to conjecture, but two factors seem to have played leading roles. Hitler, anxious to unleash his navy against American shipping in the North Atlantic, saw a declaration of war as a way both to achieve that goal and to provide some assistance to the Japanese. In turn, he hoped that the Japanese might reciprocate by invading Siberia.

Most senior German generals did not think that the declaration was a mistake. They blithely dismissed the Americans as a capitalist and materialist society incapable of fighting a long and sustained war. The American army, relatively small and certainly untested, seemed to pose little immediate threat to the growing Third Reich. Believers in the *Dolchstoß* had consistently denigrated American contributions to German defeat in World War I because of their abiding belief that their defeat had been the result of actions by domestic enemies. Crediting the Americans of 1918 would have undermined this logic. Consequently, the Germans held the American military in particularly low esteem. America's slow response to events in Europe since 1933 gave them little reason to think otherwise. The nation seemed to them completely and totally dedicated to isolation.

On the social and cultural levels, the Nazis denigrated the United States as a racially impure society whose Jews and Blacks had undermined the Nordic elements therein (a view that had significant appeal in the United States itself in the 1920s and 1930s). Nazi propaganda took aim at American art forms like jazz music, which had been popular in German cities before the Nazi rise, claiming that they were un-Aryan. One poster from later in the war, entitled "Kultur Terror," showed an American monster (complete with a Tommy Gun in one hand, Jitterbugging Blacks in a cage for a chest, and a Star of David loin-cloth) destroying the great works of Europe. A sign at the bottom reads "This monstrous country claims to save European civilization!"[2]

On the other side of the Atlantic, anti-German feelings in America were not yet at anything like a fever pitch despite the undeclared war that the American and German navies had been fighting in the Atlantic throughout 1941. Even the German sinking of an American destroyer, the *Reuben James*, in October, failed to arouse lasting popular anger despite the 115 American lives lost. After the fall of France isolationist and avowedly pro-German groups including the German-American Bund and the American First Committee faded from view. Still, it was far from clear that American society would support a major American effort in the Atlantic in place of immediate offensive action against the much more widely hated Japanese.

Social beliefs played an important role as well. Racial attitudes in the United States had changed considerably since World War I, when a wave of anti-German activity had spread across the country. The prevailing American understandings of race in the 1920s had led to the inclusion of Germans as part of the "white" race, distinct from Blacks, Mexicans, and Asians. This amalgamation largely replaced older American social divisions based on country of origin. Eugenics, which argued that "white" races shared immutable positive traits, gained tre-mendous popularity, thus reducing the divisions between white ethnic groups. The assimilation of the German-American community therefore proceeded rapidly and fully enough between the wars to ensure that no repeat of the World War I wave of discrimination against German-Americans occurred. Instead, many German-Americans (including Dwight Eisenhower, the general who led the Allied coalition that destroyed Nazi Germany), had become prominent in the military and society more generally.

Japanese-Americans, on the other hand, had long been the target of virulent racism, especially in the West Coast states of California, Oregon, and Washington. In many areas, local laws forbade the Japanese from owning property. In 1924, the National Origins Act banned further Japanese immigration to the United

States. In the same decade, the United States Supreme Court ruled that Asians could not become naturalized citizens. Long before Pearl Harbor, Japanese-Americans had been a common target for discrimination and violence. The war enabled these hatreds, resulting in America's most shameful wartime act, Executive Order 9066, signed by President Roosevelt in February, 1942. This order forcibly removed 110,000 Japanese-Americans from the West Coast on the assumption of their disloyalty. Notably, the order did not apply to Hawaii, where the Japanese formed a much higher percentage of the total population and historically faced less discrimination. No one seriously attempted to intern German-Americans or Italian-Americans, whom President Roosevelt dismissed as a "lot of opera singers."

Despite these established popular and military sentiments against the Japanese, the strategic basis for American assistance to its new European allies had been laid long before Pearl Harbor. Secret discussions between American, British, and Canadian planners from January to March, 1941 had resulted in the ABC-1 agreement. Although not binding, the agreement stipulated that if the United States found itself at war against Germany and Japan, the prevailing strategy would emphasize an active defense in the Pacific until Germany had been defeated. The enormous distances separating Japan from the United States, planners believed, would provide time and relative security.

The attack on Pearl Harbor demonstrated that the distances were considerably shorter than previously believed. Still, Pearl Harbor did not fundamentally change the ABC-1 approach. Despite the arguments of many Americans that Japan was the real enemy and that diversions into the Atlantic would serve only to rescue the British from their own mistakes, Roosevelt understood the need to ensure the survival of both Britain and the Soviet Union.[3] What soon became known as the "Europe First" strategy rapidly developed into official Allied policy. At the ARCADIA conference between Roosevelt, Churchill, and their top advisors in Washington from December 22, 1941 to January 14, 1942, the Americans and the British reaffirmed ABC-1 as their principal strategic guidance.

As recent studies have suggested, American racism against the Japanese played a paradoxical role in encouraging American efforts in Europe. Many Americans, in government and out, believed that the Japanese were neither intelligent nor courageous enough to have conducted the Pearl Harbor attack without significant help. Some American military officials quite honestly believed that the Japanese could not become pilots because of the nature of the bone structure in their ears, a supposed lack of balance caused by being carried on their mothers' backs in infancy, and their presumed night blindness. Early American news reports repeated a rumor started in Hawaii that some of the Pearl Harbor pilots were blond-haired. It soon became a common belief among many Americans that the Germans had been in on the planning of the attack, and may have even flown some of the planes. By the time the stories had been discounted, the Germans had already declared war.

These racist images contributed to what one scholar called a "war without mercy." Americans did not carefully separate war against the Japanese military from war against the Japanese more generally; thus the forced internment of even those Japanese born in the United States and accused of no crime. Numerous quotations from Americans would prove the point; two will suffice. War Manpower Commission chairman Paul McNutt told reporters in April, 1945 that he favored "the extermination of the Japanese *in toto*." Similarly, the commander of the US South Pacific Force declared "The only good Jap is a Jap who's been dead six months."[4] The immense cultural and linguistic barriers between the Americans and the Japanese only intensified the hatreds on both sides. American GIs collected Japanese skulls (and other body parts) as trophies and souvenirs. The practice became so widespread that the Commander-in-Chief of the Pacific Fleet had to issue a specific order against it, but to little effect.

American hatreds toward the Japanese played a critical role in America's entry into the European war. Unwilling or unable to believe that the Japanese could have attacked America without the help of a European power, many Americans presumed that the Japanese had become obedient servants of the Germans. The defeat of Japan, therefore, necessitated a war against their German masters as well. A week after Pearl Harbor Senators Harry Truman (who would be president less than four years later) and Scott Lucas blamed the Pearl Harbor attack on "Japan and its sinister co-criminal, Hitler" and argued that the strike on December 7 was a crime for which "not only Japan but Hitler and Mussolini must atone."[5] Roosevelt and countless newspaper editorials made the same point. Since Japan, Germany, and Italy were intimately tied together, war against one meant war against all.

The surprise Japanese strike had awakened the Americans, but they had been sleeping for too long to immediately shake off the effects of so deep a slumber. The regular army comprised fewer than 200,000 men in 1939. In 1940 Roosevelt had supported a peacetime draft to rectify this problem, but isolationist and anti-conscription forces made the fight a tough one. The Burke–Wadsworth Act authorizing the nation's first peacetime draft passed the Senate by just a single vote. Federalization of local National Guard units and the effects of conscription increased the number of army personnel to 1.7 million by the beginning of 1942, but that number was still far below the 8.4 million men under arms in Germany alone.

More importantly, few Americans had heard a shot fired in anger or knew much about soldiering. Increasing the number of men under arms would not solve the immediate problem of a lack of qualified NCOs and officers. Four of America's top commanders were veterans of the Spanish-American War of 1898 and most American ordnance was of World War I vintage. Anxious to guard their neutrality, the Americans had not carefully observed the nature of war from 1939 to 1941. Consequently, their staff colleges and planning divisions had not absorbed the tough lessons learned by the British and the Soviets in the war's early stages. One student of the American military of 1941 has noted its essential "Boy Scoutism" with field manuals focusing on the best ways to pitch tents and handle horses. It was not until 1940 that the War Department discontinued saber instruction for officers.[6]

But once awakened, America did not go back to sleep. The isolationism that had characterized the nation since its birth ended overnight. In its place came an internationalism so zealous that it could only have come from a convert. The spirit of the Neutrality Acts, the last signed just four years before Pearl Harbor, became a distant memory. As we will see, American reactions to the end of World War II differed dramatically from those to the end of World War I. Instead of retreating back across the oceans, the Americans threw themselves body and soul into internationalism. By 1945 the Americans were talking about the need for a "unilateral and active-self defense" requiring "extensive overseas bases."[7]

But before they could embark on such giant strides, the Americans had to take their first steps. Army Chief of Staff General George Marshall advocated an invasion of western Europe as soon as possible, perhaps in 1942. Marshall considered the invasion essential in order to provide a second front that could ensure Soviet survival. Just two years earlier American politicians had tried to specifically exclude the USSR from Lend-Lease aid, and several senior American officers had argued that the American military should be a force for defending the western hemisphere only. By early 1942, they were arguing for a massive invasion of western Europe; the American Army's Operations Division (headed by Dwight Eisenhower) estimated that the Americans could launch an invasion of France in 1943 with an incredible 48 divisions.

Churchill and the British, who had wished for American belligerence for more than two years, now had to find a way to curb the enthusiasm that accompanied it. Having been forced out of Europe by the Germans in Norway, France, Greece, and Crete, the British had no intention of launching an operation that most of them considered a futile suicide mission. They argued instead for an invasion of North Africa, which they would grandiosely place in a "European Theater of Operations." Semantics aside, the Americans were not at all pleased with the idea of operating in neither the Pacific *nor* in Europe. Virtually all of Roosevelt's senior military advisors (including Marshall and Eisenhower) argued against the North Africa plan, but the President overruled them.

In retrospect, the wisdom of Roosevelt's decision to approve the North Africa invasion, code-named Torch, appears obvious. The American effort in North Africa was plagued with miscommunication, incompetence, and inexperience. But an invasion of continental Europe against veteran German troops positioned close to secure lines of communication would have been a disaster. Moreover, the Allies could not have produced the 48 divisions that Eisenhower had seen as crucial to the success of a 1942 invasion of France. Neither could the Allies have produced the requisite landing craft, weapons, and air supremacy.

In one area, however, the Americans were proving themselves not just capable, but superior. Although their tactics and operations still left much to be learned, their logistics were already demonstrating the particular American genius in this area. The Torch landings involved three task forces, one of which (the Western Task Force, under Major General George Patton) left directly from Virginia. Once ashore, the Americans were able consistently to supply themselves and their British allies, thus allowing for greater freedom of recovery from their tactical mistakes. The Americans built a jeep assembly plant in Oran that could reassemble a packed vehicle in just nine minutes. The plant eventually assembled 20,000 vehicles. In just three weeks, American logisticians put together a convoy that left from three separate American states and delivered 5,000 trucks, 2,000 cargo trailers, 400 dump trucks, 80 fighter planes, 12,000 tons of coal, 16,000 tons of flour, 9,000 tons of sugar, 1,000 tons of soap, and 4,000 submachine guns. "The American Army," one general observed, "does not solve its problems. It overwhelms them."[8]

America's success in becoming the "Arsenal of Democracy" may have been its most important wartime contribution to the Allied cause. The nation was ideally suited to play such a role. Long one of the world's leading manufacturing nations, the United States had a vast complex of factories, a wealth of raw materials, and good economic relationships with almost every nation in the western hemisphere. By extending Lend–Lease aid to the nations of Latin America (Mexico, Cuba, Peru, Chile, and Brazil were all large recipients) the United States facilitated the development of economies that could be of assistance while effectively closing those economies off to the Axis nations. Moreover, the industrial plant of the United States was not subject to either bombing or sabotage, allowing it to operate and dramatically expand during the war.

The United States also possessed a large skilled workforce that, because of the depression, had been underutilized. The war brought these workers back into factories with high wages and a commonality of purpose that ensured continued production. To guarantee the continuation of these patterns, Marshall opted for a controversial policy known as the "Ninety Division Gamble." The Americans would create no more than ninety army divisions in order that conscription calls could permit the large-scale exemption of key industrial workers such as miners and specialty steel workers. The Americans would compensate for the relatively small numbers (compared to their total population) that they would field as combat troops by developing modern weapons systems in quantity and quality. The Americans also brought many previously marginalized groups into the industrial and agricultural workforces, including women, African Americans, and Mexicans.

The results of this policy were astounding. The Americans added 6,000,000 industrial workers to the labor pool during the war; General Motors alone added 750,000 jobs. In 1943 the United States by itself produced twice as many airplanes as Germany and Japan combined. The following year American industry produced 2,247 major naval vessels. The rest of the war's belligerents produced a combined 747. The same year the United States out-produced

Germany in trucks by 600,000 to 88,000. By one estimate, the Ford Motor Company alone produced more vehicles than all of Italy's industry. The Americans continued to refine their industrial process as the war continued. In 1941 a Liberty cargo ship required 355 days to build. Two years later they could consistently be built in 41 days and, as a publicity stunt, a Liberty crew built one in just 8 days.[9]

These weapons and supplies fueled not just the Americans, but greatly helped the British and the Soviets as well. Under Lend-Lease, the Soviets obtained 78,000 jeeps, 350,000 trucks, more than one million miles of telephone cable, 35,000 radios, and 400,000 field telephones. These supplies amounted to about 7 percent of total Soviet supplies, but they held a greater significance than mere numbers. American supplies were focused in areas where Soviet industry was particularly deficient, thus allowing the Soviets to play to their own strengths: producing the outstanding T-34 tank and the fearsome Katyusha multiple rocket launchers.

These supplies helped the allies to take three major steps in the autumn of 1942 and the winter of 1943. On the Russian front, the Soviets were able to hold the city of Stalingrad, then counterattack in January. Led by the talented Soviet General Georgi Zhukov, the Soviets achieved surprise and cut the Germans off from their lines of communication in the middle of winter. The Soviet destruction of the German Sixth Army proved to be a blow from which the Wehrmacht and German society never fully recovered. Thereafter the strategic initiative in eastern Europe switched to the Red Army. Now outfitted with better weapons and made more mobile by the introduction of American motor vehicles, the Soviet Union's doctrine of "deep offensive" began to make its effect felt.

The other two steps occurred in North Africa. In Egypt, a British Commonwealth force led by General Bernard Montgomery dealt the Axis a decisive blow at El Alamein in October. The Commonwealth forces enjoyed comfortable margins of 1,029 tanks to 496 and 1,451 to 800 antitank guns. Montgomery had chosen a battlefield flanked to the north by the Mediterranean Sea and to the south by the virtually impassable Qatarra Depression. Geography (plus severely limited fuel stocks) limited the Panzer Africa Army's notorious speed and ability to outflank its opponents. Montgomery could thus take maximum advantage of his army's superior resources and the excellent training regimen he had instilled.

At the other end of the continent, the Americans and British were executing the series of joint landings called for under the Torch plan. There they had to fight German, Italian, and, for a time, Vichy French forces. A daring secret landing by submarine near Algiers by American Major General Mark Clark led to a meeting with key Vichy officials, but did not result in their surrender. The Allies therefore had to oppose French forces, although these were usually overcome without extended fighting. Despite some significant reverses at the hands of the Germans, the Anglo-American force commanded by Eisenhower moved east toward Tunisia as Montgomery moved west in exploitation of his victory at El Alamein. The two armies linked up in May, 1943 and completed the elimination of Axis forces in North Africa shortly thereafter.

In January, 1943, even as the campaign for North Africa was ongoing, Roosevelt and Churchill held a major inter-Allied conference at the Casablanca suburb of Anfa. The trip was particularly arduous for Roosevelt, wracked as he was by polio and forced for security reasons to take a circuitous route from Washington to Africa. The Russians were invited, but declined because of the ferocity of the continuing struggle at Stalingrad. Charles de Gaulle, reluctantly recognized by the Allies as the leader of Free France, attended, but was furious at the perceived insult of having been invited by the British and Americans to a conference held in what he still saw as French imperial territory.

Although the Russians did not send a delegate, they were far from absent. Several of the most important decisions reached at Casablanca were designed to convince the Soviets of Allied resolve. These decisions included Roosevelt's pronouncement that only an unconditional Axis surrender would end the war, a signal to Stalin that the Allies were not interested in a separate peace or in a negotiated settlement. The Allies also announced the formation of an Anglo-American Combined Bomber Offensive to attack German industry and, they hoped, create an aerial front in Europe that would impede German war efforts.

Once again, the Americans pushed for an early invasion of France, but the logic of British arguments against such an operation proved unassailable. In the end, the Allies reached a compromise: the Allies would continue offensive action in the Mediterranean with an invasion of Sicily and mainland Italy, but they would also begin the buildup in Great Britain of the massive forces necessary to invade France in 1944. This plan was unlikely to satisfy Stalin completely, but it might pacify him long enough to give plans for the cross-Channel invasion time to develop. The Combined Chiefs of Staff, headed by the American General Dwight Eisenhower, was put in charge of planning both the Sicily invasion and the buildup for 1944. Eisenhower, ever the diplomat, ensured that key positions were held by British commanders and even succeeded in converting the skeptical and generally anti-American British Chief of the Imperial General Staff Field Marshal Sir Alan Brooke. Despite differences in outlook and pettiness from several of the Alliance's top commanders, the "cousins" were forming a *modus vivendi*.

The Grand Alliance was soon attracting other Allies as well. De Gaulle and his main anti-Vichy rival Henri-Honoré Giraud buried the hatchet between them. The two men co-chaired the French Committee for National Liberation, created in Algiers in June, 1943. This committee formed the basis for a Free French military and political effort. Connections with the Russians continued to be indirect as the Russians did not have a seat on the Combined Chiefs of Staff. Still, the Allies had formed a combined operation within just a few months of American entry. The Grand Alliance had been born.

## The Grand Alliance at war

The improvements in inter-Allied relations were occurring at the same time that those between the Axis states were significantly deteriorating. The defeat at Stalingrad had set the Axis dogs fighting amongst each another. Hitler blamed the Romanians, whose flanks Zhukov had so savagely attacked, for the disaster. Later, in a fit of repentance, he issued an order for his troops to avoid criticizing their Romanian allies, but the damage had already been done. The Italians, facing an imminent Anglo-American invasion of Sicily and the mainland, also turned on the Germans. Even the Austrians, warm enthusiasts of *Anschluß* in 1938, began to blame the excesses of the "Prussians" for the setbacks in Russia. The Axis was starting to unravel.

The invasion of Sicily furthered the deterioration of Axis fighting power. The American staff continued to recommend canceling the operation in favor of an invasion of France, only to be overruled by President Roosevelt. In May, 1943 at another inter-Allied conference in Washington, the Allies decided upon a July deadline for the Sicily operation. In exchange, the British made a commitment to launch the cross-Channel invasion in May or June, 1944. Significant strategic and political differences existed, but, unlike the Axis, the Allies were able to resolve most of them through compromise.

Nowhere is this ability for compromise better seen than in the development of the Combined Bomber Offensive. The British, anxious to reduce air crew casualties, had chosen a bombing strategy based on flying at night. This approach was safer, but it meant that bombing was notoriously inaccurate. Consequently, the RAF Bomber Command chose a strategy euphemistically called "area bombing" which aimed to inflict morale damage as much as material damage. By "dehousing" the German working class, the RAF contended, they could inflict severe damage on German industry. Unable to strike particular factories or transportation nodes, the British made a virtue out of a necessity by creating the area bombing doctrine.

The Americans disagreed with this approach. They objected to the necessarily higher civilian casualties that area bombing produced (although they later turned to the same strategy in Japan) and argued that aerial bombardment could hit targets precisely. They therefore advocated bombing missions flown by day to increase visibility and accuracy. Between the wars, the American Air Corps Tactical School had developed an "industrial web" theory of bombardment that focused on destroying key chokepoint targets such as ball bearings factories, oil refineries, and rail yards, without which the enemy could not effectively prosecute war. Attacking these objectives necessarily made targets of the civilian workforce, but the Americans were more comfortable with this approach than with area bombing (at least in Europe).

The British declined to go along with the Americans, mostly because daylight raids suffered enormous casualties. The British had never subscribed to the American belief that "the bomber will always get through." Consequently, RAF

Bomber Command's Air Chief Marshal Arthur "Bomber" Harris refused to contribute British bombers to an American plan in August 1943 to bomb the city of Schweinfurt's five ball bearing factories. As Harris predicted, the raid was a disaster, with the Americans losing 147 of the 376 bombers sent on the raid. A second attempt resulted in 60 more planes being destroyed and 142 damaged. The ball bearing plants suffered no appreciable damage to justify the heavy losses.

To resolve the impasse in air strategy, the Americans and the British compromised. Each air force would continue operations as they saw fit. The British would continue to area bomb by night and the Americans would use precision daylight bombing. The result was an around-the-clock bombardment aimed at all potential target sets inside German-controlled Europe. The appearance of an effective long-range fighter escort, the P-51D Mustang, made daylight bombing much safer and permitted much longer and deeper bomb runs. The Mustang, symbolically, was also a product of Anglo-American compromise: the air frame was built by the United States-based North American Aviation Corporation and the engine was the powerful Merlin built in Great Britain by Rolls Royce.

Competition between the "cousins" could produce results as beneficial as compromise. The invasion of Sicily involved a joint Anglo-American Fifteenth Army Group, commanded by British Field Marshal Sir Harold Alexander. British commanders Admiral Sir Andrew Cunningham and Air Chief Marshal Sir Arthur Tedder, working under the American Eisenhower, commanded the sea and air arms, respectively. The two ground commanders, the British General Montgomery, in charge of the Commonwealth Eighth Army, and the American Patton, in charge of the newly-formed United States Seventh Army, disliked one another intensely. Each sought the glory of being named the man who liberated Sicily and each instilled in his men a desire to best their ally for the credit for the capture of Sicily. Alexander's orders to Patton to cover Montgomery's flank as the latter advanced did little to mollify the American's massive ego. Patton believed that the British were condescending to the Americans and delegating to them a second-class role.

Patton and Montgomery thereafter fought two wars: a shooting war against the Axis defenders, whose low morale diminished their fighting power, and a cold war against one another for access to supplies, highways, and ports. Ordered to protect Montgomery's approach to the key port of Messina, Patton instead "became obsessed with roaring into the city ahead of Montgomery." He told a division commander, "The prestige of the US Army is at stake. We must take Messina." He was less concerned with armed resistance from Italian defenders than he was with beating his British rival to the punch. Patton won the honor of accepting the Axis surrender in Messina, with the British commander grudgingly congratulating him on a "jolly good race."[10] The pettiness between the two commanders had not been the Alliance's finest moment, but the rivalry had contributed to the rapid clearing of the island in less than one month.

The Sicilian campaign also led to the collapse of the first Axis government. Even as increasing numbers of Germans arrived to defend the Italian mainland, the Grand Fascist Council deposed Mussolini, imprisoning him on July 26, 1943. The week before, 500 Allied bombers had attacked Rome, underscoring the change in Italy's fortunes and signaling the rapid approach of Allied armies. In September, Allied forces landed at Salerno on the Italian mainland, just 50 kilometers from the key port city of Naples. Despite promises from Italian Army Chief of Staff Marshal Pietro Badoglio to his German allies that "we will fight [on] and never capitulate," the Italians signed a surrender shortly after the Salerno landings.[11]

Italian society had been on a war footing longer than any other European power, beginning with the invasion of Abyssinia (Ethiopia) in 1935. Mussolini's ill-fated decision to send three of his best divisions to the Russian front had cost the nation some of its most valuable and important troops in a theater far from home. Perhaps most importantly, Italian society had never embraced the lust for conquest that German society had, resulting in a half-hearted imperial effort and the early onset of war weariness. A relatively poor country among the major powers, Italian industry collapsed under the demand to produce war materiel. Italian agriculture also suffered badly from the absence of farmers. At several points during the war, Mussolini had to demobilize large parts of his armed forces in order to ensure that the harvest could be brought in and Italy could avoid famine.

The downturn in Italian fortunes was increasingly blamed on the megalomania of Mussolini. The Taranto raid of 1940 had created some anti-British bitterness, but by 1943 few Italians had any desire to wage war against the Anglo-Americans. Many Italians, especially in Sicily, had family who had emigrated to the United States. The warm reception that Sicilians and Calabrians gave to the "invading" British and Americans made an Italian surrender inevitable, as Badoglio quickly came to understand. A cartoon by the famous American war correspondent Bill Mauldin showed a GI and a barefoot Italian civilian sharing a bottle of wine and listening to the radio. The American cheerfully turns to the Italian and proclaims, "You hear that Fernando? Italy surrendered! You ain't a enemy no more!"[12]

But the Italian surrender did not mean the end of the war for Italy. Germany had decided to fight for Italy, with or without the Italians. Daring German paratroopers rescued Mussolini from captivity and delivered him to Munich, where he proclaimed an Italian Social Republic (RSI) in northern Italy. The Germans soon delivered him to Salò, the seat of the new rump state. From there, Mussolini railed against the corruption and decadence of the Italian monarchy that had deposed him and urged Italians to rally to him. Some military units remained loyal to the new regime, but it soon became apparent that the RSI was an even more complete puppet of the Nazis than the previous Mussolini regime had been. A wave of strikes in Turin and Milan demonstrated that support for the RSI was thin indeed. The Germans responded by deporting

100,000 northern Italian workers to Germany and seizing the gold reserves of the Bank of Italy. The Italian monarchy replied with a declaration of war against Germany, leading to a series of reprisals and the threat of civil war between supporters of Mussolini and King Victor Emmanuel III.

To meet the Allied advance, German forces rapidly established a series of defenses known as the Gustav Line between Rome and Naples. The Germans hoped to keep Allied forces far enough to the south to prevent the Allied use of Italian air bases for air strikes at southern Germany. The result was a tough, slow slogging match through the Apennine Mountains that belied Churchill's description of Italy as Europe's "soft underbelly." Allied forces, including Free Polish and Free French units, failed to breach the Gustav Line despite courageous charges reminiscent of World War I. A hastily planned amphibious landing just south of Rome at Anzio failed to improve the situation appreciably. The Allies did not enter Rome until June 5, 1944. German troops retreated to another line of defenses and managed to hold key cities including Milan and Venice until the final days of the war.

The arrival en masse of German forces in Italy also led to the deportation of Italy's Jewish community. Roberto Benigni's 1997 award-winning film *Life is Beautiful* made famous the sufferings of Italy's Jewish community under German rule. Benigni's own father, although not Jewish, had been deported from Italy for his opposition to Mussolini. Italy, like most other Fascist nations in Europe, had passed anti-Semitic laws; a 1938 law was based on the dubious proposition that Italians were "Aryans," but Jews were more properly considered African than European. Nevertheless, Mussolini maintained open friendships with many Jews and had protected his nation's Jews from Hitler's Final Solution. Italian anti-Semitism never took on the murderous tone that its German counterpart had, in part because Italy's Jewish population never exceeded one-tenth of 1 percent. Even during the promulgation of anti-Semitic laws, Mussolini exempted families of Italian war veterans, early members of the Fascist party, and other "exceptional" Jewish families.

After September, 1943, however, Italy's Jews found themselves the targets of German military and SS units. Although the Germans had to plan for the defense of northern Italy, they nevertheless devoted substantial resources to rooting out and killing Italy's relatively small Jewish population. Germans also began seizing Jews in the portion of southeastern France under Italian control, previously an important haven for Jews who had been living in France in 1940. Mussolini encouraged his military commanders to stall and frustrate German plans to deport Italian Jews to death camps, but he and his military officials were in a weak position to impose their will on the German occupiers.

One of those deported was Primo Levi, raised in a secular family and the grandson of an Italian baroness. He had graduated first in his class at the University of Turin in chemistry, but was unable to teach or pursue an advanced degree because of a codicil in the 1938 law that forbade Jews from becoming academics. Five years later, when Mussolini's regime was replaced by an occupying German force, Levi attempted to contact a resistance group, but the Germans arrested him and deported him to Auschwitz. Out of his railroad convoy of 650 people, only 24 survived the war. Levi was one of the survivors because, due to his knowledge of chemistry, he was sent to work as a slave laborer at the synthetic rubber plants of I. G. Farben Laboratories. A sympathetic civilian passed him the soup that Levi credits with keeping him alive. After the war, Levi wrote several books, most notably *Survival in Auschwitz*, about his experiences. But depression and survivor's guilt plagued him his whole life. In 1987 he committed suicide in his hometown of Turin.

Germany's decision to assume the defense of Italy coincided with another major reversal in Russia. In July, 1943 (as Anglo-American forces were conquering Sicily) the Red Army defeated a major German offensive aimed at the salient of Kursk southwest of Moscow. The Soviet victory at Stalingrad had given Stalin enough confidence to allow his generals more latitude in planning to meet and defeat future German attacks. He abolished the hated commissar system, sending 122,000 of the political officers to serve as riflemen in infantry divisions. New stocks of weapons and better intelligence about German intentions were also decisive. Soviet support for the war rose to new levels. Hundreds of thousands of civilians volunteered or were coerced into constructing 3,000 miles of tank ditches and planting 400,000 mines. This effort allowed the Red Army not only to survive German attacks on both the southern and northern shoulders of the Kursk salient, but to counterattack as well, inflicting another serious blow to German fortunes in Russia.

The victory at Kursk led to a remarkable social transformation in Russia: the reestablishment of organized religion. The rise of the Bolsheviks after 1917 had led to the official closing of churches and the establishment of atheism as official state doctrine. From the early days of World War II, however, the church had been a symbol of both Russian determination and resistance to the occupiers. On the very day of the invasion, while Stalin remained stunned and silent, Metropolitan Sergel had broadcast a radio appeal to the Soviet people calling for a defense of the motherland. The church became a major source of fundraising for both military hardware and civilian relief efforts. The war thus led Stalin, a former disgruntled seminary student, to shelve his plan to eliminate the church from Soviet life.

Rather than close the church, Stalin soon took steps to reinstitute it officially into Soviet life. On September 4, 1943, as the Soviets were still basking in the glow of the Kursk victory, Stalin received senior members of the church at the Kremlin. Stalin reestablished the office of patriarch, which Peter the Great had replaced with a government bureaucracy in the eighteenth century, giving the aged Sergel (who died in 1944) the office. Religious journals reappeared and Stalin even supported the limited teaching of theology. In return Sergel and his senior clergymen agreed to use the church to support Russian nationalism and continued efforts to win the war.

Final victory depended in large part upon the success of the Anglo-American buildup for the 1944 cross-Channel invasion. Once the Allies had established a front in France, Germany would face Anglo-American fronts on the west and the south as well as a resurgent Russia in the east. In order to increase the odds of the success of the invasion (code-named Overlord), thousands of men and women from all over Europe and America had to be assembled and trained in Great Britain. The appearance of so many foreigners caused significant tensions, but the money and resources the foreigners (most notably the Americans) brought with them helped Britons to supplement their allotment of both necessities and luxuries.

Food rationing in Great Britain began in 1940 and did not officially end until 1954. Scores of common food items simply disappeared from store shelves. Paul Fussell relates the story of an American soldier who gave an orange to a young English girl who had never seen one.[13] Public feeding centers known as "British Restaurants" assumed the role of feeding thousands of Britons for five shillings or less per meal. Thanks to American assistance and growing Allied success in the Battle of the Atlantic, Britain was much better off than most continental nations. Most Europeans had to make do with what they could grow, procure from local farmers, or obtain with ration cards. Wealthier Europeans had the option of buying on the black market.

The men preparing for Overlord, however, had so many supplies that a common joke wondered why Britain did not sink under the weight of all the materiel. The massive invasion force included 200,000 men, 6,000 ships, 13,000 vehicles, and 5,000 fighter aircraft. One hundred and sixty-three air bases had been specially constructed to maintain supporting air operations. Heavy bombardments of French transportation nodes were designed to isolate the Normandy beaches by destroying the canals, bridges, and roads that German reinforcements might use. In order to disguise the exact location of Overlord, Allied bombers struck all across France. These raids necessarily involved killing French civilians, a prospect that haunted both Churchill and Roosevelt. Allied air crews were therefore instructed to minimize French casualties as much as possible while inflicting maximum damage on German military resources in northern France.

Overlord, launched on June 6, 1944, also depended on the help of the French resistance to hinder German response times. Allied estimates suggested that 100,000 resistance figures and 40,000 members of the paramilitary resistance group known as the maquis, were able to help. The British Special Operations Executive and the American Office of Strategic Services (forerunner of the CIA) trained these men and women and delivered supplies to them. They also set up a code system to communicate with French groups via BBC radio using the French poem "Chanson d'Automne." The BBC's broadcast of the first verse indicated that the invasion was imminent. The second verse indicated that the invasion was just 24 hours away and that resistance figures should begin sabotage operations against German targets. Savage German torture and infiltration operations had divined the general outlines of the plan, but higher headquarters did not place enough faith in intelligence reports to make much use of them.

The success of Overlord also depended on the strength of Allied logistical ability and the maturation of Allied fighting power. The Allies built two portable harbors known as Mulberries (the outlines of one can still be seen outside Arromanches) to facilitate the uninterrupted flow of supplies in the event that the Germans destroyed the harbor facilities in Cherbourg and Le Havre. To ensure the continued supply of much-needed oil, the Allies created the misnamed PLUTO (Petroleum Line Under the Ocean) to transport oil across the English Channel from Britain to France.

Overlord witnessed one of the finest examples of joint warfare in military history, with overall commander Eisenhower again naming British commanders for air (Air Marshal Sir Trafford Leigh-Mallory), sea (Admiral Sir Bertram Ramsey), and ground (Montgomery) operations. The Americans, British, and Canadians each had their own beaches to capture and their own chains of command once ashore. This system functioned much more smoothly than the confused command structures of Allied operations in Italy.

Although the breakout from the Normandy beachheads took longer than anticipated, Allied forces were approaching Paris by early August. Eisenhower initially favored bypassing Paris in favor of devoting all resources to pursuing the retreating Germans, but a rising by railway workers and police in the city in mid-August led to a reconsideration. On August 23, Eisenhower released Major General Philippe Leclerc's Second Armored Division to head for the city, leaving the honor of liberating the French capital to a French unit. The German commander, General Dietrich von Choltitz, defied Hitler's order to destroy the city, surrendering it on August 25. An Allied landing in southern France that month began the liberation of Provence and Burgundy against light opposition and such ecstatic local reception that the operation received the nickname "the champagne campaign."

Across France the liberation was accompanied by fierce reprisals against collaborators and officials of the Vichy regime. But exact definitions of collaboration were difficult to identify, because thousands of Frenchmen had passively or actively assisted the Germans in one fashion or another. Public reprisals and vengeance therefore tended to focus on the most extreme cases and on obvious targets, such as women who had had sexual relations with Germans. These "horizontal collaborators" often had their heads shaved in public and their property confiscated. The problem of collaboration (what one scholar has called "the Vichy syndrome") continues to haunt France and many other nations across Europe.[14]

The two operations in France created the second front for which the Russians had pleaded, but the Russians took care of their own business that summer as well. On the third anniversary of the German invasion of Russia (June 22, 1944) the Russians launched a massive assault against German Army Group Center that involved 118 infantry divisions, 2,715 tanks, and 1,355 heavy assault guns.

The operation (code-named Bagration) cleared much of the Ukraine and White Russia of German forces and opened the way for the Red Army to enter Poland. By August 23, the Red Army sat on the banks of the Vistula River just outside Warsaw.

Virtually all Europeans now knew that the war was entering its final stages. The Germans, though not yet beaten, were yielding ground on all fronts. On July 20, a group of German generals attempted, but failed, to assassinate Hitler in the hopes of replacing him with a more orderly and rational military system. In the wake of the assassination attempt, Hitler became increasingly paranoid and mistrustful of all but his most sycophantic generals. Eastern Germans, aware that the vengeful Russians were coming closer and closer, began to tell one another, "Enjoy the war. The peace will be hell."

## To the Elbe

The alliance between the capitalist, democratic states of Britain and the United States on the one hand and the authoritarian, communist Soviet Union on the other hand had always been a marriage of convenience at best. Churchill's often-quoted phrase, "If Hitler invaded hell I would make at least a favorable reference to the devil in the House of Commons", sums up the relationship rather well. Longstanding ideological differences had complicated the relationship of the Bolshevik state to the western democracies; the events of 1939 and 1940 only compounded these problems. Britons remembered that the Soviets had provided some of the economic assistance that had enabled Blitzkrieg warfare in the west against France and the Low Countries. The Soviets had themselves invaded Poland in 1939 in defiance of an Anglo-French alliance with the Poles. The unprovoked Soviet invasion of Finland only increased tensions.

Although the Roosevelt Administration had recognized the Soviet government in 1933, the United States also harbored its doubts. American distrust of the Soviets went so far as to lead to their exclusion from the initial Lend-Lease legislation. Roosevelt sent one of his closest advisors, Harry Hopkins, to Moscow for the express purpose of establishing a working relationship with Stalin and the Soviet regime. This personal link helped to solve many problems, especially those connected with Lend-Lease details, but it did not remove the fundamental suspicion that lingered throughout the war.

As Richard Overy has recently argued, the ironic and uncomfortable truth is that democracy was saved by the exhortations of Soviet Communism.[15] In order to accommodate this odd alliance, the British and Americans undertook a propaganda campaign designed to convince their people to accept "Uncle Joe" and his Red Army as full partners in the war for freedom over tyranny. For the duration of the war, it was "[b]etter not dwelt upon too much" that an alliance with Stalin (and several other unsavory characters) undermined the democratic principles that the west claimed it was fighting for.[16] As the end of the war in

Europe came into sharper view, these contradictions cast a shadow over a post-war world in which victory and triumph would have to be shared between two competing ideologies.

From the Soviet side, the picture was scarcely more rosy, western economic aid notwithstanding. Massive economic assistance did not allay all of the Soviet government's ideological suspicions about the nature of capitalism and democracy. Stalin accused the British and Americans of intentionally delaying their opening of a second front in France in order to bleed the Red Army dry, thus guaranteeing the capitalist states a dominant role in post-war Europe. He did not accept Anglo-American arguments that the North African or Italian fronts constituted second fronts nor was he willing to accept the Combined Bomber Offensive as a substitute for a land invasion of France. He, too, saw the Alliance (as he had seen the Nazi–Soviet Pact of 1939) as little more than an emergency arrangement between irreconcilable systems.

Even before the Allies entered the final stages of victory, signs of conflict emerged. As the Red Army approached Warsaw, the clandestine Polish Home Army took the enormous gamble of rising against the Nazis despite the Poles' lack of proper military equipment; only 15 percent of their 36,000 members had access to weapons. Nevertheless, in the first half of 1944 they had been increasingly active in support of the advancing Russians. They had damaged almost 7,000 locomotives, 19,000 railway trucks, and 4,300 military vehicles. They had also destroyed almost 5,000 tons of gasoline and blown up 38 railway bridges. These achievements are all the more remarkable given that many Poles saw the advancing Soviets as enemies every bit as much to be feared as the Germans.

The plight of the Poles generated significant sympathy in the west. The German invasion of Poland, after all, had been the trigger that had brought France and Britain into the war in 1939. The defeated Poles had fought valiantly in the face of overwhelming odds against both the Germans and the Russians; many had escaped through Romania to France and Britain to continue the fight. They had been responsible for providing Britain with the vital Enigma machine that enabled cryptographers to decipher the crucial intelligence known collectively by the code-name Ultra. This intelligence had helped Britain concentrate air resources in the Battle of Britain and had helped the Royal Navy secure lines of communication during the Battle of the Atlantic. Even as the Soviets advanced toward Warsaw, Free Polish units were fighting with the Allies in Normandy, where they played a role in the bloody struggle to close the Argentan–Falaise pocket northwest of Paris, and in Italy, where the courageous Second Polish Corps seized Monte Cassino Abbey, a key stronghold in the Gustav Line. That fall, the Polish Parachute Brigade participated in Montgomery's failed Market-Garden offensive. The Poles were, therefore, full members of the Allied coalition, even as their state was under enemy occupation.

The Soviets had grudgingly recognized a Polish government in exile established in London first under the widely-respected General Władysław

Sikorski and, after his death, under the less charismatic Stanislaw Mikołajczyk. Britain reluctantly agreed to draw the Soviet–Polish border well west of the line favored by most Poles. In exchange, Churchill expected Stalin to recognize the Polish government in London as the legitimate and legal representative of the Polish people. Stalin, however, became increasingly unwilling to negotiate with the "London Poles." Instead, the Soviet dictator created a Lublin Committee of Polish officials more to his liking. This move threatened to make Poland a puppet state of the Soviet Union after the war, but there was little that the western Allies could effectively do to pressure the Soviets in an area soon to come under their military control.

As the Lublin Poles versus London Poles debate reached an impasse, the Polish Home Army's commander-in-chief, General Tadeusz Komorowski, ordered his men to rise up and seize the resources of Warsaw. He hoped that having the city in the Home Army's control would increase his power relative to the Soviets. The western Allies hurriedly tried to air drop supplies to the heroic men in Warsaw, but the distances proved too great. To the west's great dismay, Stalin ordered the Red Army to halt outside the city rather than enter it to come to the aid of the Poles. The fighting inside Warsaw went on for 63 days, with every street and every building the scene of intense fighting. The Germans responded with typical ferocity, executing as many as 40,000 civilians in just five days. More than one-quarter of the city's population was killed and 83 percent of its buildings destroyed during the rising, which the Germans finally extinguished on October 1. Warsaw suffered more damage than any other European capital.

Stalin's failure to help the Poles radically changed the tone of the Alliance. The Soviet leader had even refused (with one exception) American aircraft permission to land at Soviet airfields after making supply drops over Warsaw. Whether due to Soviet unwillingness to assist them or not, the failure of the western Allies to provide real assistance to the Home Army undermined the legitimacy of the London Poles. The Home Army itself was destroyed. Many westerners accused Stalin of intentionally letting the cream of the Warsaw resistance be slaughtered in order to facilitate his control over a Polish satellite after the war.

The tragic ending of the Warsaw rising fueled western desires to, in Churchill's phrase, shake hands with the Soviets as far east as possible. If the Allies could get deep into Germany, perhaps even into Berlin itself, before the Soviets did, they might dramatically increase their bargaining position after the war. This logic contributed to a daring gamble by Montgomery to land 20,000 paratroops and glider troops behind German lines. These forces would capture three bridges in Holland (Operation Market) then the Allies would follow up with an armored advance linking the bridges together and placing Allied troops over the Rhine River before the onset of the winter of 1944–1945 (Operation Garden).

Bad weather, bad luck, and bad intelligence turned the operation (launched on September 17, 1944) into a failure. Dutch resistance members had tried to warn the Allies that the Germans had moved two elite SS Panzer units into the drop area; these units were, by an unfortunate coincidence, training to repel an airborne invasion. Although photo reconnaissance confirmed the Dutch resistance's intelligence, the Allies did not alter their plans. When the operation began, the Dutch government in exile, operating in London, called for a general strike to assist the Allied effort. Allied forces captured two of the three targeted bridges, but failed to capture the third, on the lower Rhine River at Arnhem, and soon pulled the survivors back to a salient around the city of Nijmegen.

Holland's suffering thus continued. As a nation, it represented both the best and the worst of European reactions to Nazism. A Germanic nation with cultural, ethnic, and linguistic ties to the Third Reich, Holland contributed 25,000 volunteer soldiers to the Wehrmacht, most of whom fought in Russia. They were part of the *Volksdeutsche* units composed of men viewed by the Nazis as ethnically German. Holland's was the largest per capita contribution of military volunteers to the German military of any occupied nation.

On the other hand, the Dutch resistance had been active throughout the war, using Holland's large printing industry to produce and distribute thousands of opposition newspapers, forged ration cards, and false identity papers. Many Dutch citizens also courageously risked their own lives to protect Jews, most famously in the case of the family of Anne Frank. The Dutch Queen, Wilhelmina, broadcast regularly to her subjects via the London-based Radio Orange, becoming a symbol of freedom and resistance to her oppressed peoples. It was over Radio Orange that she urged a strike in support of Market-Garden. Once the offensive had been halted, the Germans retaliated by deporting 50,000 Dutch men as forced laborers to Germany and by sharply reducing coal and food supplies to the civilian population. During the winter of 1944–1945 an estimated 16,000 Dutch civilians died of cold and hunger. Many were reduced to eating tulip bulbs. It was cruel treatment for the nation that had been the first to deliver food stocks to starving Germans in 1918.

The failure of Market-Garden and the surprise German Ardennes offensive, popularly known as the Battle of the Bulge, that began on December 17, 1944 slowed the Allied advance to Berlin considerably. The following month the Russians entered Germany proper. Hundreds of thousands of German refugees, many recently resettled on seized Slavic lands as a result of *Lebensraum* policies, headed west. This mass migration enabled post-war diplomats to draw a generous western boundary for Poland. Unlike the Polish state created after World War I, the new Poland, "slid to the west," would not contain a sizable ethnic German minority.

The Russian advance brought with it a terrible revenge for the German crimes committed in Russia. Most first-line units acted with a reasonable degree of professionalism, motivated as they were by pushing ever further westward and defeating the German military formations in front of them. Second- and third-line troops, however, looted, pillaged, and raped as they advanced. The rapes were a crime both against women and against the men who failed to protect them. The relative comfort of German homes, with amenities including electricity and indoor plumbing, contrasted sharply with the austere life familiar to Russians in both war and peace. Russian officers, struck by the contrast in living styles, did little to discourage their men's appetites for destruction. The catharsis exacted a dreadful price, releasing the tensions caused by nearly four years of Russian misery at German hands. SS units contributed to the anguish by destroying anything of value to the Russians as they retreated, often killing scores of women and children in the process.

Shortly after the first Russian units entered Germany, Stalin, Churchill, and Roosevelt met at the Crimean city of Yalta to discuss the future of Germany and Europe. The conference met from February 4 to 11, 1945. The eventual defeat of Germany seemed sufficiently imminent to arrange for a division of the country into zones of occupation. The Allies developed such a plan, which included a separate occupation zone for each of the three major Allied powers and one for France. The Soviet Union also agreed to the terms by which the Red Army and Air Force would enter the war against Japan; in return the Allies reluctantly agreed to recognize the transformation of the pro-Soviet Lublin Committee into a Provisional Government of National Unity. This decision effectively placed a post-war Poland into a Soviet sphere of influence, confirming by diplomacy what had become a military reality.

One of the most significant consequences of the conference was the demonstrable appearance of what would become known as the superpower system. By this time, the ailing Roosevelt (who died in April) had determined that cooperation with the Soviets in the post-war world would be vital to world peace. In order not to antagonize the notoriously paranoid Stalin, Roosevelt refused to meet with Churchill in private. That decision, along with France and Germany's fate being decided without a representative of either nation being present, symbolized the dramatic shift in power from 1939 to 1945. Most of the key decisions were reached by the Americans and the Soviets.

Another symbolic step also came from Yalta. The British, Americans, and Soviets agreed to create a multi-national body to replace the defunct League of Nations, this one to be named the United Nations. The idea had first emerged in 1941, but the exigencies of winning the war had pushed it to secondary importance. Roosevelt insisted that this new body convene and hold its regular meetings in the United States, a move that at once announced America's desires to the world that it would be a full participant in global affairs after the war and at the same time announced to the American people that their new global responsibilities would not end with the German and Japanese capitulations. This time, the American legislature voted overwhelmingly for the United States to not only join, but fund, the new organization. There would be no return to isolation from European affairs.

The unity that the three powers showed at Yalta revealed to German commanders the unlikelihood of splitting the Grand Alliance, especially after the Germans found a copy of the Yalta agreements in a crashed American cargo plane. German units that faced the Russians especially hoped to make peace with the British and Americans in the hopes of creating a joint effort against the Red Army. This bit of fancy gave them an excuse to make contact with the western powers, as most hoped to surrender to the Americans or the British, not the vengeful Red Army. The Germans hoped to put as pleasant a face on the end of the Thousand Year Reich as they could in the hopes of forging good relations with the western powers.

The chances of such an eventuality, at least in the short term, were slight. The Americans and British, needing Soviet help against the Japanese, had no intention of signing a separate agreement with the defeated Germans. The German massacre of 86 American POWs near the Belgian town of Malmédy on the first day of the Ardennes Offensive led to a war of increasing ferocity. Rumors (correct as they turned out) circulated among American units that the Germans were employing the ruse of disguising themselves in American uniforms. Although these units did not dramatically alter the combat on the western front, they increased Allied hatred and suspicion of their German enemy. Elite German and American units took increasingly fewer prisoners as the war went on, a dramatic change from the relatively lawful conduct of the war in North Africa.

German behavior against civilians also multiplied the developing antipathy between the Germans and the British and Americans. In June, 1944 in the French city of Oradour-sur-Glane, a quiet agricultural town far from the battle front, German forces prepared to evacuate after hearing about the Normandy landings. Before doing so, they placed all the women and children of the small town in the church and placed all the men in barns. They then set all of these buildings on fire and shot anyone who fled from the flames. A total of 642 unarmed civilians died; a German sweep of the town found no arms at all. The French government decided not to rebuild the town after the war. It remains largely as it was on the day of the massacre as a memorial to the horrors of the German occupation.

Anti-German sentiments continued to rise as the war approached its final end. Shortly after Yalta, two events occurred that further infuriated the western powers. In early March the Germans unleashed their V-1 flying bombs on London. These pilotless aircraft carried an 850 kg high explosive warhead and had been used to strike Allied facilities (especially ports) in Belgium and Holland. Notoriously inaccurate, the decision to use them against English cities fanned Allied hatred of the Germans. Churchill ordered the preparation of plans to evacuate 10,000 women and children per day out of the capital in part because of uncertainty about the progress of German "secret weapons" that might have included gas or even atomic warheads. Eventually, the Germans fired 10,000 V-1s at England, with three in four actually making the crossing over the English Channel. More than 2,400 struck targets in London; one landed as far away as Manchester. The V-1s killed 6,184 people and wounded almost 18,000 more. The V-2 rocket, propelled by alcohol and liquid oxygen, killed

2,700 more Londoners. Hitler's public rantings about more secret weapons kept the nerves of civilians and military personnel alike on edge until the end of the war.

The second event occurred on April 12, when American generals Eisenhower, Patton, and Bradley, accompanied by journalists and photographers, entered the Ohrdruf death camp. What they saw was enough to make even the battle-hardened Patton physically ill. The photographs and newsreels stunned a world inured to suffering by more than five years of total warfare. Since 1942 the Allies had known that the Germans were herding Jews and other perceived enemies into camps, but few people dared to guess the magnitude of the evil. The stunned American generals ordered GIs to march through the death camps to remind them of the evil they were fighting. They also ordered German civilians to march through the camps. In one case, the mayor of an adjoining town went home and committed suicide, either out of guilt or fear of retribution.

In the coming weeks, the Allies liberated camps that were several times larger than Ohrdruf. They also uncovered evidence of horrifying medical experiments. The Nazis had actually increased the speed and scale of the killing in the war's final weeks in the hopes of eradicating the remaining Jews of Europe and, at the same time, hiding the evidence of their many crimes. The Russian liberation of the massive Polish death camps of Treblinka, Auschwitz-Birkenau, and Chelmo, among others, provided more evidence of the depths of German barbarity. The Allies also liberated slave labor camps and uncovered mass graves. The full sins of the German regime thus became more obvious with each step the Allies took toward Berlin.

Anti-German sentiments soon became reflected in official policy. The Allies agreed that they had to conduct war crimes trials themselves and not, as they had done after World War I, allow the Germans to conduct them themselves. In May, 1945, the new American president, Harry Truman, ordered American Supreme Court Justice Robert Jackson to prepare the legal groundwork for war crimes tribunals. The Soviets quickly agreed to the idea of such trials and favored the mass execution of top Nazi officials.[17] Justice Jackson helped to convene a conference on war crimes in London in July and August. This conference resulted in the London Agreement that established legal procedure for the tribunals and decided upon the selection criteria for the judges.

On April 25, three events occurred, which, together, signaled that the end was finally at hand. In San Francisco, the United Nations Conference opened, the culmination of four years of work designed to create an international agency. The work of creating a post-war international order thus began. The two-month conference involved representatives from 50 nations, with the United States, France, Britain, China, and Russia assuming permanent seats in the new body's Security Council. The unity of the meeting was marred slightly by disagreements over who should hold the seat for Poland; as a compromise of sorts, it sat vacant for the duration of the conference.

In Germany on the same day, Russian forces completed their encirclement of Berlin. The Americans had already cancelled plans to land an airborne division in the city, thus freeing the way for the Russians to capture it. Inside Berlin, essential services were running only intermittently and riots were commonplace. SS head Heinrich Himmler made one last appeal via Switzerland to arrange a surrender to the Americans and British only, but the western powers stayed true to their agreement with Stalin and refused. Five days later, the Hammer and Sickle of the Soviet flag flew over the Reichstag building; five days after that Hitler committed suicide.

The third event of April 25 occurred a little more than 100 km southwest of Berlin on the Elbe River. There American and Russian soldiers shook hands. Four days later British forces under Montgomery joined them. On May 6, German Army Chief of Staff Alfred Jodl came to Eisenhower's Reims headquarters to negotiate a surrender. Eisenhower told him, in language that had first been officially introduced more than two years earlier at Casablanca, that no terms except unconditional surrender were acceptable. Jodl agreed. May 8, 1945 became V-E (Victory in Europe) Day; the war to destroy Nazi tyranny was over. The recovery of Europe, and with it an entirely new paradigm of warfare, was about to begin.

## Further reading

Irish journalist Cornelius Ryan interviewed many important participants and wrote three readable books on operations at the end of the war. *The Longest Day* (New York: Simon and Schuster, 1959) covers the D-Day operation; *A Bridge Too Far* (New York: Simon and Schuster, 1974) discusses Market-Garden; and *The Last Battle* (New York: Simon and Schuster, 1966) reviews the battle for Berlin. Antony Beevor, *The Fall of Berlin, 1945* (New York: Viking, 2002) is a more recent treatment.

Paul Fussell's *Wartime: Understanding and Behavior in the Second World War* (Oxford: Oxford University Press, 1989) is a social and cultural look at the British and American experiences. J. Glenn Gray's *The Warriors: Reflections on Men in Battle* (New York: Perennial, 1959) offers wonderful insights into the nature of war. Michael Howard, *The Mediterranean Strategy in the Second World War* (Greenwood, CT: Praeger, 1968) analyzes the disagreements and compromises of the Anglo-American alliance. Several of the essays in Martin Blumenson, *Heroes Never Die: Warriors and Warfare in World War II* (New York: Cooper Square Press, 2001) are also useful.

On the Holocaust, several wonderful books are available. For accounts by those who survived see the works of Primo Levi and Elie Weisel. For historical coverage, see Christopher Browning, *Ordinary Men: Reserve Police Battalion 101 and the Final Solution in Poland* (New York: Perennial, 1992) and his *The Path to Genocide: Essays on Launching the Final Solution* (Cambridge: Cambridge University Press, 1995). Daniel Jonah Goldhagen, *Hitler's Willing Executioners:*

*Ordinary Germans and the Holocaust* (New York: Vintage, 1997) is more controversial, but is worth reading. See also Robert Abzug, *Inside the Vicious Heart: Americans and the Liberation of Nazi Concentration Camps* (Oxford: Oxford University Press, 1987) and Richard Rhodes, *Masters of Death: The SS Einsatzgruppen and the Invention of the Holocaust* (New York: Knopf, 2002).

# 7

# WAR AND SOCIETY IN EUROPE, 1945–1989

## Reckoning with World War II

Shortly after V-E Day, Winston Churchill summed up the meaning of the end of the war in the eloquent manner to which millions of Europeans had become accustomed. His words reveal the ambivalence with which many Europeans looked at their future and therefore they deserve long quotation:

> I wish I could tell you that our toils and troubles were over. . . . On the continent of Europe we have yet to make sure that the simple and honorable purposes for which we entered the war are not brushed aside or overlooked in the months following our success, and that the words "freedom," "democracy," and "liberation" are not distorted from their true meaning as we have understood them. There would be little use in punishing the Hitlerites for their crimes if law and justice did not rule, and if totalitarian or police Governments were to take the place of the German invaders. . . . I told you hard things at the beginning of these last five years; you did not shirk, and I should be unworthy of your confidence and generosity if I still did not cry: Forward, unflinching, unswerving, indomitable, till the whole task is done and the whole world is safe and clean.[1]

Churchill had good reason for curbing his enthusiasm. Allied victory had destroyed Nazism, but it also had left the continent in almost as dangerous a state in 1945 as in 1939. The physical devastation alone was almost incomprehensible. The war left such a wake of destruction in its path that exact statistics are nearly impossible to calculate, even sixty years later. In 1945 Europe had to reckon with millions of dead, millions of refugees, an industrial infrastructure in ruins, and serious shortages of housing and food. Brian Bond's estimate of 11,000,000 refugees (called "displaced persons" in the official lexicon) seems a reasonable estimate, although even that figure may be too low.[2] Memories of the great influenza and typhus epidemics at the end of World War I were a haunting reminder of the consequences of such terrible conditions; those epidemics had killed more people than the combat of 1914–1918 had.

Economists, moreover, worried that without the massive government spending that had characterized the war years, the continent might revert back to pre-war depression depths. Victory on the battlefield notwithstanding, the world of 1945 posed tremendous challenges for European society.

Foremost among the challenges, the hatreds and suspicions that had created the unprecedented horrors of the twentieth century did not end with V-E Day. Anti-German sentiment remained (quite naturally) high across the continent. The post-war strength of the Russians also frightened many Americans and Europeans who had little desire to see German mastery of Europe replaced by Soviet hegemony. Furthermore, a shattered and humiliated France needed to be reconstituted, satisfactory boundaries for the states of eastern Europe fixed, and a role for the United States in European affairs determined. Peacemaking appeared to be an even more daunting task than it had been in 1919. The failure of the Versailles Treaty signed in that year was a reminder of how important the first year after the war would be in determining the future peace and stability of Europe.

To further complicate this process, many of the men who led Europe in war did not lead it in peace. The last major inter-Allied conference held at the Berlin suburb of Potsdam from July 17 to August 2, 1945 symbolized the change. The American contingent was led by the nation's new president, a relatively unknown Missouri senator and World War I artillery officer named Harry Truman. When he arrived at Potsdam, he had been president for just three months. Previous to the conference he had served as vice-president for only 87 days before Franklin Roosevelt's death. Roosevelt had not taken Truman into his confidence, and did not even inform him of the American development of an atomic bomb. The new president was inexperienced in European security problems, even though the United States had committed itself to playing a major role in post-war Europe. On the issue of the Soviets, however, the new president had a clear vision. Truman's attitude toward growing Soviet power was marked by much greater suspicion than his predecessor's had been. He was infuriated by Soviet treatment of eastern Europe, especially in Poland, where he believed that the Soviets had reneged on agreements made at Yalta.

Great Britain, too, had a new leadership. The end of the war meant a new round of British elections, the first since the war had begun. Nine days into the conference, Churchill's deputy prime minister Clement Attlee's Labor Party won a majority of seats in those elections. Atlee immediately replaced Churchill both as prime minister and as chief of the British delegation at Potsdam. Churchill, the great war leader, abruptly stepped aside. Attlee and Truman formed the core of Anglo-American leadership in the immediate post-war years. Attlee remained prime minister until 1951. Truman won reelection in 1948 and remained in office until replaced by former Allied Supreme Commander Dwight Eisenhower in 1953.

At Potsdam, the leaders agreed on the "removal of Germans from Poland, Czechoslovakia, and Hungary" and fixed the Polish borders. These steps merely confirmed realities on the ground as hundreds of thousands of German refugees had moved west to avoid the prospect of life under Soviet control. This mass migration meant that the elaborate ethnicity problems of Danzig (which took on the new Polish name of Gdansk) and the Polish Corridor that had plagued the interwar years would not reemerge. The German migration also allowed millions of ethnic Poles to leave Russian-controlled territory. National and state lines now overlapped more uniformly as Poland "slid to the west". Symbolically, even Hitler's famous Wolf's Lair command post at Rastenburg, in pre-war East Prussia, fell under Polish control in a city renamed Ketrzyn.[3]

Similar patterns existed across eastern and central Europe. An estimated 3,500,000 ethnic Germans left the reconstituted state of Czechoslovakia, most of them forcibly expelled. On a smaller scale, thousands of ethnic Slovaks left Hungary and thousands more ethnic Hungarians left Czechoslovakia. Polish officials opposed the mass return home of Jewish Holocaust survivors; many of them left for the United States or for the British Mandate of Palestine (which, in 1948, became the state of Israel). As a result of these patterns, within a few years of the end of the war, Poland, Czechoslovakia, and Hungary all had less than 5 percent of their populations constituted of ethnic minorities.[4] Ethnic boundaries in Eastern Europe stopped posing the massive social problems they once had. This readjustment has played a major, and heretofore not fully examined, role in maintaining peace in Europe since 1945.

With the borders of eastern and central Europe thus being adjusted, the societal reconstruction of the new Germany sat foremost on the agenda at Potsdam and in the minds of virtually all Europeans. Many plans developed, all with the central idea of preventing Germany from starting another continental war. Stalin wanted the Germans to pay reparations even harsher than those imposed after World War I. All of the powers agreed to occupation zones for the Soviet Union, Great Britain, France, and the United States in order to ensure the denazification of German society. At Soviet insistence, the powers agreed to impose their own reparations out of their individual spheres of occupation. American Secretary of the Treasury Henry Morgenthau had advanced a plan in 1944 to deindustrialize and demilitarize Germany. In its place, he envisioned the establishment of several agricultural states. Roosevelt and Churchill agreed to the plan at the Quebec Conference in September, 1944 but by the time of Potsdam Morgenthau's plan had little support.

Rebuilding Germany proved a daunting task. Few Europeans were willing to trust that German society could be pacified on its own. Nevertheless, the western powers did not envision a long-term and large-scale occupation both because of the high costs involved and because of the general desire to return to normalcy. Removing the Nazi elite therefore remained a primary part of the plan to rebuild German society. The United States, the Soviet Union, Great Britain, and France decided upon a series of international war tribunals stretching from November, 1945 to October, 1946 that tried twenty-two members of the Nazi regime's top leadership. Three officials were acquitted, seven received prison terms ranging from ten years to life, and twelve received death sentences. The latter category included military leaders such as Luftwaffe chief Hermann Göring, Head of German Armed Forces High Command (OKW) Wilhelm Keitel, and OKW Chief of Operations Alfred Jodl (a controversial West German court decision posthumously exonerated him of his crimes in 1953). Others condemned to death included Alfred Rosenberg, one of the chief architects of Nazi racial ideology; Julius Streicher, founder of the vehemently anti-Semitic newspaper *Der Stürmer*; and Martin Bormann, whose anti-Semitism and anti-clericalism had strongly influenced Hitler.

The Allies hoped that by conducting these trials they could purge Germany of its most pernicious influences. Churchill's reference to Hitlerites in the passage that began this chapter is indicative of this mentality. The trials also reinforced the rhetorical division between "Germans" and "Nazis." In effect, by blaming the highest officials of the latter, the reinstatement of the former into the community of European nations might be made easier. American General George Patton reflected these ideas when he told reporters that joining the Nazi party in the 1930s was essentially no different from an American joining the Republican or Democratic parties. By this logic, a thorough purge of German society would not be necessary. Remove the Nazis, the argument ran, and the Germans could again become good neighbors. Germany was, in this view, like a patient suffering from a curable disease. Once the doctors had removed the malignancy, the patient would be ready to return to a normal life.

This plan appealed to western leaders anxious to avoid an intensive and costly occupation. It also had enormous flaws, not least the implication that twenty-three men (including Hitler) were responsible for the crimes that had killed millions. The search for other German war criminals continued, often by organizations not directly connected to the Great Powers. In 1960, Israeli agents located and captured Adolph Eichmann, then living in a German immigrant community in Argentina. During the war, Eichmann had headed the German Race and Resettlement Office, which oversaw the implementation of the Final Solution. The agents smuggled him out of South America and brought him to Israel, where he was tried and executed. The same agents nearly captured the notorious chief medical officer from Auschwitz, Josef Mengele, who was also living in Argentina. His gruesome medical experiments on camp victims had made him a particularly sadistic and sought-after figure. After his narrow escape, he fled to Paraguay, where it is believed he died in 1979.

Similarly, Italy had imprisoned an SS officer, Herbert Kappler, whom an Italian court found guilty of the 1944 murder of 335 Romans in retaliation for a bomb that killed 23 German soldiers. In 1977 Kappler escaped from a military hospital, where he was being treated for cancer, to northern Germany. The West German government refused to extradite him to Italy, citing humanitarian and legal grounds; West Germany's constitution prohibited extradition, in part to protect Germans accused by foreigners of war crimes. A tense standoff ensued and rumors soon spread that an Italian hit squad had been sent to Kappler's home. Kappler supporters responded by detonating bombs outside the Italian embassy in Paris and at the scene of the massacre thirty-three years earlier. The impasse remained until Kappler succumbed to his cancer in 1978. The Kappler case served as a visible reminder of how easily old wounds could be reopened, even three decades later.

One of the most immediate problems centered upon the creation of a native German leadership that could be both reliable to the Allies and legitimate in the eyes of the German people. Finding effective German military and civilian leaders untainted by association with Nazism proved to be nearly impossible. Inevitably, some former Nazi party members had to be reincorporated into German society. Others deemed useful to the developing Cold War were protected by the Americans or the British. They included Wernher von Braun, the German rocketry expert whose research had been critical to the V-1 and V-2 programs. The Americans made him a naturalized citizen and allowed him to work for the United States government in the hopes that he could boost America's own ballistic missile program.

The Americans also protected Klaus Barbie, the notorious head of the Gestapo in Lyons. He had been personally responsible for the torture and death of Jean Moulin, the French Resistance's greatest hero. Despite French desires to try him, the Americans gave Barbie a job in counterintelligence and then helped him to relocate to Bolivia. In 1983 France extradited him and four years later sentenced him to life in prison. American officials claimed not to have known about the extent of his crimes.

Rebuilding France proved to be just as difficult as rebuilding Germany. French society at the end of the war remained deeply divided along several lines. The most obvious, but at the same time the most difficult to define, was the line between "resisters" and "collaborators." Finding efficient French officials not linked to either the German occupation or the Vichy government under Pétain proved to be a thorny problem. The imprisonment of the aged Pétain and the execution of henchmen such as Pierre Laval did not put the matter to rest. Collaboration, in one form or another, reached so deeply into French society that dealing with it after 1945 became a national "neurosis" that continues to impose itself on French self-identity.[5]

Facile attempts to blame the Nazis for all of France's wartime problems did little to make the problem go away. The anti-Semitic policies of Vichy had much more to do with French anti-Semitism than with its German counterpart. The crimes committed by Frenchmen against other Frenchmen further fractured historical memory of "Les Années Noires" (the dark years). The result was a grand "oublie" or national forgetfulness centered on an attempt to place the ambiguity of the war safely in the recesses of memory. A recent campaign to place posters around Paris commemorating de Gaulle, Moulin, and Philippe Leclerc reflected these tensions. Above photographs of the three men were the words "Ceux Qui Ont Dit 'Non'" (Those Who Said No). Exactly what they said no to (fascism, Vichy, Germany, collaborators, or crimes against humanity, to name just a few possibilities) remained up to the viewer.

As late as 1997 the war rudely intruded on French society once again. In that year a former French cabinet official, Maurice Papon, was arrested and tried on charges of having deported 1,560 Jews (including 223 children) from Bordeaux where he was alleged to have headed Vichy's Service for Jewish Questions. Unlike the German Gestapo agent Klaus Barbie, Papon was a Frenchman, and his case thus struck to the heart of the question of French culpability in German crimes. His connection to Vichy was a common one for French officials; even the reputation of long-time Socialist President François Mitterand was sullied by his early political links to Vichy. Papon's trial brought back to the surface all of the contradictions and shame of the war years. His ability to escape prosecution (and even to serve in French governments) for half a century only added to the anguish.

Papon's trial became one of the longest and most publicized in French history. The defendant argued that he had merely followed instructions from his superior, who was by then dead and unable to corroborate his testimony. The Nazi war crimes trials had already invalidated this defense so Papon switched tactics. He claimed to have had no knowledge of the death camps and therefore of the fate to which he sentenced the Bordeaux Jews when he turned them over to German officials. After almost six months of deliberations, Papon was found guilty and sentenced to ten years in prison. Then 87 years old, Papon's sentence was as good as a death sentence. Cases like these proved that the issues of collaboration and resistance could not be so easily and quickly discarded.

Collaboration was not the only problem with which French society had to reckon. Even France's resistance was deeply divided. Communists and socialists (including Moulin) had formed the core of many French Resistance cells. De Gaulle, however, loathed the communists and was determined to keep them out of a post-war French government. His doctrinaire anti-communism was one of the principal reasons that the United States and Britain supported him during and after the war. The communists, however, saw de Gaulle's rise to power as an example both of the nefarious behavior of western capitalist states and of the ability of the bourgeoisie to forget the workers' contributions and deny them access to political power. These tensions remained just under the surface of French society, and eventually exploded during the crisis of May 1968.

One other clear fault line existed, that between de Gaulle and his own armed forces. The majority of the new Fourth Republic's senior officers came neither from Resistance leaders nor from de Gaulle supporters, but from former military officials of the Vichy government. Generals Jean de Lattre de Tassigny and Alphonse Juin, both of whom later fought alongside the Allies, had originally sworn their allegiance to Pétain. Future French generals in the war in Algeria such as Jacques Massu, Maurice Challe, and Raoul Salan, had all been officers in the Vichy army. In their eyes de Gaulle had been disobedient in June, 1940 when he resisted what was then the legal government of France. They continued to look at de Gaulle after the war as "the most conspicuous example of the insubordinate officer whose bad example was abundantly rewarded." Given France's tortuous history of civil–military relations and its two "dirty wars" after 1945 in Indochina and Algeria (discussed later in this chapter), this division proved to be quite serious.[6]

The problems of eastern Europe were even more serious, as this region had fewer economic resources upon which to rebuild. These nations also had to contend with a Soviet colossus that had no intention of allowing unfriendly governments to take root. Having faced devastating western invasions in 1812, 1914, and 1941, Josef Stalin planned to protect the USSR by establishing a *cordon sanitaire* of states under the control of the Soviet Union. He also planned to exact the reparations to which he had been entitled as a result of the agreements made at Potsdam. As insurance, the Soviet Union kept 2,000 German POWs from World War II until hostilities between the two nations were formally ended in 1955, two years after Stalin's death.

Poland became an early example of Soviet intentions. In June, 1945 the Poles formed a government of national unity. Its name belied its structure and purpose. Sixteen of the twenty-one cabinet posts went to members of the pro-Soviet Lublin Committee. The new government soon revoked Polish citizenship from 75 Polish officers who remained in London as the core of a second Polish government in exile. Soviet officials initiated a brutal campaign of harassment and fraud prior to the elections of 1947. These elections yielded a highly improbable 80 percent majority for the communists. The results ousted the former head of the London Poles, Stanislaw Mikołajczyk, as deputy prime minister. He soon fled to London in fear for his life. When Churchill published his memoirs in 1953 he cited the inability of the Soviets and the western powers to settle the issue of Poland satisfactorily as one of the most serious consequences of the end of the war.

To western eyes, Poland's plight symbolized Soviet perfidy. Through the years of Soviet occupation, Poles maintained as much independence of thought and action as was possible under the circumstances. Poland had eastern Europe's highest rate of church attendance, indicating that doctrinaire Soviet atheism could not dent traditional Polish adherence to Roman Catholicism. The selection of a Polish cardinal to become Pope John Paul II in 1978 served as a symbol of Polish independence of thought, if not action. Polish drives for independence from the Soviets in 1956 and again in the 1980s seriously weakened Soviet control of eastern Europe.

Soviet occupation of eastern Europe held other immediate and far-reaching consequences. Throughout most of their area of control, the Soviets collectivized agriculture, thus ending an economic system that had been the backbone of the region for centuries. This policy removed the base of power for eastern Europe's social elites, most notably the Prussian Junkers, whose large estates were now under Soviet control. The Soviets replaced these old elites with Soviet satraps and bureaucrats. They also attempted to lessen the role of religion in the societies under their control and to cut off eastern European economies from the capitalist states of the west.

The Soviets were willing to commit to a much longer and larger physical occupation of eastern Europe than the British and the Americans were in western Europe. The USSR also continued to force reparations from the new nation of East Germany well into the 1950s. The result was further impoverishment of a region that had always been economically behind the states of the west. The Soviets did encourage the industrialization of some sectors of the eastern European economy, but these reforms were clearly state-guided and limited in their achievements.

Yugoslavia was one of the region's few states that escaped falling within the Soviet orbit. An April, 1945 treaty of friendship between Stalin and Tito established the latter as the leader of Yugoslavia. Tito, the dynamic former head of the anti-Nazi partisans, also had significant western support. He soon established a state based largely on Soviet models, but he resisted a Soviet occupation. Nevertheless, his new state faced crushing problems of its own. During the war the various competing nationalities of Yugoslavia had fought one another, making World War II as much a story of civil war as of war against Germany. The war resulted in the virtual elimination of Yugoslavia's Jewish, Turkish, and Roma minorities. Tito attempted to rally the remaining core nationalities of Yugoslavia behind loyalty to the state rather than to one's ethnicity. Himself a Croat, Tito established his government's capital in the Serbian city of Belgrade. As a result of Tito's firm leadership, the various internecine quarrels of the region remained largely muted until after Tito's death in 1980 (see the Conclusion).

The rapid establishment of different systems in Europe, one supported by the Soviets and one by the British and Americans, ended any chance for postwar cooperation between the erstwhile Allies. As early as February, 1946 Joseph Stalin had begun making speeches in which he predicted a future of irreconcilable conflict between the Soviets and the western capitalist states. In the same year, while at a small American college in Truman's home state of Missouri, Churchill delivered his famous "Iron Curtain" speech that rhetorically divided the continent between the free states of the west and the oppressed states of the east. Soon, each step in the long, tortuous process to rebuild Europe came to be seen not as the conclusion of World War II, but as the beginning of a developing conflict between the west and the east for control of Europe.

Before turning to the Cold War, however, it is important to look at a series of parallel wars. These wars involved the European powers in struggles against independence-minded native groups in colonial possessions from Angola to Indochina. Sometimes these struggles had associations with the Cold War, but more often than not their principal roots lay in the discredited system of imperialism and the efforts of European powers to maintain their empires. In the course of doing so, they inflicted great misery upon their former colonial subjects and, in one case, nearly brought their own nation to civil war.

## "The dirty wars" for empire

The end of warfare in Europe in 1945 did not mean the end of warfare for European society. Even before the year was over, European societies had to face the desires of peoples in European colonies across the globe to resist a return to the *status quo ante bellum*. The very same month that Japan surrendered unconditionally to the Allies, indigenous groups in the Dutch East Indies proclaimed the independence of the new nation of Indonesia. Between 1945 and 1974 virtually all of the major European powers that possessed overseas colonies had to decide whether to fight to retain their empires or to allow them to dissolve peacefully. In those cases where the European power chose war, it rarely saw gains commensurate with the financial and human expenditures. In the process, war came home to Europeans once again, with terrible human, economic, and political costs.

European colonialism had been based for decades upon the preeminence of the west's vastly superior military power. In the post-war world, that power was increasingly designed around large-scale conventional (and in some cases nuclear) forces to deter the Soviet Union. As the Europeans soon discovered, this emphasis proved to be less relevant to waging the kind of small unit guerrilla wars fought after 1945. The wars after 1945, therefore, shared more of the characteristics of Britain's frustrating Boer Wars than with the larger patterns of the two world wars. With the Soviet threat conditioning much of Western Europe's military procurement priorities, moreover, there was, in most cases, little funding available for counterinsurgency warfare.

Furthermore, the Europeans' principal ally, the United States, was in most cases opposed to the reestablishment of European colonialism. The Americans were, on principle at least, opposed to colonialism of all kinds; soon after the war the United States granted independence as promised to its only large pre-war colony, the Philippines. The tenet of "national self-determination," espoused by President Woodrow Wilson in his Fourteen Points and again at the Paris Peace Conference of 1919, had served as a source of inspiration to anti-imperialists the world over. The Americans, after all, had been among the very first peoples to distance themselves successfully from their European colonizer. In this vein, the United States threatened to cut off the flow of post-war aid to the Netherlands if the Dutch government did not make progress in negotiating a peaceful settlement with independence-minded groups in Indonesia. The United States also refused to support France's war in Algeria (1954–1962) and actively encouraged the peaceful resolution of conflicts in Kenya, Malaya, and elsewhere.

The American anti-imperial mindset was both idealistic and self-interested. American opposition to the concept of imperialism was genuine and a traditional part of American foreign policy, the experience of the Philippines notwithstanding. The Americans also did not want to see their European allies waste time, treasure, and lives on what they saw as an outdated quest for empire.

They preferred to see continental defense spending be focused instead on the developing Cold War because they believed that deterring the Russians was the most pressing European security issue. Reestablishing empire also meant re-establishing imperial trade preference policies, which the Americans opposed because it put their own economic goods at a severe disadvantage.

The lack of American interest in supporting these European wars for empire meant that they were fought outside the general pattern of twentieth-century alliance warfare. Many Europeans defended the efforts of their militaries with the argument that their indigenous enemies were communist-inspired. Although in some cases these contentions held a grain of truth, this argument did not gain sufficient support to allow states to define these wars in terms of a defensive anti-communist struggle. As a result, the use of NATO or UN assets was out of the question. The only exception to this pattern was the American-led war in Korea (1950–1953). There, the absence of a Soviet representative to the UN Security Council in 1950 (the USSR was then protesting the lack of a seat for the People's Republic of China) allowed the United States to create an alliance under the auspices of the United Nations. The Soviets, then boycotting the UN Security Council, could not block the creation of the alliance with their veto.

The one notable exception to the general lack of American support for European wars after 1945 was in French Indochina, known today as the nations of Laos, Cambodia, and Vietnam. Powerful native groups, led by a Vietnamese nationalist named Ho Chi Minh (a pseudonym meaning "he who enlightens"), were determined to resist the return of French colonial rule to the region. Ho had attempted to represent the Vietnamese people at the Paris Peace Conference of 1919, but had been turned away. He later turned to Leninism and Marxism as guiding influences. These ideologies, too, were anti-imperial, albeit for differ-ent reasons from those of Woodrow Wilson and the Americans.

Ho Chi Minh's connections to communism led the Americans to support the French war in Indochina. Thus Vietnam became an exception to American unwillingness to help Europeans regain their colonial holdings. In reality, Vietnam, like most other anti-colonial struggles, was more a nationalist war than a communist war. Ho Chi Minh had initially sought (and received) American support, but he had later turned to China and the Soviet Union when American intentions to support the French became clear. His communism was therefore a nationalist vehicle through which he hoped to remove first the French then the Americans from his native soil.

Many Asians had also been influenced by the ease with which the Japanese, an Asian power, had humbled the Europeans, most notably the French in Indochina and the British in Malaya and Singapore. Although most Asians later came to distrust the Japanese as much as they had the Europeans, the humilia-tion of the latter at the hands of the former proved to be profound. This loss of prestige played an enormous role in undermining the civilizing justification that colonizing powers had used to support their rule. The experiences of World

War II in Asia shattered the illusion of Europeans as naturally superior. "The white man," Ho said in 1945, "is finished in Asia."

Partially because of that very humiliation in World War II, France looked to reestablish its colonial empire. Doing so would both quickly return France to the status of first-class world power and help to rebuild the shattered French economy. Initially the French, like the Dutch in Indonesia, had the support of the British. Britain saw most clearly that the age of empires was over; as early as 1931 the British had restructured the empire into a Commonwealth of relative equals. They did not commit large military resources to maintaining India by force and were careful to apply military force only in conjunction with social and political reforms to assist friendly regimes in Malaya and Kenya. Still, the British believed that the return of European rule, envisioned as a temporary expedient, would provide for a stable transition from empires to the establishment of independent successor states.

France, on the other hand, saw the reestablishment of its empires as central to its post-war fate. Nevertheless, the war in Indochina did not return the French nation to glory. From 1947 to 1954 the French army fought an opponent so skilled and determined that any long-term French possession of the colony was impossible. The costs of the war mounted until France spent more money on the fighting in Indochina than they received in Marshall Plan aid. At the height of the war, France had more than 150,000 men in Indochina. This situation was sustainable for seven years only because the Americans, seeing Ho Chi Minh as a communist agent, funded an increasing share of the war. But American money could not win the war alone. France had to remain in a state of military mobilization to meet the needs of self-defense and prosecute the war in Indochina. Alone among the western great powers, France had as large an army in 1957 as it had had in 1945 (1.2 million men).[7]

Moreover, the war grew increasingly unpopular at home. That unpopularity made the dispatch of conscripts to Indochina politically unfeasible and militarily unreliable. Instead, the French used colonial troops and enlisted dislocated Europeans in the Foreign Legion to fight a war that many Frenchmen would not. More disturbingly, the military showed signs of disdain toward government efforts to resolve the problem in Indochina peacefully. Badly wounded by the humiliation of 1940–1945, the French army had placed a symbolic importance on Indochina far out of proportion to the colony's economic, political, or military importance. This military emphasis stood in marked contrast to the desires on the part of most Frenchmen to end the war, even if it meant losing the colonies of Indochina.

The Indochinese situation came to a head in 1954 at the French base of Dien Bien Phu in northwestern Vietnam. The Americans, ironically given their own future war in Vietnam, refused to intervene militarily, leaving the French forces isolated. The military defeat of the French garrison at Dien Bien Phu in July coincided with a conference held at Geneva, Switzerland and a new round of French elections. From 1947 to 1954, France suffered 90,000 casualties in Indochina, a figure no doubt smaller than the casualties suffered by the Indochinese themselves, but far greater that the price than French society was prepared to pay. The new French Prime Minister, Pierre Mendès-France, agreed to withdraw French forces from Indochina and to temporarily divide Vietnam into two nations at the 17th parallel. The French phase of the war in Indochina was ending and the American phase was beginning.

The agreement might have given France a period of peace, but soon afterwards events in Algeria conspired to keep war at the forefront of European society. Just six months after the fall of Dien Bien Phu, a group representing the National Liberation Front of Algeria (FLN) attacked French military and police units across the colony. The incident was the start of a nasty, unpopular war in Algeria from 1954 to 1962. All told, it meant that France hardly knew a complete month of peace from May, 1940 until July, 1962.

France was already war weary from the experience of 1940–1945 and then from the war in Indochina. Nevertheless, France believed that it could not back down in Algeria. Unlike Indochina, Algeria was a fully constituted part of France, complete with voting representation in the French parliament. French influence had penetrated so deeply into Algerian society that, despite its Muslim majority, Algeria was the world's largest producer of wine. To most Frenchmen, Algeria was as much a part of France as Provence or Normandy, and Algiers as much a French city as Nice or Toulon. Moreover, Algeria had a large population of Europeans who had settled there over the decades and who considered themselves both French and Algerian. Most of the so-called *pieds noirs* saw no distinction between the two identities. The *pieds noirs* community, although poor, included such French luminaries as the writer Albert Camus, whose most famous work, *The Stranger,* was set in Algeria. Even Pierre Mendès-France, who had ended France's war in Indochina, argued for military action in Algeria on the grounds that Algeria *was* France.

The French war in Algeria, then, was destined to be fundamentally different in character from that just concluded in Indochina. Because of the physical proximity and intimate links between Algeria and French society, the French deployed considerable military resources to the war against the FLN. Unlike Indochina, the French did deploy conscripts to Algeria. At the height of operations there, the French army had 500,000 men stationed in Algeria. At first most Frenchmen saw the war as necessary to protect the *pieds noirs* and French economic interests in Algeria. But the 1956 assassination of the mayor of Algiers by FLN agents radically changed the tenor of the war. French army units and the FLN soon engaged in a mutual war of atrocity characterized by a spiraling exchange of reprisals. The French army, believing itself fighting barbarians, soon turned to torture as a routine instrument of intelligence gathering and intimidation.

The degradation of the war in Algeria, and the army's rather boastful attitude toward its brutality, rapidly undermined popular support for the war. The army itself soon intruded uncomfortably into politics, seizing a plane carrying the

FLN leader Ben Bella without government approval. The government's inability to contain the war, or their own generals, led to a succession of ministerial changes and threats to the viability of the Fourth Republic itself. In May, 1958, arguing that the French government was not giving the army enough resources to win the war, General Raoul Salan, with wide *pied noir* support, declared the creation of a Committee of Public Safety, demanded the resignation of Prime Minister Pierre Pflimlin (who favored negotiations with the FLN aimed at giving Algeria self-determination within the French Union), and took political control in Algiers.

Salan's insubordinate behavior posed a direct and serious challenge to the authority of the French government. Salan was no ordinary officer. A loyal republican before 1958, he had once been the youngest general in France and became an important aide to Indochina commander Marshal Jean de Lattre de Tassigny. In 1952, Salan became commander-in-chief of French forces there. Still, his Indochina experience left him bitter at the French government and increasingly concerned about the honor of the army. Many Frenchmen began to fear that Salan was planning a much more ambitious takeover. Rumors soon spread that his elite paratroopers were planning a landing in mainland France evocative of Francisco Franco's *coup de main* from Morocco against the Spanish government in 1936.

To resolve the crisis, France turned again to Charles de Gaulle. Fearful of a coup from its own army, the French National Assembly dissolved the Fourth Republic in June, 1958 and gave de Gaulle a grant of special powers to govern for six months. He replaced Salan with Air Force General Maurice Challe, who had once been responsible for providing Eisenhower's staff with a complete copy of the German order of battle at the time of the D-Day landings. He soon turned the military tide in Algeria with mobile commando units, air support, and paratroopers. Challe believed that he had established the foundation upon which France could destroy the FLN, pacify Algeria, and win the war.

De Gaulle, however, saw the situation differently. To him, Algeria was one issue, and not even the most important issue, facing France. When his six months of special powers expired, France would need a new constitution and a more stable system for dealing with crises. In order to resolve the most pressing crisis, de Gaulle opened up negotiations with FLN in 1960, infuriating the French officers who believed that by doing so de Gaulle was rendering mean-ingless the sacrifice of those Frenchmen who had died in Algeria. The *pieds noirs* soon formed their own paramilitary organization, the OAS, which reacted to de Gaulle's negotiations with strikes and a wave of deadly terrorist incidents in Algeria and in France itself. The OAS and disloyal officers of the French army hatched at least four plots to assassinate de Gaulle, a remarkable demonstration of the tensions that Algeria caused.

An even more serious situation arose in April, 1961 when Salan, Challe, and others attempted to seize the government in Algiers. They believed that the government in Paris was dooming Algeria and the *pieds noirs* to a future of terror if the FLN took control of part or all of the Algerian government. They were also unable to face the prospect of yet another humiliating French defeat. Civil war seemed to be a genuine possibility. That France did not descend that deeply was in large part because the revolt failed to generate support from the mass of the French army in Algeria, most of whom were conscripts who had much greater affection for the government than for the generals. Nevertheless, more than 14,000 officers and men were implicated in the plot. Challe made a last stand in front of a crowd in Algiers, but, symbolically, his microphone failed and the crowd did not rally to him. He gave himself up and, like Salan, was imprisoned. Both men received life sentences, but were given amnesties in 1968.

After the plot, public discontent with the war and attendant behavior by the army soared. Referenda in Algeria showed that 75 percent of Algerians favored independence, although the vast majority of *pieds noirs* did not. Still, it was obvious that France could not keep up the fight. Opinion polls in France itself showed three in four Frenchmen wanted to grant Algeria independence and remove all French troops. In the summer of 1962 the OAS and FLN agreed to a cease fire. One month later Algeria declared its independence from France. Almost one million *pieds noirs* left Algeria and came to France.

France's experience with wars of national liberation was by far the most violent among the nations of western Europe, but it was not the only one. Portugal, a relatively poor nation by western European standards, decided to fight to retain its sub-Saharan African colony in Angola and to protect the 330,000 Portuguese who had migrated there. From 1961 to 1974 the Portuguese fought a repressive war similar in broad outline to those fought by France in Indochina and Algeria. The Portuguese, in possession of western weaponry, inflicted severe casualties on the forces of the Frente Nacional de Libertação de Angola (FNLA). Despite the FLNA's links to the Soviet Union and Communist China, the Portuguese did not receive substantial aid from the United States. The Americans did not wish to create another potential military crisis while their war in Vietnam remained ongoing.

Even without American support, Portuguese military units largely succeeded in breaking up guerrilla units and turning the tide of the war in their favor. Battlefield success notwithstanding, the thirteen-year war placed tremendous strains on Portuguese society, which was then also fighting a less intense war in Mozambique (1962–1974). At its height, the small nation of just 9,000,000 people had 150,000 troops deployed to Africa and was spending 40 percent of its annual budget on defense. Both of these figures were proportionately higher than the equivalent figures for America's war in Vietnam, fought at roughly the same time. Despite having suffered 11,000 casualties in Africa, by 1974 the Portuguese military had virtually succeeded in destroying the military power of the FLNA and the two other main Angolan guerrilla groups. They had also made significant progress in Mozambique.

Still, the wars were unpopular both inside and outside the military. More importantly, they were not producing any obvious benefits to Portuguese society commensurate with the costs. In 1974, a general and former African colonial governor, António de Spínola, overthrew the Portuguese government in a coup. His action was reminiscent of the political crisis in Algeria in 1961, except that his actions succeeded in seizing power. Once in office, he responded to the army's dissatisfaction with pacification efforts in Africa and ended the costly and divisive wars there. Later, he even used the army to suppress rioting by Angola's white settlers. He then withdrew the Portuguese military from Africa and opened the way for Angola and Mozambique to become independent nations, although Angola continues to be extremely unstable.

The Spínola coup underscored the dangers that militaries posed to the very societies they served. Rumors in France in the mid-1970s suggested that the army might rebel against the "first prospect of a Socialist/Communist dominated government," though in the end the military stayed loyal when the socialist François Mitterand became president in 1981.[8] Also in 1981 the Spanish army staged its own coup, temporarily seizing the Spanish parliament and holding hostage 350 legislators and the entire cabinet. Only the personal intervention of King Juan Carlos, who appealed to generals not to support the coup, saved the government. The following year the King had to act again to foil a second coup attempt.

The combination of the frustrating conclusions of the wars for empire and the political meddling of European militaries into civilian affairs combined, by the 1980s, to greatly reduce the prestige and status of armed forces in the eyes of most European citizens. Britain's less overtly political military establishment and its successful and popular Falkland Islands War against Argentina in 1982 made it an exception to this pattern, although its own frustrations in Northern Ireland created tensions. But the "dirty wars" in Africa and Asia were only part of the story. European militaries and societies had to deal as well with the developing struggle of ideologies known as the Cold War. In this conflict they were, at various moments, both active participants and spectators.

## The Cold War and European society

The Cold War was unique in the history of European warfare in two ways. First, and most obviously, the two sides did not actually go to war. Instead, the American-led NATO alliance (created in 1949) and the Soviet-led Warsaw Pact (created in 1955) fought one another through non-military and indirect means. Most notably, the two sides paid, trained, and supported forces throughout the world that were friendly to their own ideology and hostile to that of their opponents. In this way, the Cold War fueled conflicts in Asia, Africa, Latin America, and the Middle East. On the European continent itself, both sides built massive nuclear and conventional forces, but never used them. The Cold War's economic, political, social, and cultural impacts, however, radically changed the face of European society.

Second, the Cold War reduced many of the traditional powers of Europe to the ranks of second-string players. This pattern was most obvious in the cases of France, Germany, and Italy. Great Britain emerged as a relatively strong military power, but much of that power derived from continuing close association with the United States. In eastern Europe, the nations of the Warsaw Pact surrendered much more autonomy to the Soviet Union than did the NATO nations to the United States, but in almost all cases, the nations of Europe had ceased to be masters of their own military fates. This state of affairs was the natural consequence of half a century of warfare, but it came as a great psychological blow to many Europeans nevertheless.

Each nation reacted differently to this dilemma. Some, like Britain, largely accepted the new world order in return for such benefits as increased security through NATO. By virtue of having established a close working relationship with the Americans during World War II, the British were able to retain and build upon that relationship. They became a crucial part of the NATO command structure and maintained their role as the United States' most important ally.

The closeness between the "cousins" also led Britain to become the largest single beneficiary of one of the Cold War's first economic policies, the Marshall Plan. Named for General George C. Marshall, the former American Chief of Staff during World War II, the plan dispensed $13.7 billion of aid (approximately $130 billion in today's dollars) to fifteen western European nations from 1948 to 1952. Marshall, acting as President Harry Truman's secretary of state, devised the program to help rebuild the shattered economies of Europe. His ideas derived from essential American altruism; he won *Time* magazine's Man of the Year Award (his second) and the Nobel Peace Prize for his efforts. The Marshall Plan also had a political dimension, as Marshall feared that hunger and economic dislocation would prove fertile ground for communist expansion as it had after World War I. By rebuilding European economies, he hoped, Europe could move forward into a stable, democratic, and pro-American future.

Great Britain, the largest recipient of wartime Lend-Lease aid, also became the leading recipient of post-war aid. France, Italy, West Germany, and Holland each received more than $1 billion in aid. The Marshall Plan achieved its aim of relieving much of the immediate suffering of Europe, but it quickly forced nations to choose sides in the brewing American–Soviet rivalry. The United States offered aid to the nations of eastern Europe, but the Soviets heavily pressured them not to accept it. Czechoslovakia's foreign minister, Jan Masaryk, went to Moscow to try to convince the Russians to allow his nation to accept desperately needed Marshall Plan aid, but soon learned that he could not escape the Russian noose being drawn around eastern Europe. "I went to Moscow [he said in June, 1947] as the foreign minister of an independent, sovereign state; I returned as a Soviet slave."[9]

The Russians suspected (correctly) that the Marshall Plan was part of a long-term American plan to induce the states of eastern Europe to accept capitalism and democracy. The Soviets therefore saw the plan as a hostile American act that needed to be resisted. The plan also envisioned a restructured and rebuilt West Germany as an integral part of a new European economy, an idea that the Soviets found repugnant. The USSR therefore ordered client states and Communist Party cells in France and Italy to reject participation in the program. Soviet pressure had little bearing in the west, but it condemned the east to decades of economic stagnation and continued backwardness.

Even supporters of the Marshall Plan in the west understood that by accepting American aid, the nations of western Europe would find themselves being drawn ever more deeply into the American orbit. The American dollar soon became an important common currency on the continent, and the Americans encouraged Europeans to spend much of the aid money with American firms. Wartime damage to European industry and agriculture was so extensive that many products were simply unavailable in Europe and had to be purchased in the United States in any case. American aid was also a reflection of a desire to create stable, democratic political structures. Italy did not receive aid until post-war elections returned a massive Christian Democratic majority and aid to France was temporarily suspended on one occasion because of American fears of political unrest.

Dependence on the new superpowers was further enhanced by the desires of the Americans and Soviets to maintain a visible, powerful presence in European affairs. For the Soviets, this presence would provide them with a buffer zone in the event of another invasion from the west. Control of the governments in eastern Europe further assured the Soviets that the militaries of the region would not be used in joint operations aimed at them as Romania and Hungary had been in World War II. Stalin and his close associates were determined to maintain as strict a control over bordering states as possible. Lacking the economic and political leverage of the United States, the Soviets had to turn to their military and an occupation of the eastern European states.

For the Americans, the defense of Europe took on a critical importance as well. American officials were unwilling to allow a Soviet domination of Europe to replace the recently deposed Nazi one. Having fought so long and hard to liberate the continent, the American government did not wish to abandon it to aggressive Soviet expansion. As opposed to the common American mood in 1919, the American people generally supported a large post-war presence in Europe. The Americans, therefore, did not retreat back across the Atlantic Ocean in 1945. Instead, they retained a major presence through their zones of occupation in Germany and Austria and through the numerous World War II bases that remained open and operating in the post-war world.

Two events further solidified the American desire to maintain a military presence in Europe. The first was the Soviet Union's decision to close the Allied sector of Berlin to rail and road traffic in 1948. This decision isolated Germany's capital city, divided into Allied and Soviet zones, deep inside East Germany. The Americans and British responded with Operation Vittles, a series of airlift flights over the Soviet zone of occupation to West Berlin. By the end of the year, the operation succeeded in flying in 4,500 tons of food and fuel to the beleaguered city every day. On Easter Sunday, 1949, the Allies flew 1,398 flights and brought in a record 13,000 tons of supplies. That spring, as the NATO charter was drafted and signed, the Soviets lifted the Berlin blockade, thus allowing overland convoys to return to the city.

The Berlin Airlift demonstrated how much European society had changed in the four years since the end of World War II. The very same American and British pilots and planes that had once dropped bombs on a hostile Germany in order to aid the Soviet war effort were now risking war with the Soviets in order to feed the population of West Berlin. The residents of the city, recently the targets of the Grand Alliance's military forces, were now depicted in the west as the heroic resisters of the evil Soviet state. The common thread in this ironic situation was the American and British desire to prevent one single European power (first Germany, then the USSR) from dominating the continent. In this way, the Cold War was consistent with British policy dating back at least to the Napoleonic Wars, if not earlier. American participation, however, was novel and fundamentally changed the nature and definition of European security arrangements.

The second event, oddly enough, occurred far from both Europe and the United States. The North Korean invasion of South Korea in 1950 seemingly reinforced the dominant American belief that communism was international and monolithic. A communist intervention anywhere in the world, therefore, must have ties to China (communist-controlled since 1949) and Moscow. Using this logic, the Americans developed a policy of containing communism. In 1947 President Truman had issued his Truman Doctrine, which pledged assistance to any nation "resisting attempted subjugation by . . . outside pressures," an obvious reference to the USSR. Initially Truman used the Doctrine to support anti-communist governments in Turkey and Greece, but the Doctrine's language opened up the possibility of much wider application.

Partly in order to give some force to the Truman Doctrine, the Americans spearheaded the creation of a peacetime alliance, the North Atlantic Treaty Organization, formed in 1949. A popular witticism held that the alliance's purpose for western Europe was to keep the Americans in, the Germans down, and the Russians out. While the joke had some validity, NATO was really an expression of the dominance of the idea of collective security and joint military operations that had been developing since at least 1914. In this case, the alliance system had evolved from an instrument of war, as it had been in the two world wars, to an instrument of deterrence. The NATO charter specified that an attack on one member state would constitute an attack on them all.[10] The obvious implication was that any Russian incursion into western Europe would provoke an American declaration of war.

By the time of the Korean crisis in 1950 the Americans already had a plan in place for a massive buildup of military force in Europe under NATO auspices.

In April of that year, the National Security Council presented Truman with Memorandum Number 68 (better known as NSC 68), which proposed a much greater military role for the United States in Europe. Given American assumptions about global communism, the North Korean incursion into South Korea in June appeared (erroneously) to be one step in a Soviet-led struggle for world mastery. As a result, the United States intervened in Korea and followed the goals of NSC 68. During the years of the Korean War (1950–1953) the Americans built up large forces in Europe, adding 285,000 men to American forces on the continent even as they were fighting a war in Asia.

European reactions to this American buildup were mixed. While many Europeans were grateful for the protection and deterrence value that the American forces provided, the increased American presence and differing views on how best to protect and defend western Europe caused tensions within European society. To cite one example, the United States supported a rearmed West Germany as a vital part of NATO. Anti-German sentiment in Europe remained quite high, especially in France and the Low Countries. The American plan to rebuild West German armed forces, and even place Wehrmacht officers in NATO commands, therefore met with considerable resistance. The Europeans also fell noticeably short of their agreement at Lisbon in 1952 to boost their own conventional forces to match the American buildup resulting from NSC 68.

These shortcomings revealed themselves in the joint French–British–Israeli operation in the Suez in 1956. Because of a relative lack of attention to military modernization in the years since World War II, the British and French had difficulty developing efficient plans and executing operations. They therefore failed to achieve their goals of seizing the Canal Zone and enacting regime change in Egypt. The Suez operation revealed important flaws in the equipment, doctrine, and tactics of French and British military forces. The contrast for Britain, only a decade before one of the world's most powerful militaries, was especially striking. The sight of Danish and Norwegian UN peacekeepers taking over from British and French positions symbolized the changing fortunes of the fighting prowess of two of Europe's traditional great powers.[11]

Nor did Britain and France receive much help from the Americans. The United States saw the Egyptian crisis as relatively minor in the face of the larger Cold War and was therefore anxious to maintain some level of control over the foreign policy of its European allies. They feared that a relatively minor incident could spark the general war with the Soviets that American forces were designed to deter. The Americans thus reacted angrily to Britain and France's cooperation with the Israelis to invade Egypt in 1956. The Americans had not been consulted in advance and saw the operation as an outdated expression of European imperialism. They were also concerned about the possible repercussions of western powers humiliating Egypt, which had close relations to the Soviet Union. The Americans placed tremendous political and financial pressure on the British and French to abandon the operation, much to the latter's anger.

172

The United States also saw the French and British focus on Suez as a distraction to a developing situation in Hungary that the Americans viewed as much more important than Suez. Hungary had taken the bold and courageous step of declaring its neutrality in the Cold War and repudiating the Warsaw Pact. The Soviets had reacted to a similar demonstration in Poland with troops and tanks, killing dozens. In Hungary, they deployed a massive force of fifteen army divisions and 4,000 tanks. Over the two weeks of fighting more than 3,000 Hungarians were killed and as many as 200,000 Hungarians fled into Austria. Although the Hungarians had sought western support, the Americans decided not to risk a confrontation with the Soviets. Instead, they stayed true to their doctrine of containing communism where it then existed. They also chose not to respond with force to a Soviet incursion by 500,000 troops into Czechoslovakia in 1968. Even had they chosen to diverge from the policy of containment, it is unlikely that the Americans, distracted as they were by their own war in Vietnam and social unrest at home, could have noticeably altered the situation.

The power of the United States and the Soviet Union underscored the decline in the fortunes of nations like France and (West) Germany. As a result, the rivalry between these two nations, which had played such a dominant role in guiding the fortunes of the continent for decades, quickly abated. The two nations were now together in the same military alliance and, through organizations such as the European Coal and Steel Community (formed in 1951), shared close economic ties as well. Throughout the 1950s relations between France and West Germany steadily improved as economic, political, and cultural ties increased.

In 1958, West German Chancellor Konrad Adenauer visited Charles de Gaulle at the latter's private country home. The two men soon developed an important personal friendship that helped to guide Franco-German reconciliation. In 1963, de Gaulle and Adenauer signed a treaty of friendship known as the Elysée Treaty. France and West Germany agreed to consult one another regularly on questions of foreign policy and to hold biannual meetings on a variety of international and domestic questions. Later that year the two leaders made a symbolic joint appearance at the massive cemetery at Verdun. In that ceremony, the two nations symbolically buried the hatchet between them and pledged to work together to resolve future European disputes.

For de Gaulle, warm relations with West Germany were part of a plan to distance France from what he saw as a hegemonic United States, and a Great Britain that was too fully dependent on American aid. Cooperation with West Germany was thus the bedrock on which he hoped to create an independent Europe. France also took steps to disengage from NATO, pulling its troops out of the alliance's command structure and demanding the removal of American forces stationed in France. Both of these steps were completed by 1966. The French developed their own nuclear *force de frappe* (strike force) independent of the NATO alliance and potentially aimed, as de Gaulle rather indelicately put it, "to all points of the compass."

Warmer relations with France allowed West Germany to undertake an initiative of its own, called Ostpolitik. In 1970 West Germany signed a non-aggression treaty with the Soviet Union and a similar agreement with Poland. The agreements together recognized the borders of eastern Europe as fixed, although West German Chancellor Willy Brandt still hoped for the eventual reunification of West and East Germany. In 1972 the two German states normalized relations and agreed on a method to allow limited travel between East and West Berlin. Two years later the discovery of an East German agent in Brandt's inner circle forced the Chancellor's resignation and put an end to his Ostpolitik policies. Still, the initiative demonstrated the ability of European states to pursue their own agendas within the framework of the Cold War.

On a broader level, the Cold War stood in contrast to the developing commercialism and economic growth of western European and American society. In what the French called the "Thirty Glorious Years" from the mid-1940s to the mid-1970s, standards of living rose sharply even amid fears of nuclear war. The specter of the Cold War seemed to many Europeans an unwelcome intruder during a pattern of general economic prosperity. The maintenance of conscription in most European states brought the burden of military service to young Europeans and Americans in peacetime, furthering the interruption of life courses and removing young men from school or the beginnings of their working careers.

As a new generation of Europeans came of age in the 1960s and 1970s, the Americans appeared to be a less attractive model than they had been in the 1950s. The Vietnam War, the Watergate scandal, and American racial violence undermined the moral high ground upon which the Americans had built their justification for global leadership. An American initiative to deploy neutron bombs and, later, Pershing II missiles on European soil in the 1970s and 1980s furthered these tensions. The missile deployments were designed to protect Europe from the new Soviet SS-20 intermediate range missiles introduced the previous year. To many Europeans, however, the Pershing II deployments represented not security, but a dangerous proliferation of first-strike weapons. Mass demonstrations across the continent opposed the American plan even though it had the support of most European governments. The later deployment of Tomahawk cruise missiles prompted similar demonstrations.

Although few saw it at the time, events in the late 1970s and early 1980s seriously undermined the superpower system and led to several direct challenges to it. The humiliating seizure of American hostages in the Iranian capital of Tehran in 1979 undermined the image of American power. The frustrating and inconclusive Soviet invasion of Afghanistan the following year produced a similarly weakened global image for the USSR. A strike by Polish dock workers in Gdansk took advantage of Soviet preoccupations in central Asia and placed Poland again in the forefront of European affairs. Led by the charismatic labor organizer Lech Walesa, the Solidarity movement soon grew to 10,000,000 members and became both a trade union and a center of anti-Soviet activity. A vigorous Soviet and Polish effort to destroy the movement sent it underground but could not diminish its stature and its influence.

In the early 1980s, American President Ronald Reagan supported a massive increase in both American defense spending and in American military presence worldwide, most notably in western Europe. Reagan envisioned assuming the defense of western Europe under American protection. This decision seemed to many Europeans to further both the marginalization and militarization of the continent. The implementation of these ideas sparked a new round of anti-Cold War protests, some of them distinctly anti-American in character. Popular culture also reflected a weariness with the Cold War and its fundamental assumptions. In 1985, British pop music superstar Sting released one of the best-known examples of this new attitude, his song "Russians," noting that "the Russians love their children too."[12] An anti-war song by the West German band Nena entitled "99 Luftballons" became a major hit on both sides of the Atlantic in 1984.

Also in the mid-1980s, Mikhail Gorbachev assumed control of the Soviet Union. His rise to power marked a dramatic change in Soviet attitudes. He promoted policies of *glasnost* (openness) and *perestroika* (reconstruction) to allow the USSR to reduce defense expenses and focus on the enormous domestic problems faced by Soviet society. He quickly developed close working relationships with British Prime Minister Margaret Thatcher and, more improbably, Reagan. In 1986 Reagan and Gorbachev met at Reykjavik, Iceland and preliminarily agreed to massive cuts in the two sides' nuclear arsenals. Gorbachev even proposed that both sides agree to decommission all of their nuclear weapons within fifteen years. Although the summit failed to produce the broad agreement that many had predicted, it was a critical watershed. Reagan made an historic visit to Moscow in 1988. When asked if he still held to his famous statement that the Soviet Union was an "evil empire," the old Cold Warrior answered, "No. . . . I was talking about another time and another era."[13]

Perhaps most importantly, Gorbachev's rule meant a much more lenient Soviet presence in eastern Europe and massive changes inside the Soviet Union itself. At the end of 1988 Gorbachev told the United Nations that he envisioned large-scale Soviet troop withdrawals from eastern Europe and the eventual end of the Warsaw Pact. Across Europe, people began to take matters into their own hands. In Hungary, border guards cut down the barbed wire that separated Hungary from neighboring Austria, opening an important pathway to the west that had been sealed since 1956. Shortly thereafter, Soviet troops completed a peaceful withdrawal from Hungary and Poland held its first free elections.

These activities signaled massive changes, but no one predicted what came next. Motivated by an East German government announcement that it would grant passes to any East German wanting to visit the west, crowds began to gather near the very symbol of the Cold War, the Berlin Wall. West Berliners came to the wall, too, to cheer on their East German counterparts and encourage total strangers to come to the west with or without a government pass.

175

Soon people on both sides brought out hammers and chisels and began to chip away at the monstrous, ugly barrier. Incredibly, the East German police did nothing to stop them. Mass demonstrations broke out spontaneously all across eastern Europe. Repressive governments such as that of Romania's Nicolae Ceausescu soon fell under the weight of popular activity.

The Cold War was over. With it came a spontaneous outpouring of emotion that led many Europeans to predict an unbridled future of economic prosperity without militarism. But human history, especially European history, is not so pliable. Even as the celebrations continued, the breakdown of the superpower system was planting the seeds for the next round of conflict.

## Further reading

On guerrilla warfare generally see Edward E. Rice, *Wars of the Third Kind: Conflict in Underdeveloped Countries* (Berkeley: University of California Press, 1988) and John Shy and Thomas W. Collier, "Revolutionary War," in Peter Paret, ed., *Makers of Modern Strategy from Machiavelli to the Nuclear Age* (Princeton: Princeton University Press, 1986). For individual wars of independence, see Alistair Horne's *A Savage War of Peace* (London: Macmillan, 1977) on Algeria and, although it has some factual errors, Bernard Fall, *Street Without Joy* (New York: Schocken, 1972) on France's war in Indochina. Anthony Clayton's work, notably *The Wars of French Decolonization* (London: Longman, 1994) and *Frontiersmen: Warfare in Africa Since 1950* (London: UCL Press, 1999), are also valuable.

Henry Rousso, *The Vichy Syndrome: History and Memory in France since 1944* translated by Arthur Goldhammer (Cambridge: Harvard University Press, 1991) is indispensable on French reactions to World War II. On the Cold War see Jeremy Isaacs and Taylor Downing, *Cold War: An Illustrated History, 1945-1991* (New York: Little, Brown, 1998), a companion to a Cable News Network series and Walter LaFeber, *America, Russia, and the Cold War, 1945-1992* (New York: McGraw Hill, 1993), now in its seventh edition.

# CONCLUSIONS

The end of the Cold War in 1989 produced two monumental changes in the nature of European defense and security arrangements. First, and most obviously, the enormous military power of the Soviet Union was gone. With a rapidity that seems all the more remarkable in retrospect, the Soviet/Bolshevik menace that had influenced European history for more than 75 years had disappeared. In the years immediately following the end of the Cold War, Russia turned much of its focus away from defense and toward its massive domestic problems. Events in the 1990s, most notably a war in the breakaway republic of Chechnya (1994–1996) also distracted Russian attention. As a result, Russia played a much reduced role in the defense plans of European states. The absence of a Russian threat truly revolutionized the nature of European politics and defense. Expenditures on defense dropped dramatically and many European states ended conscription.

The second change emerged naturally from the first but had much more ambiguous consequences. The United States remained a superpower, but now had no rival to contain. Put another way, mostly by people suspicious of American motives, there was no longer any power capable of containing the United States. In the initial hopes for a post-Cold War peace dividend, American defense expenditures dropped, although never as sharply as those in Europe. Even with reduced military budgets, however, the American military system's staff work, technology, and support infrastructure had no rival. By the mid-1990s, American defense expenditures were again on the rise. Most European states did not follow suit.

As a consequence of these changes, the bipolar system of the Cold War had become a unipolar system dominated by the United States, now the world's only superpower. These transformations seemed on the surface to promise a more peaceful continent, as Europe would no longer be a potential battleground of NATO and Warsaw Pact forces. With the end of the Cold War, many hoped that peripheral conflicts such as Vietnam and Afghanistan would end as well.

Predicting exactly what the new world might become nevertheless remained difficult. Some argued that with monarchy, fascism, and now communism discredited, the European continent could look forward to a future characterized by liberal democratic states. One scholar, Francis Fukuyama, argued that the end of the Cold War would produce what he called "the end of history," meaning that liberal democracy would become the only universal and coherent political aspiration of man. A universal consumer culture and the development of multi-national institutions, he contended, would bring the peoples of the world closer together. The world could thus look forward to a future that would be shared, not contested.[1]

This approach struck many critics as being far too simplistic a vision of the future and far too optimistic an interpretation of human nature. American political scientist Samuel Huntington argued that the bipolar world would be replaced by a small handful of civilization centers identified by shared ethnic, religious, and cultural ties. His argument implied that the nations of western Europe and the United States would continue to move closer to one another because of their shared "western" cultural systems and their shared concerns about Islamic fundamentalism and the rise of new powers such as China. Russia, Huntington's thesis implied, would move toward the west because of the same concerns, although its ties to Eastern Orthodox culture would continue to dis-tinguish it from western Europe. Huntington's vision was more pessimistic than Fukuyama's, as he posited a future filled with conflict between the eight major civilizations.[2]

Huntington's vision of close "civilizational" relations between western Europe and the United States has not fully come to fruition. In both the Bosnia crisis and the Second Persian Gulf War of 2003, Europeans often saw them-selves as offering a different model from the American one. The emergence of America as the world's lone superpower has thus had ambiguous results for Europe. Great Britain and the states of eastern Europe have moved closer to the United States while traditional allies such as France and Germany seem to be drifting further away. The abiding closeness between the trans-Atlantic cousins is hardly surprising and fits nicely into Huntington's central thesis. No two great powers share more cultural and civilizational ties than the United States and Great Britain. The willingness of many eastern European states to associate themselves with American military policy, however, suggests a more complex continent (to say nothing of the rest of the world) than the one that Huntington envisioned.

The breakup of the Soviet Union into numerous smaller republics posed more obvious challenges both to early theoretical concepts and to the realities of international security. To cite one example, during the Cold War, the Soviets deployed nuclear weapons in several republics, based upon strategic need. The rapid collapse of Soviet authority left many of these republics, then in the process of becoming states in their own right, as significant nuclear powers. Ukraine alone possessed 176 strategic nuclear missiles in 1990. Ukraine's retention of these missiles would have made it a major nuclear power. Belarus and Kazakhstan faced similar situations. Kazakhstan by itself would have become one of the world's five largest nuclear powers.

European and American defense experts also worried that nuclear warheads from the former Soviet Union might be sold or transferred to (or even stolen by) states or terrorist groups interested in acquiring them. The successor states to the Soviet Union all faced enormous financial and defense pressures. Furthermore, their procedures for maintaining and guarding their nuclear weapons often failed to meet international security standards. Compounding the dangers, their nuclear commodities represented an easy source of cash and influence if they chose to so use them. The risks of nuclear proliferation loomed over the Soviet Union's peaceful demise and threatened to write a deadly footnote to an otherwise joyful story.

While this issue caused great concern, none of the post-Soviet states had much interest in remaining nuclear powers. They understood that as long as they retained nuclear weapons on Russia's border, Russia would be likely to see the need to continue to exercise a great deal of control over them. As non-nuclear states, they believed, they would pose a much lower threat to Russia and their future relationship with their larger neighbor would be correspondingly less confrontational. Retention of nuclear weapons also threatened their relationships with the states of the west. The developing states of the former Soviet Union understood that the western states (especially the United States) had the financial and technological capability to greatly assist in their development. Their continued status as nuclear powers, however, reduced chances of receiving that aid because all the western states favored non-proliferation of nuclear weapons.

Ukraine's process of nuclear disarmament followed a similar path to that of Belarus and Kazakhstan. Thus Ukraine can serve as an example for all three. In July, 1990 the Ukrainian Parliament (the Rada) issued a nearly unanimous (355 votes to 4) statement declaring its intention to become a sovereign state. The declaration also stated that the Ukraine would not accept, produce, or acquire nuclear weapons. Working with Russia and the United States, Ukraine signed the Trilateral Accord in 1994. Ukraine agreed to transfer all of its nuclear warheads, at American expense, to Russia for the expressed purpose of rapid decommissioning. By the end of the year Belarus and Kazakhstan had signed similar agreements, resulting in the transfer and destruction of more than 900 warheads. The nuclear proliferation threat had passed peacefully.

At the same time, the United States and Russia agreed on massive cuts to their own nuclear forces. The START II agreement, signed by Presidents George Bush and Boris Yeltsin, set ambitious targets for cutting nuclear stockpiles. From 1993 to 2003 the two sides were to cut by two-thirds their holdings of nuclear warheads, with the United States agreeing to remove the vast majority of its weapons still remaining in Europe. The United States also agreed to help finance the Russian dismantling and decommissioning program, committing nearly $500 million for the purpose of purchasing Russian weapons-grade uranium. The Americans pledged to downgrade the Russian uranium to non-weapons grade. As a confidence building measure, the two sides agreed not to aim their existing warheads at one another. Great Britain joined in the agreement as well, greatly reducing the threat of an accidental nuclear launch.

If the threat of nuclear weapons had abated, the threat of war in Europe had not. In 1991 war broke out in the former Yugoslav republic of Slovenia. The constituent elements of Yugoslavia each sought to take advantage of the vacuum created by the decline of Tito (who died in 1980) to carve out autonomous, ethnically homogenous states. As long as Tito ruled the nation with a firm hand, the centrifugal forces pulling Yugoslavia apart were kept in check. Even in death, his role as the Father of Yugoslavia served as an important symbol of unity. After he withdrew from public life, no single person or group emerged to fill the role of unifier of Yugoslavia. Attempts to rotate the presidency of Yugoslavia among various ethnicities predictably failed to bring unity.

At the same time, the collapse of the Soviet Union removed another potential force for cohesion. Yugoslavia had been one of the few states of eastern Europe that had avoided falling into the Soviet orbit. As long as the Soviet Union existed, many Yugoslavs saw unity as a way to retain their autonomy. With the Soviet menace gone, that motivation disappeared. So, too, did American subsidies designed to keep Yugoslavia out of the Soviet sphere of influence. Cold War politics soon faded, only to yield to the traditional ethnic hatreds of the Balkans.

As a consequence of its troubled past, Yugoslavia posed special problems for the entire European continent. Its history is rife with ethnic conflict and bloody wars. Early in the twentieth century the Balkans had been Europe's tinderbox, prompting Bismarck's comment that the next war would begin with "some damn fool thing in the Balkans." The First and Second Balkan Wars in 1912 and 1913 had seriously undermined the security of Europe. It was in the Bosnian city of Sarajevo that Archduke Franz Ferdinand's assassination had triggered World War I. Yugoslavia stood little chance of dividing itself peacefully as Czechoslovakia was then in the process of doing. The outbreak of hostilities in Yugoslavia, therefore, had ominous continental and international implications. Russia's abiding interest in the Balkans and its ongoing ethnic and religious connections to the region's most powerful group, the Serbs, complicated an immensely difficult issue even further.

International media coverage of the violence in Yugoslavia increased the tensions. The influence of televised images of civilian suffering led to a phenomenon that some have called the "CNN effect." The intense and almost instantaneous barrage of images led policymakers to take a greater interest in the Yugoslav civil war than they might have otherwise. Most western media sources depicted the Serbs as the clear aggressors in the conflict. Statements by Serbian leaders that they sought "ethnic cleansing" in Yugoslavia furthered the growing anti-Serbian sentiment in the west. Public opinion in several western states demanded action to prevent a genocide.

Containing and eventually stopping the bloodshed in Yugoslavia provided Europe with a major challenge immediately after the end of the Cold War.

Efforts by European Union politicians to define the Yugoslav problem as an EU issue led to the initial exclusion of the United States and Russia from direct involvement. For their part, the United States and Russia were willing to allow the EU to play the lead role in Yugoslavia, because neither nation wanted to involve itself directly into this intricate region. EU diplomacy worked well in Slovenia and Croatia in 1991 to contain and reduce tensions in these two provinces, leading some Europeans to gain confidence in their own ability to resolve future security issues through continental means.

Nevertheless, the international attention focused on Yugoslavia made conflicts there, the first major regional conflicts to erupt inside Europe since 1945, a concern outside of western Europe. A conflict with international dimensions, many argued, needed an international solution. The United Nations was the obvious place to find such a solution, but the UN was ill-equipped to solve the problems of Yugoslavia for several reasons. First, its structure was designed to ensure peace only after a cease-fire arrangement was in place and the parties involved had agreed to a UN deployment. In Yugoslavia neither of these conditions applied. Second, the UN peacekeeping forces appeared to many (especially the Serbs) to be agents of western powers, thus threatening the impartiality upon which peacekeepers must necessarily rely. Finally, and most portentously, Russia, a permanent member of the UN Security Council, continued to support the Serbs, jeopardizing any long-term UN viability in the region. Shadows of 1914, when Russia supported Serbia in the face of what it saw as outside aggression, loomed ominously.

Despite these problems, in June, 1992, the United Nations adopted a resolution calling for the deployment of a United Nations Peacekeeping Force (UNPROFOR) to Bosnia. At first, the nations contributing forces to UNPROFOR sought to keep their presence small because none of their national security interests were directly threatened. Because the war for them was "not a war of necessity but a war of choice" they also aimed to keep costs (both human and economic) as low as possible.[3] Great Britain's initial contribution to UNPROFOR was just 1,800 troops. By 1994 there were less than 23,000 UN troops in Bosnia, enough to catalog and witness the slaughter of 200,000 people, but not enough to stop it with any consistency.

The intricacies of the situation in Yugoslavia quickly revealed the limitations of the United Nations. Aware of its inability to guard all of Bosnia, the UN designated several Bosnian cities as safe zones and authorized the use of air strikes to prevent further Serbian gains. The Serbs reacted by seizing UN personnel to use as human shields, installing surface-to-air missile systems, and brazenly destroying the "safe zone" of Srebenica in July, 1995. Serbian forces massacred the town's 40,000 residents within sight of a small UNPROFOR detachment (consisting of Dutch soldiers), which was powerless to take action. At the time of the massacre, the UN had just 7,000 troops dedicated to protecting safe zones including Srebenica, when by its own estimate it needed at least 34,000 troops to implement the policy effectively.

The atrocity at Srebenica marked a "watershed" in western attitudes toward the wars in Yugoslavia, removing "all pretense of impartiality" in Washington and most European capitals.[4] Thereafter the United States began to take a much greater interest in events in Yugoslavia and lost confidence in the ability of the Europeans and UNPROFOR to solve the problem on their own. Because UNPROFOR would need NATO (and therefore American) assets to complete a withdrawal, the events at Srebenica forced the United States to make a critical decision: allow UNPROFOR to be placed in an untenable operational position or use American assets to change the situation on the ground. It was in this vein that British General Sir Michael Rose noted that Srebenica forced the United States across the "Mogadishu line" that separated peace-keeping from peace-enforcement. The United States was coming closer to committing itself to the latter, and that commitment would mean the direct military involvement of American forces.[5]

Consistent with the military history of Europe in the twentieth century, the United States soon played a large role, both on its own accord and as part of NATO. In 1995 NATO, led mainly by the United States, began the largest military campaign of its history. Designed as an alliance to deter Soviet expansion, NATO instead charged itself with damaging the Serbian military's ability to conduct offensive operations in order to force the Serbs to accept a diplomatic solution. This operation, code-named Deliberate Force, had, as its name implied, a specific mission and a specific endpoint.

As a result, NATO forces were severely limited in their operations. They were not, for example, authorized to strike civilian targets. Moreover, because they were in Yugoslavia to protect civilians, NATO forces became hyper-sensitive to reports of inadvertent civilian casualties (what the military euphemistically calls collateral damage). Fears of negative publicity that might undermine support for the mission also played on the minds of policymakers. Deliberate Force therefore presented the odd contrast of a Serbian military killing its enemies at will with NATO military units gently trying to use force without causing any unintended damage at all. NATO forces designed for a total war against the Soviet Union had to fight a delicate limited war that achieved its mission but imposed minimal casualties.

Deliberate Force thus provided an entirely new and untried model for NATO in the post-Cold War era. In the absence of a Soviet-style menace that needed to be deterred, NATO proponents argued that the alliance could serve as a mechanism to enforce morality and establish and maintain European stability. NATO forces, however, were not designed for such a mission. Despite powerful air strikes (in two weeks NATO flew 3,500 air sorties and fired 100 cruise missiles) the Serbs appeared to be consolidating their hold on power in many areas. Only a major advance by NATO-supported Bosnian and Croatian ground forces in summer, 1995 involving 200,000 men (the largest ground offensive in Europe since World War II) forced the Serbs to attend the Dayton Peace Conference sponsored by the United States.

The wars in Yugoslavia from 1991 to 1995 (which might accurately be called the Fourth Balkan War[6]) thus challenged the fundamental presumptions that had guided Europe since 1945. Collective security arrangements in the UN and NATO had proven themselves unequal to the task of stopping blood-letting inside Europe. Efforts by the European Union to solve the crisis without asking for American help had also failed. Although the events of Yugoslavia seemed to provide a dark vision into the future, in many ways they were a hark-ening to the past: a European conflict had been solved (or at least ameliorated) by active cooperation between the United States and the powers of Europe. Consequently, the Dayton Accords produced a joint peacekeeping force for Bosnia, that included forces from the United States, Canada, Great Britain, Russia, France, and Spain.

These wars also showed the limits of Francis Fukuyama's notion that man's ultimate quest lay in the establishment of liberal democratic states. The war in Yugoslavia showed that more traditional goals, such as national self-determination, irredentism, and the simple butchery of one's long-time foes, still dominated. If there was an "end of history" along the lines Fukuyama suggested, there was scant evidence of it in the Balkans. Instead, quite the reverse appeared to be true: the region's long and troubled history was guiding both its present and its future.

On the surface, the Fourth Balkan War seemed to prove many of the key tenets of Huntington's thesis: Yugoslavia's timeless wars were in part a function of the often uneasy coexistence of Catholics, Orthodox Christians, and Muslims in a relatively small territory. Nevertheless, the "clash of civilizations" had an ironic twist. NATO's military forces, almost all from overwhelm-ingly western and Christian states, acted in defense of Muslims against the aggression of a Serbian-dominated, and thus Eastern Orthodox-dominated, Yugoslavia.

The outbreak of further Serbian aggression in Kosovo in 1998 forced NATO once again to intervene in order to prevent the genocide of Muslims, this time Kosovar Albanians. Kosovo has long been a region coveted by both Albanians and Serbs. Franz Ferdinand's 1914 visit to Sarajevo occurred on St. Vitus Day, the anniversary of a 1389 Serbian defeat at Kosovo Polje near the city of Pristina. Serbian patriots, including members of the Black Hand terrorist group, were enraged by the timing. Kosovo remained central to modern Serbian notions of nationalism and therefore reemerged as a battleground and rallying cry when central authority in Yugoslavia collapsed.

Because the problems of the Balkans remained central to Europe, the nations of Europe once again took action under the aegis of NATO. In late September, 1998 NATO warned Serbian leader Slobodan Milosevic that his forces must stop "repressive actions" against the population of Kosovo and "take immediate steps to alleviate the humanitarian situation." When Milosevic took no action toward fulfilling these demands by the following March, NATO began air strikes on Serbian targets.

NATO military pressure achieved its political goal, although the absence of large-scale NATO ground forces prohibited a quick resolution of the suffering. The air strikes lasted for 78 days, leading Serbian forces to withdraw from Kosovo in favor of a NATO peacekeeping force. Working under the name Operation Allied Force, five NATO nations (Italy, Germany, Great Britain, France, and the United States) divided Kosovo, with each nation responsible for peacekeeping operations in its own sector. The operation represented the largest deployment outside their borders for Italy and Germany since World War II. It thus marked the return of a (newly unified) Germany to European military operations. Once again, the model of US–European cooperation achieved its goal of stopping the killing, although the presence of NATO forces will likely remain a feature of Balkan politics for some time to come.

European states engaged in peacekeeping operations across the globe. These missions allowed several states in Europe to play a military role without fighting wars. Through peacekeeping they have contributed to UN operations and utilized their military strength to help maintain peace worldwide. Some states have made peacekeeping an integral part of their military identity. In November, 1998 Poland, Finland, Austria, Ireland, and France all contributed more soldiers to UN peacekeeping operations than either the United States or Great Britain. Poland's contribution to UN peacekeeping operations is the largest of any nation in the world.

War fighting and peacekeeping in the former Yugoslavia promised a new identity for NATO. Nevertheless, the demise of the very entities the alliance was created to deter, namely the Soviet Union and the Warsaw Pact, left open some serious questions. First, and most fundamentally, did it make sense to maintain an alliance that had fulfilled its main mission? With the Soviet Union gone and all sides rapidly reducing stockpiles of nuclear weapons, NATO seemed to have lost its reason for being. Many Europeans argued that dismantling NATO was the natural and logical next step to follow on the demise of the Warsaw Pact.

Second, what were the consequences for Russia of keeping NATO strong? Opponents of maintaining a strong NATO argued that Europe could not move forward into a future of cooperation as long as an alliance built to deter, and if necessary fight, Russia continued to exist. The persistence of instability and the rise of ultra-nationalist groups inside Russia made others wary of dismantling a counterweight to the massive Russian giant.

Third, would an expansion of NATO bring greater or lesser security to the European continent? Proponents argued that a larger alliance meant greater security because member states could call upon the resources of the alliance to resolve disputes. Opponents contended that an expansion of NATO that included large numbers of former Warsaw Pact nations would threaten Russia. Because collective security is the cornerstone of NATO, moreover, a local conflict between a member state and a non-member state ran the risk of becoming general. If, for example, Poland joined NATO and were attacked by Belarus, all NATO members would be treaty-bound to come to Poland's aid. Opponents of expansion called into question the willingness of NATO member nations to put their soldiers' lives at risk to fight for the nations of eastern Europe.

These fears notwithstanding, three former Warsaw Pact members joined NATO in 1997. The addition of Poland, the Czech Republic, and Hungary revolutionized the nature of European defense, bringing the states of western and eastern Europe into closer contact with one another. The lack of demonstrated opposition by Russia to these changes led to a second round of expansion. In 2002 NATO invited Bulgaria, Estonia, Latvia, Lithuania, Rumania, Slovakia, and Slovenia to join the alliance. These changes, once confirmed by the member states, will bring NATO right to the Russian border.[7] The creation of the European–Atlantic Partnership Council of NATO forged links with twenty-seven non-member nations, including Russia and thirteen other former Soviet republics. This council's mission is to ensure that relations between NATO and the non-member European states remain smooth.

NATO thus continues to grow even though its exact mission remains unclear. During the height of the Cold War, a popular aphorism, as previously noted, proposed that NATO's purpose was to keep the Russians out, the Americans in, and the Germans down. Neither the first nor the third mission now seems necessary and many Europeans question the need for the second. NATO continues peacekeeping operations in the former Yugoslavia and maintains a large collective presence in Europe. Nevertheless, the alliance's future remains unclear. Events in the Middle East, most notably European opposition to the Second Persian Gulf War, have recently placed the alliance under increased strain due to intense disagreements among member states. Whether NATO can survive such open dissent on an extra-European issue remains to be seen.

The Middle East has emerged as the most consistent area of competition and cooperation for Americans and Europeans since the end of the Cold War. Iraq's invasion of Kuwait in August, 1990 appeared to bring the Europeans and Americans closer together. Both sides quickly agreed that a military response to Iraqi aggression and the threat to the world's oil supply were both appropriate and necessary. Their military action met with general support, if not much enthusiasm, from European society. On the operational and tactical levels, the training, weaponry, and doctrine of American and western European military forces were well-suited to fighting the large conventional forces of Iraq. The first major global conflict since the end of the Cold War therefore witnessed Europe and America acting in general accord.

That accord held together even during the buildup phase (Desert Shield, 1990–1991) and the war itself (Desert Storm, 1991). Fourteen European nations contributed combat forces or support personnel to the coalition, which had broad international and UN support. France and Great Britain contributed the largest European contingents by far, including air, sea, and land assets. These forces fought under unified chains of command ultimately controlled by American generals and admirals under General Norman Schwarzkopf. They therefore fit the much larger World War II pattern established under American General Dwight Eisenhower and, less perfectly, in World War I under French General Ferdinand Foch.

The First Persian Gulf War had minor direct impacts on European society because casualties were minimal and the forces engaged were volunteer professionals. Furthermore, the coalition kept its military objective limited. It aimed to remove Iraqi forces from Kuwait, not to overthrow the regime of Saddam Hussein. The war was therefore short and coalition forces returned home rather quickly. Moreover, the Americans bore the majority of the manpower and financial responsibility for the war, keeping the costs and risks to Europe small.

Despite the relatively harmonious experiences of Desert Shield and Desert Storm, the experiences of the 1990s led European states to conclude that important flaws existed in their military system. The experiences of European militaries in the former Yugoslavia and the Persian Gulf combined with the uncertain future of NATO have therefore begun to yield major changes. European military and political leaders disliked their almost total reliance on American military and diplomatic power to resolve these crises. The sharp reductions in European military budgets in the 1990s had led to a massive disparity in forces. Budget cuts notwithstanding, the United States upgraded its communications systems, satellite navigation, and precision weapons, leaving Europe lagging behind. In 2001, for example, only 10 percent of European aircraft could deliver precision munitions and only Great Britain possessed cruise missiles or stealth technology. Moreover, European militaries were almost entirely dependent upon American reconnaissance, transportation, and command structures.

Faced with their relative powerlessness to act without the Americans, European states revived the notion of a European Defense Force, first suggested in 1948. In 1998, France and Britain agreed to improve the European Union's defense infrastructure and the following year fifteen European nations approved the concept of an international rapid reaction force to deal with humanitarian crises inside Europe such as Kosovo. In 2000, the EU voted to create the Eurocorps, a 60,000 soldier-strong force supported by 400 aircraft and 100 ships. In theory, the force, headquartered in the EU capital of Strasbourg, could deploy within 60 days and remain in the field for as long as one year.

Some European nations, most notably France, saw the Eurocorps as a way for the EU to act independently of the United States. Instead of asking for American help, the Eurocorps could theoretically mobilize and deploy to a crisis area by itself. The EU could therefore affirm itself as the arbiter of major problems in Europe and avoid what one French diplomat called "monopoly domination" by the United States. In order to achieve that level of effectiveness, however, the Eurocorps will need a massive infusion of money and technology. The EU states have committed to those expenditures on paper, but have yet to translate that promise into a genuine support structure for the Eurocorps.

The Eurocorps thus represents the military end of the unification of Europe that has been ongoing for nearly half a century. It remains doubtful whether the various diplomatic, economic, and political goals of the EU member states can be sufficiently rationalized to create one military force that will satisfy all of them. Moreover, not all EU member states use the same military hardware. Most western states use a blend of American and European military products, while France uses almost exclusively French-produced fighters and many eastern states remain heavily dependent on older Russian-built systems. How such a mutually incompatible military force might operate in a crisis remains unclear.

To further compound the problems that face a joint EU military presence, not all member states have the same goals in mind. Great Britain and others have seen the Eurocorps as a complement to, not a counterweight for, NATO. From the onset of the first serious discussions about joint European defense, the British have feared that their commitment to the Eurocorps might jeopardize the close relationship between the United States and Europe. More pragmatically, the British are aware that it will take years for the Eurocorps to be in a position to operate truly independently of the United States. Until that day should arrive, the Eurocorps will have to depend on NATO (and thus the United States) for most of its planning, intelligence, and support assets. NATO also retains primary responsibility for defending Europe against any outside threats.

Therefore, unless and until Europe can agree on how to upgrade its military hardware and support systems, the Eurocorps will remain more a political issue than a military one. The obvious overlap of NATO and the EU will also ensure that the two bodies will not diverge. Currently, Great Britain contributes one-fourth of the military elements of the Eurocorps, a factor that is likely to prevent any joint European military force from becoming an instrument opposed to American policy. The Bush Administration, which first reacted coolly to the Eurocorps concept, has recently embraced it much more warmly, a clear indication that problems of relating the Eurocorps to NATO have been resolved.

All of these problems moved to the background in the wake of the shocking terrorist attacks on the World Trade Center and Pentagon on September 11, 2001. Terrorism, of course, had struck at European states and American targets overseas for decades. The events of September 11, however, were the largest and most audacious ever carried out on American soil. The response from Europe was immediate and wholly supportive of the United States. For the first time in memory, the United States was a victim, not a protector.

NATO reacted by invoking its collective security clause (Article 5 of the NATO Charter) for the first time in its history. Article 5 pledged that

> The Parties agree that an armed attack against one or more of them in Europe or North America shall be considered an attack against them all and consequently they agree that, if such an armed attack occurs,

187

each of them . . . will assist the Party or Parties so attacked by taking forthwith, individually and in concert with the other Parties, such action as it deems necessary, including the use of armed force, to restore and maintain the security of the North Atlantic area.

Article 5 had been designed to assure Europeans that a Soviet invasion of western Europe would bring a military response from the United States. Instead Article 5's first invocation was at the behest of Europeans in support of the United States. In effect, the nations of NATO were officially declaring that they viewed the attacks on the United States as attacks on them all. In Britain's case, the link was more than rhetorical. Sixty-seven Britons died in the terror attacks, making September 11 the bloodiest day in the history of anti-British terrorism.

The NATO nations backed up their rhetoric with action. More than 200 European military personnel from thirteen nations deployed to the United States. These forces supported the operations of AWACS (Airborne Warning and Control System) air platforms as part of Combat Air Patrol missions in the United States. These aircraft acted as flying radar stations to support American fighter aircraft patrolling the skies over major American cities. Nine European nations contributed forces to Operation Enduring Freedom, which attacked the Al Qaeda terrorist organization and its Taliban sponsors in Afghanistan.[8]

Operation Enduring Freedom marked the high point of European–American cooperation. With shared goals and shared determination, the forces of more than a dozen nations worked together to eliminate Al Qaeda's Afghanistan safe haven. They also cooperated in dismantling the terrorist group's assets world-wide. France alone deployed more than 2,000 personnel to the Middle East in support of these operations, marking one of that nation's largest overseas emergency deployments since the end of the Algerian War in 1962. Italy's deployment of 3,000 personnel and Germany's of almost 4,000 personnel represented significant overseas operations for those nations as well.

Since then, European–American relations have become more contentious. European society vocally opposed the Bush Administration's invasion of Iraq in 2003. A majority of Europeans disagreed with the Administration's argu-ment that an invasion was the only way to ensure that Saddam Hussein's military did not possess weapons of mass destruction. Widespread demon-strations across Europe opposing the war called into question any possibility of a coalition war.

France and Germany, working at times with Russia, led the European oppo-sition to the war. Since France and Russia hold permanent seats on the United Nations Security Council, they both held the power to block a UN resolution authorizing force. Debates between French and American diplomats became especially confrontational and, at times, public opinion in both nations became heated. France and Germany, building on their close relationship since the 1960s, sought to provide a model of independent statesmanship for other European nations to follow.

Not all nations saw the advantages of following France and Germany, however. The governments of Great Britain and Spain became early supporters of operations in Iraq, despite public opposition in both nations. Several eastern European nations supported the United States as well, despite veiled threats from French President Jacques Chirac that their pro-American policies would threaten their future acceptance into the European Union. The comments of American Defense Secretary Donald Rumsfeld that a division exists between the old Europe and the new Europe might indicate a greater American willingness to work with the latter at the expense of its traditional military relations with the former.

From 1898 to 2003 the European continent has undergone a remarkable transformation. Europe began the twentieth century as the world's most belligerent, most volatile, and most heavily armed region. It begins the next century relatively calm, mostly stable, and comparatively disarmed. As support for operations in places such as Sierra Leone, Kosovo, and Afghanistan showed, Europeans remain willing to support limited military deployments in order to prevent humanitarian crises or if national interests are directly involved. As opposition to the Second Persian Gulf War demonstrated, however, the existence of significant pacifist elements shows that nations cannot commit military force as easily as they did a century ago.

To be sure, the former Yugoslavia remains a point of great concern and will likely continue to need an outside military presence for years to come. Still, no inter-state competition presently threatens war on the continent and the absence of European colonies means that overseas deployments are significantly lower now than they were a hundred years ago. Europe's apparently peaceful present and future are due in large part to the lessons Europeans have learned from their horrifically violent past. For that future to remain peaceful, it is necessary to confront and understand the demons of Europe in the twenty-first century. Only by doing so can one understand where they came from and gain insight into preventing their return.

# NOTES

## INTRODUCTION

1  Examples include Brian Bond, *War and Society in Europe* (Oxford: Oxford University Press, 1986) and Geoffrey Wawro, *Warfare and Society in Europe, 1792–1914* (London: Routledge, 2000).
2  See my *Foch: Supreme Allied Commander in the Great War* (Dulles, VA: Brassey's, 2003).
3  R. L. DiNardo and Daniel Hughes, "Germany and Coalition Warfare in the World Wars: A Comparative Study," *War in History* 8 (Spring, 2001): 166–190. Holger Herwig, *The First World War: Germany and Austria* (London: Edward Arnold, 1997) covers the alliance relationship between these two nations.
4  See Peter Schrijvers, *The Crash of Ruin: American Combat Soldiers in Europe During World War II* (New York: New York University Press, 1998).
5  This book is a sequel of sorts to Wawro, *War and Society in Europe*. I have overlapped my account with his in order to explain more fully the outbreak of World War I.

## 1  FROM FASHODA TO SARAJEVO

1  Quoted in Paul Marie de la Gorce, *The French Army: A Military-Political History*, translated by Kenneth Douglas (New York: George Braziller, 1963), 63.
2  Samuel Williamson, *The Politics of Grand Strategy: Britain and France Prepare for War* (Cambridge, MA: Harvard University Press, 1969), 1.
3  Quoted in J. M. Bourne, ed., *Who's Who in World War One* (London: Routledge, 2001), 304.
4  Brian Bond, *War and Society in Europe, 1870–1970* (Gloucestershire: Sutton Publishing, 1998), 80.
5  Eugen Weber describing the sentiments of Jules and Paul Cambon in *France Fin de Siècle* (Cambridge, MA: Harvard University Press, 1979), 106.
6  Quoted in Dennis Showalter, *Tannenberg: Clash of Empires* (Hamden, CT: Archon Books, 1993), 56.
7  Quoted in Jeremy Popkin, *History of Modern France*, second edition (New York: Prentice-Hall, 2001), 185.
8  See Bond, *War and Society*, 64, 69.
9  Quoted in Richard Holmes, *The Little Field Marshal: Sir John French* (London: Jonathan Cape, 1981), 182.
10  See Gerd Krumeich, *Armaments and Politics in France on the Eve of the First World War:*

*The Introduction of Three-Year Conscription, 1913–1914*, translated by Stephen Conn (Oxford: Berg Publishers, 1984).

11 See John Horne, *Labour at War: France and Britain, 1914–1918* (Oxford: Clarendon Press, 1991).

12 Hew Strachan, *The First World War: To Arms!* (Oxford: Oxford University Press, 2001), 133.

13 Quoted in de la Gorce, *The French Army*, 97.

14 Quoted in Colin Nicolson, *The Longman Companion to the First World War: Europe 1914–1918* (London: Longman, 2001), 86.

15 Quoted in Strachan, *To Arms!*, 173.

16 See Robert Doughty, "French Strategy in 1914: Joffre's Own," *Journal of Military History* 67 (April 2003): 427–454.

17 Geoffrey Wawro, *Warfare and European Society, 1792–1914* (London: Routledge, 2000), 197.

18 Wawro, *Warfare and European Society*, 212.

19 Quoted in Nicolson, *The Longman Companion*, 71.

20 See J. F. V. Keiger, *Raymond Poincaré* (Cambridge: Cambridge University Press, 1997), chapters six and seven.

21 Quoted in Nicolson, *The Longman Companion*, 91.

22 Engels and Moltke quoted in Stig Förster, "Images of Future Warfare, 1871–1914," in Roger Chickering and Stig Förster, eds., *Anticipating Total War: The German and American Experiences* (Cambridge: Cambridge University Press, 1999), 343–376, quotations at 347.

23 Quoted in Richard Watt, *Dare Call it Treason* (New York: Dorset, 1969), 29.

## 2 WORLD WAR I, 1914–1917

1 Quoted in Samuel Williamson, *The Politics of Grand Strategy: Britain and France Prepare for War* (Cambridge: Harvard University Press, 1969), vii.

2 John Gooch, *The Plans of War: The General Staff and British Military Strategy, c. 1900–1916* (New York: John Wiley, 1974), 280–283.

3 Quoted in Williamson, *Politics of Grand Strategy*, 331.

4 John Horne and Alan Kramer's *German Atrocities: A History of Denial* (New Haven: Yale University Press, 2001) is a great starting point for study of this issue.

5 Much of this discussion comes from Michael Neiberg, *Foch: Supreme Allied Commander of World War I* (Dulles, VA: Brassey's, 2003), chapter three.

6 Quoted in Holger Herwig, *The First World War: Germany and Austria-Hungary, 1914–1918* (London: Arnold Publishing, 1997), 137.

7 Alistair Horne, *The Price of Glory: Verdun 1916* (London: Penguin, 1962) is the classic narrative account of this battle. For a more analytic treatment see Ian Ousby, *The Road to Verdun: World War I's Most Momentous Battle and the Folly of Nationalism* (New York: Doubleday, 2002).

8 Horne, *Price of Glory*, 119.

9 Steinbrecher quoted in Jay Winter and Blaine Baggett, *The Great War and the Shaping of the Twentieth Century* (New York: Penguin, 1996), 186.

10 Roger Chickering, *Imperial Germany and the Great War, 1914–1918* (Cambridge: Cambridge University Press, 1998), 111.

11 Quoted in Philip Warner, *Passchendaele* (London: Wordsworth, 1987), 2.

## 3 WORLD WAR I, 1917–1919

1 Quoted in John S. D. Eisenhower and Joanne Thompson Eisenhower, *Yanks: The Epic Story of the American Army in World War I* (New York: Free Press, 2001), 114.
2 Edward M. Coffman, *The War to End All Wars: The American Military Experience in World War I* (New York: Oxford University Press, 1968), 158.
3 See Gary Sheffield, *Forgotten Victory: The First World War, Myths and Realities* (London: Headline, 2001).
4 Harold Nicolson, *Peacemaking, 1919* (New York: Grossett and Dunlap, 1965), 58.
5 Quoted in Richard Watt, *The Kings Depart* (New York: Barnes and Noble, 2000), 42.
6 Nicolson, *Peacemaking*, 62.
7 Quoted in G. B. Noble, *Policies and Opinions at Paris, 1919* (New York: Howard Fertig, 1968), 191.
8 Nicolson, *Peacemaking*, 77.
9 Quoted in Nicolson, *Peacemaking*, 24.
10 "Marshal Foch Says What He Thinks of Bolsheviki and Boches," *Literary Digest* 63 (December 20, 1919): 86–92, quotation at 92.
11 David Stevenson, "War Aims and Peace Negotiations," in Hew Stachan, ed., *The Oxford Illustrated History of the First World War* (Oxford: Oxford University Press, 1998), 204–215.
12 Nicolson, *Peacemaking*, 41.
13 Quoted in Watt, *Kings Depart*, 11.
14 Nicolson, *Peacemaking*, 32 and 371.
15 Quoted in Watt, *Kings Depart*, 464.
16 Quoted in Arno J. Mayer, *Politics and Diplomacy of Peacemaking: Containment and Counterrevolution at Versailles, 1918–1919* (New York: Alfred A. Knopf, 1967), 222.

## 4 THE INTERWAR YEARS, 1919–1939

1 See chapter eight of J. F. V. Keiger, *Raymond Poincaré* (Cambridge: Cambridge University Press, 1997).
2 Quoted in Holger Herwig, "Clio Deceived: Patriotic Self-Censorship in Germany after the Great War," *International Security* 12 (Autumn, 1987), 12.
3 See the relevant essays in Manfred F. Boemeke, Gerald D. Feldman, Elisabeth Glaser, eds., *The Treaty of Versailles: A Reassessment after 75 Years* (Cambridge: Cambridge University Press, 1998).
4 Quoted in Jeremy D. Popkin, *A History of Modern France* (Upper Saddle River, NJ: Prentice Hall, 2001), 206.
5 Quoted in Paul Marie de la Gorce, *The French Army: A Military-Political History* (New York: George Braziller, 1963), 231 and 231–232.
6 Raymond Carr, *The Spanish Tragedy* (London: Phoenix, 2000), 48.
7 Quoted in Carr, *Spanish Tragedy*, 147.
8 George Orwell, *Homage to Catalonia* (New York: Harcourt Brace Jovanovich, 1952), 4.
9 Orwell, *Homage*, 182.
10 Orwell, *Homage*, 36.
11 Orwell, *Homage*, 56.
12 Brian Bond, *War and Society in Europe, 1870–1970* (Gloucestershire: Sutton Publishing, 1998), 147.

## 5 WORLD WAR II, 1939–1942

1  Gerhard Weinberg, *A World at Arms: A Global History of World War II* (Cambridge: Cambridge University Press, 1994), 109.
2  Williamson Murray and Allan R. Millett, *A War to be Won: Fighting the Second World War* (Cambridge, MA: Harvard University Press, 2000), 63.
3  François Kersaudy, *Norway 1940* (Lincoln: University of Nebraska Press, 1990), 9.
4  Quisling quoted in Kersaudy, *Norway*, 40.
5  Martin Allen, *Hidden Agenda: How the Duke of Windsor Betrayed the Allies* (New York: M. Evans and Company, 2000) alleges that the Duke actively aided the Nazi advance into France in 1940 and maintained close relations with German authorities thereafter.
6  Winston Churchill, *The Second World War*, volume 2, *Their Finest Hour* (London: Folio Society, 2000), 95–96.
7  Churchill, *Their Finest Hour*, 130.
8  See Tami Davis Biddle, *Rhetoric and Reality in Air Warfare: The Evolution of British and American Ideas About Strategic Bombing, 1914–1945* (Princeton: Princeton University Press, 2002).
9  Churchill, *Their Finest Hour*, 453.
10  Quoted in Churchill, *Their Finest Hour*, 453.
11  Quoted in John Bierman and Colin Smith, *The Battle of Alamein: Turning Point, World War II* (New York: Viking, 2002), 15.
12  Quoted in Antony Beevor, *Stalingrad: The Fateful Siege, 1942–1943* (New York: Penguin, 1998), 16–17.
13  Beevor, *Stalingrad*, 15.
14  Winston Churchill, *The Second World War*, volume 3, *The Grand Alliance* (London: Folio Society, 2000), 485.

## 6 WORLD WAR II, 1942–1945

1  King's 1932 Navy War College thesis argued that Britain "must be considered a potential enemy and a powerful one." See Mark Stoler, *Allies and Adversaries: The Joint Chiefs of Staff, the Grand Alliance, and U. S. Strategy in World War II* (Chapel Hill: University of North Carolina Press, 2000), 8.
2  "Cultural terror," in Peter Paret *et al.*, *Persuasive Images: Posters of War and Revolution from the Hoover Institution Archives* (Princeton: Princeton University Press, 1992), 173.
3  Stoler, *Allies and Adversaries*, 70.
4  John Dower, *War Without Mercy: Race and Power in the Pacific War* (New York: Pantheon, 1986), 55 and 79.
5  Quoted in Richard Hill, *Hitler Attacks Pearl Harbor: Why the United States Declared War on Germany* (Boulder, Colorado: Lynne Rienner Publishers, 2003), 86.
6  Paul Fussell, *Wartime: Understanding and Behavior in the Second World War* (New York: Oxford University Press, 1989), 6.
7  Stoler, *Allies and Adversaries*, 258.
8  Rick Atkinson, *An Army at Dawn: The War in North Africa, 1942–1943* (New York: Henry Holt, 2002), 413–415.
9  See chapter six of Richard Overy, *Why the Allies Won* (New York: Norton, 1995).
10  Martin Blumenson, "The Race to Messina," in *Heroes Never Die: Warriors and Warfare in World War II* (New York: Cooper Square Press, 2001), 471–480, quotations at 479.

11 Macgregor Knox, *Hitler's Italian Allies: Royal Armed Forces, Fascist Regime, and the War of 1940–1943* (Cambridge: Cambridge University Press, 2000), 193.

12 Bill Mauldin, *Bill Mauldin's Army: Bill Mauldin's Greatest World War II Cartoons* (Novato, CA: Presidio Press, 1979), 110.

13 Fussell, *Wartime*, 205.

14 See Henry Rousso, *The Vichy Syndrome: History and Memory in France Since 1944*, translated by Arthur Goldhammer (Cambridge, MA: Harvard University Press, 1991).

15 Overy, *Why the Allies Won*, chapter one.

16 Fussell, *Wartime*, 179.

17 Gerhard Weinberg, *A World at Arms: A Global History of World War II* (Cambridge: Cambridge University Press, 1994), 834–835.

## 7 WAR AND SOCIETY IN EUROPE, 1945–1989

1 Winston Churchill, *The Second World War*, volume 6, *Triumph and Tragedy* (London: Folio Society, 2000), 431–432.

2 Brian Bond, *War and Society in Europe, 1870–1970* (London: Sutton, 1984), 197.

3 Martin Gilbert, *The Second World War: A Complete History* (New York: Owl Books, 1989), 711.

4 Steven Béla Várdy and Emil Niederhauser, "East Central Europe," in Peter Stearns, ed., *The Encyclopedia of European Social History*, volume 1 (New York: Scribners, 2001), 396. The figure for Czechoslovakia is for the Czech Republic. The figure for Slovakia is roughly 14 percent, most of them Hungarians.

5 That phrase comes from Henry Rousso's masterful study, *The Vichy Syndrome: History and Memory in France since 1944*, translated by Arthur Goldhammer (Cambridge, MA: Harvard University Press, 1991).

6 See Alistair Horne, *The French Army and Politics, 1870–1970* (New York: Peter Bedrick, 1984). The quotation comes from R. O. Paxton on page 72.

7 Horne, *The French Army and Politics*, 73.

8 Horne, *The French Army and Politics*, 90.

9 Quoted in Jeremy Isaacs and Taylor Downing, *The Cold War, 1945–1991* (New York: Little, Brown, 1998), 52.

10 The original member states were: Belgium, Canada, Denmark, France, Holland, Iceland, Italy, Luxembourg, Norway, Portugal, the United Kingdom, and the United States. Turkey and Greece joined in 1951. West Germany joined in 1955. Spain joined in 1983.

11 A good short introduction to the Suez Crisis is Derek Varble, *Suez Crisis 1956* (Oxford: Osprey, 2003).

12 Sting, "Russians," from *The Dream of the Blue Turtles*, A & M Records, 1985.

13 Quoted in Isaacs and Downing, *The Cold War*, 370.

## CONCLUSIONS

1 See Francis Fukuyama, *The End of History and the Last Man* (New York: Free Press, 1992).

2 See Samuel Huntington, *The Clash of Civilizations and the Remaking of World Order* (New York: Touchstone Books, 1998). The eight civilizations he identified

were: Western (meaning Western European and the United States), Eastern Orthodox, Latin American, Islamic, Japanese, Chinese, Hindu/Indian, and African.

3 That phrase comes from Warren Chin, "The Transformation of War in Europe, 1945–2000," in Jeremy Black, ed., *European Warfare, 1815–2000* (London: Palgrave, 2002), 192–241, quotation at 199.

4 Laura Silber and Allan Little, *Yugoslavia: Death of a Nation* (London: Penguin, 1995), 351.

5 Silber and Little, *Yugoslavia*, 351. An American-led UN operation from 1992 to 1994 to ensure the safe delivery of food in Somalia ended disastrously. UN forces quickly extended their initial mission to include actively disarming local warlords. In doing so, many believed, they lost the image of impartiality needed to effectively operate peacekeeping missions. Ensuing combat in the city of Mogadishu killed hundreds, including eighteen Americans, and led President Clinton to limit the roles that American peacekeepers should assume in the future. The episode seemed to demonstrate that the United States had little desire to participate in future peacekeeping missions.

6 The first occurred in 1912–1913, the second in 1913 (see Chapter 1). World War I's Balkan phase might accurately be understood as the Third Balkan War.

7 In 2003, the United States Senate voted unanimously to approve all seven applicants for NATO membership. All but Slovenia had supported the American-led war in Iraq earlier in the year.

8 They were: Great Britain, France, Denmark, Holland, Germany, Norway, Italy, Greece, and Turkey. Germany, Denmark, Britain, and Norway sent Special Forces units as well as air, naval, and conventional forces.

# INDEX